D1292343

Christian Unity and Religion in New England

Collected Papers in Church History
of Roland H. Bainton

Collected Papers in Church History

SERIES THREE

Christian Unity and Religion
in New England

By Roland H. Bainton

Beacon Press   Boston

Copyright © 1964 by Roland H. Bainton
All rights reserved

Published simultaneously in Canada by S. J. Reginald Saunders
and Co., Ltd., Toronto

Library of Congress catalog card number: 64-13530

Printed in the United States of America

Acknowledgments

Grateful acknowledgment is made to the following for permission
to reprint the articles comprising this volume: Abingdon Press,
from *Religion in Life;* The Bethany Press, from *The Sage of
Bethany;* The Christian Century Foundation, from *The Christian
Century; Christianity Today;* Columbia University Press, from *The
Constitution Reconsidered; Bulletin* of the Congregational Library
of the American Congregational Association; Guilford College;
Harvard Divinity School from the *Harvard Divinity School Bulle-
tin;* The New Haven Association of Congregational Christian
Churches and Ministers; *Quarterly Journal of Studies on Alcohol;*
Sci-Art Publishers, from *The Albert Schweitzer Jubilee Book;
Theology Today;* The University of Michigan Press, from *Religion
and the State University;* World Council of Churches, from *The
Ecumenical Review; Zeitschrift für Kirchengeschichte.*

BR
530
.B34

6 5 3 8 3

To

Raymond P. Morris
Commissariat extraordinary to the scholars' army.

Foreword

In the preface to this the third volume of my collected essays a word of appreciation is in order to the Beacon Press for having undertaken and brought to completion an enterprise which evidences a concern for scholarship rather than a quest for affluence. I am deeply grateful for the care which has been expended in the effort to make something of a unity out of materials necessarily diverse.

This volume falls into two parts. The first has to do with problems of the reunion of the churches, the second with the religious history of New England. The essays in this latter portion are miscellaneous and scarcely call for comment. Those on church unity may well leave the reader wondering where I stand. My comments may well appear ambivalent. They are. Unity in the spirit is a Christian absolute, but institutional unity is contingent upon circumstances. There are strategic considerations. If one union produces two schisms then three churches will replace two. But even if unions are nearly unanimous there are still pros and cons. Obviously on the mission field the atomization of Protestantism has been confusing and harmful. In western lands a multiplicity of denominational churches in the villages and suburban areas imposes a heavy and needless economic burden. In the field of religious education mergers increase the size of the constituency and by insuring a larger distribution of published materials make possible a superior product at a lower price. On the other hand, would one wish a single Protestant agency for the creation and testing of new educational materials? When several major bodies are engaged in friendly competition the range of ideas and experimentation is extended, and this advantage may well offset the financial gain from consolidation.

Bigness of itself offers opportunities and dangers. If the churches come together they can offer a united front to the secular and non-Christian world. But in so doing they will run the risk of developing bureaucracy, and of reducing the scope of popular participation in the decisions and administration of the Church. Latitude for diversity in the life of the Christian community is to be safeguarded, but no one polity will automatically insure it or preclude it. Even Rome, with its high degree of centralization, has allowed diversity in the monastic orders, whereas churches with a congregational polity sometimes find ways to stifle variety.

The sum of the matter is that the entire situation is complicated and every proposed union must be considered separately. I have favored the union of the Congregational-Christian and the Evangelical-Reformed. They have a common Reformed tradition. They are relatively small and their strength lies in different geographical areas so that the remnant of each in the territory of the other can provide a larger fellowship. But approval of this union does not entail endorsement of any and every other union. All separation is not scandal and sin. There are times when protests are necessary, and if the protestors are ousted the sin at any rate is not on their side. Moreover, a division may be unifying, because, although it rends the structure, it may revivify the spirit. On the other hand, obviously there is no point in continuing schisms long after the point for which the dissenters contended has been achieved.

The breath of friendliness blown by Pope John provides a new atmosphere for Catholic-Protestant discussions. But, as a leader of the World Council has remarked, thus far we have been engaged not in a dialogue, but in a dialogue about a dialogue. We have still to come to grips with the issues which divide, and with them these articles are concerned.

R. H. B.

Contents

I.   The Unity of Man and the Unity of the Church

1. The Unity of Mankind in the Classical-Christian Tradition

One world is the cry of our generation. By it we mean not merely to assert the fact of globalism, but to voice an aspiration for the spiritual unity of mankind. We differ as to how it is to be achieved. Some are occupied in the drafting of blueprints for the external. Others regard all plans as fatuous apart from a change in values. Albert Schweitzer long ago told us that the disease of our time is moral and the cure lies in no new formula but in that balance of self-fulfillment and self-effacement in harmonious living which is the core of the classical-Christian tradition. To some extent this ideal has received historical embodiment, notably in the Roman Empire and in Christendom, a somewhat amorphous entity hovering between an idea and an area. Christendom meant Christianity and Europe, but not the whole of either. The Byzantines and the Russians, though Christian, were scarcely included. The Jews and the Arabs, though European, were left out. Christendom was Christian Europe.

This paper will seek to trace the course of Christendom with an eye to its contribution to the unity of mankind. The ingredients of Christendom are classical and Christian, and they lie in the realms alike of idea and of the concrete. The Greeks developed the concept of cosmopolitanism; the Romans established the *Pax Romana*, in which were further elaborated the ideals of peace and humanity.

Cosmopolitanism was built up actually by an expansion of loyalties. First came the Greek city-state. Then the association of Hellenes who, possessed already of a common culture, were first made conscious of their unity by a common foe. The Persians

First published in *The Albert Schweitzer Jubilee Book,* ed. A. A. Roback (Cambridge, Mass., 1945) .

taught the Greeks to think of themselves as Hellenes.[1] The concept which accompanied this stage of development was that of concord (ὁμόνοια).[2] It meant not universal harmony but only pan-Hellenic unity. Wars between the Greeks were inappropriate. Their conflicts indeed should not be dignified by the name of war, but rather should be called "disturbances," to be conducted with a mitigation of asperities. Such were the views of Plato and Aristotle, who never divested themselves of the restrictions of provincialism.[3]

The one who expanded Hellenism until it became a name for culture rather than for race was Alexander the Great. By some he is credited with being the first to conceive of the unity of mankind.[4] His actual program, however, did not exceed the attempt to form a ruling caste compounded of Macedonians and Persians, and among the populace the stimulation of commerce and the planting of cities with Greek nuclei throughout the East.[5] Unmistakably after Alexander we meet with genuine cosmopolitanism. Earlier in Greece the term had been coined in the mint of Diogenes and the connotations were negative. To be cosmopolitan was to be deracinated. After Alexander cosmopolitanism came to be conceived in terms not of the eradication but of the expansion of loyalty in concentric rings from the family to the city-state and to the world. Another approach was made by Stoicism, which conceived of unity among men not as being built up by stages from the bottom but as already existing and needing only to be recognized throughout the universe as a whole. The world is one; harmony is the law of its being. The heavens above, the earth beneath, and even the animals are integrated by an all-pervading Reason which is intelligence in man and meaningfulness in the world. Animals of the same species

---

[1] J. B. Bury, *The Hellenistic Age* (Cambridge, 1923), p. 24, where a change in the meaning of barbarian is discovered in the seventh book of Herodotus. The subject is more fully treated by Julius Jüthner, *Hellenen und Barbaren* (Leipzig, 1923).

[2] Hans Kramer, *Quid valeat ὁμόνοια in litteris graecis* (Göttingen, 1915).

[3] Plato, *Rep.* V. 469-471. Aristotle's advice to Alexander to emancipate the Greeks and enslave the barbarians is recorded in Plutarch, *Mor.* 329B.

[4] W. W. Tarn, "Alexander the Great and the Unity of Mankind," *Proceedings of the British Academy*, XIX (1933), 123-166.

[5] Helmut Berve, "Die Verschmelzungspolitik Alexanders des Grossen," *Klio*, XXXI (1938), 135-168.

do not devour each other. How much less should men?[6] They will be able to live in peace if they order their lives in accord with the law of nature, a concept vague in content but vast in import of a moral order of the universe higher than the laws of states, self-validating through the Nemesis which overtakes those who violate the structure of the cosmos. Justice and good faith are among its ingredients.[7]

The Greeks were never able to give concrete embodiment to their ideal. The nearest approach was interstate arbitration in which they excelled all the peoples of antiquity. Such continuous peaceful settlement of disputes was, however, intermittent and impotent to save the Greeks from devouring one another.[8] Nor did the empire of Alexander correspond to his ideals. Hellenism was disseminated but the peoples of the East were never so united as were to be those of the West.[9]

Unification, in fact, was to be the work of Rome. She was able to achieve it partly because she did not intend to. Of real imperialism at Rome before Julius Caesar one cannot properly speak. The earlier expansion was gradual and grudging, motivated by a desire for security.[10] Rome was aided by a policy epitomized in the words "concord" and "magnanimity." The first was the Greek

---

[6] Viktor Engelhardt, *Weltbürgertum und Friedensbewegung*, I (Berlin, 1930); Moses Hadas, "From Nationalism to Cosmopolitanism in the Greco-Roman World," *Journal of the History of Ideas*, IV, 1 (1943), 105-111; Hugh Harris, "Greek Origins of the Idea of Cosmopolitanism," *International Journal of Ethics*, XXXVIII (1927), 1-10; Julius Kaerst, *Die antike Idee der Oekumene* (Leipzig, 1903); Johannes Mewaldt, "Das Weltbürgertum in der Antike," *Die Antike*, II (1926), 177-187; Max Mühl, *Die antike Menschheitsidee* (Leipzig, 1928); Karl Reinhardt, *Kosmos und Sympathie, neue Untersuchungen über Poseidonius* (Munich, 1926).

[7] Auguste Bill, "La morale et la loi dans la philosophie antique," *Études d'histoire et de philosophie religieuses (Strasbourg, Université)*, XVIII (1928); Walther Ekstein, "Das antike Naturrect in sozialphilosophischer Beleuchtung," *Schriften der soz. Gesell. in Wien*, II (1926).

[8] A. H. Raeder, *L'arbitrage international chez les Hellenes* (New York, 1912); Jackson Harvey Ralston, *International Arbitration from Athens to Locarno* (Stanford University Press, 1929); Frank M. Russel, *Theories of International Relations* (New York, 1936); M. N. Tod, *Greek International Arbitration* (Oxford, 1913).

[9] Karl Holl, "Das Fortleben der Volksprachen in Kleinasien in nachchristlicher Zeit," *Gesammelte Aufsätze*, II, 12 (Tübingen, 1928).

[10] Towney Frank, *Roman Imperialism* (New York, 1914).

homonoia, and meant no more than unity at home, with the discouragement of all uprisings like those of the Gracchi, even though in the interests of justice.[11] Magnanimity, however, applied to those without. The word itself exhibits an interesting development. To begin with the *magna anima,* the quality of the great soul, (μεγαλοψυχία) was the courage of the warrior. Under Stoic influence it came to be the imperturbability arising from the mastery of the passions. Cicero voiced the new meaning when he exhorted Julius Caesar to forgo the revenge of a Marius or a Sulla by treating his vanquished rivals with largeness of spirit, with magnanimity. The word had thus become a synonym for clemency, to whom as a goddess the Senate under Julius Caesar erected a temple.[12] To this divinity Rome had long paid homage and she had her reward. At the approach of Hannibal the Italians declined to throw off the yoke and by the end of the Republican period the Samnites, Bruttians, Umbrians and the other Italians had all become neo-Romans.[13]

There was one exception to Roman clemency, namely Carthage. Her demolition was fraught with ill alike for Italy and for Africa. Before the event, Scipio Nascica foretold that the elimination of the foe would leave Rome a prey to internal dissension.[14] In the ensuing disorders Sallust discerned the fulfillment of his prediction and the explanation of Roman degeneracy.[15] In Africa the reduction of the Punic population left a residue of resentment. The like was not true elsewhere. Despite the brutality of the conquests, Spain and Gaul became cordially Roman; and for that matter, in Africa, the Roman element was more Latin than Rome herself. Coincident with the western was the eastern expansion of

[11] Eiliv Skard, "Zwei religiös-politische Begriffe Euergetes-Concordia," *Det Norske Videnskapsakademi Oslo,* hist.-filos.-Kl. II, 2 (1931).

[12] Helfried Dahlmann, "Clementia Caesaris," *Neue Jahrbücher für Wiss. und Jugendbildung,* X (1934), 17-26; Arthur Elias, *De notione vocis Clementia* (Königsberg, 1912); Ulrich Knoche, "Magnitudo animi," *Philologus,* Suppl. Bd. XXVII, 3 (1935).

[13] Michael Rostovtzeff, "Horace," *Yale Review* (Autumn, 1936), 101-118.

[14] Matthias Gelzer, "Nasicas Widerspruch gegen die Zerstörung Karthagos," *Philologus,* LXXXVI (1930-1931), 261-299.

[15] Georg Schörner, *Sallust und Horaz über den Sittenverfall und die sittliche Erneuerung Roms* (Erlangen, 1934).

Rome. Although her conquests engendered temporary bitterness —witness the butchery of Romans by Mithridates—yet many peoples welcomed the termination of their dissensions through the imposition of a single sway. The rule of Rome was accepted as a boon by all save the Jews, who were celebrated in antiquity not for avarice but for their turbulence. They alone were permanently unreconciled to Rome.[16]

Two concepts received development under the *Pax Romana.* They were peace and humanity. The concept of peace among the Greeks and Romans was at first negative. For the Greeks *peace* was the absence of war; for the Romans *pax* was a pact to abstain from fighting. But peace for the Greeks soon came to be esteemed as the bestower of plenty. Prior to the fourth century, she had become a goddess, accompanied in art by a cornucopia.[17] The poet Philemon hailed her as

> The bestower, dearest Zeus, of every treasure,
> Weddings, kindred, children, friends,
> Wealth, health, wheat, wine, and pleasure.[18]

Peace as an ideal was associated with the prevalent notion of the Golden Age lost through the fall of man.[19] Hesiod portrayed its progressive deterioration from the age of gold characterized by

---

[16] Ernest A. Baumann, *Beiträge zur Beurteilung der Römer in der antiken Literatur* (Rostok, 1930); Luigi Castiglioni, "Motivi antiromani nella tradizione storica antica," *R. Ist. Lombardo di Scienze,* Rendiconti Ser. 2, 61 (1928), 625-639; Harald Fuchs, *Der geistige Widerstand gegen Rom in der antiken Welt* (Berlin, 1938).

[17] Michael Rostovtzeff, *A Social and Economic History of the Hellenistic World,* 3 vols. (Oxford, 1941), 1358-1359; bibliographical notes; εἰρήνη in Gerhard Kittel, *Theologisches Wörterbuch zum Neuen Testament,* II (1933–); *Pax* in W. H. Roscher, *Ausführliches Lexikon der griech. und röm. Mythologie* (Leipzig, 1886-1937); Bruno Keil, EIPHNH, *Berichte Sächs. Gesell. der Wiss.,* philol.-hist. Kl. LXVIII (1916); Wallace E. Caldwell, "Hellenic Conceptions of Peace," *Columbia Univ. Studies in Hist., Econ., & Public Law,* LXXXIV, 2 (1919); Harald Fuchs, *Augustin und der antike Friedensgedanke* (Berlin, 1926); Wilhelm Nestle, "Der Friedensgedanke in der antiken Welt," *Philologus,* Suppl. Bd. XXXI, 1 (1938).

[18] *Comicorum Atticorum Fragmenta,* ed. Theodor Kock (Leipzig, 1884), Philemon, Fr. 71.

[19] Arthur O. Lovejoy and George Boas, *Primitivism and Related Ideas in Antiquity* (Baltimore, 1935).

peace and plenty.[20] In Roman letters the great popularizer of the theme was Ovid.[21] This whole tradition was embodied in fact and in symbol in the *Pax Romana*. Then for the first time at Rome peace became a goddess with her altar, the *Ara Pacis* adorned with a cornucopia.[22] Virgil celebrated the age of Augustus as the restoration of the Age of Gold.[23] Emperors as the makers of peace were styled the sons of God.[24]

Another concept developed by imperial Rome was that of humanity. The idea was elaborated by a group of aristocrats in the circle of Scipio Africanus, the conqueror alike of Carthage and of Hellas, who became himself the captive of the Greeks and patronized distinguished fugitives. Among them the Stoic Panaitios undertook to reconstruct Stoicism as a code for conquerors. The key word was humanity, which meant not softness but civility, good breeding, the cultivated life, the epitome of the ideal of self-fulfillment.[25] Under the *Pax Romana* humanity was further humanized. For Seneca it meant that man is sacred to man.[26] Humanity became the sister of peace. Seneca combines the themes when he writes, "We punish murderers and what shall we say of wars and massacres which we laud because they destroy whole nations? ...

[20] *Erga*, 109-120, 276f.

[21] *Metamorphoses* I. 98. Cf. *Fasti* I. 719f; *Pont. Ep.* IX. 39, 40.

[22] Viktor Emil Gardthausen, *Augustus und seine Zeit*, 4 vols. (Leipzig, 1891-1904) ; Michael Rostovtzeff, *History of the Ancient World*, 2 vols. (Oxford, 1928) , II, plate XXXVII.

[23] T. R. Glover, *Studies in Virgil* (London, 1904) ; Wilhelm Weber, "Der Prophet und sein Gott, eine Studie zur vierten Ekloge Virgils," *Beihefte zum alten Orient*, III (1925).

[24] Hans Windisch, "Friedensbringer-Gottessöhne," *Zeitschrift für die neuentestamentliche Wissenschaft*, XXIII (1924), 240-260.

[25] Richard Harder, "Nachträgliches zu Humanitas," *Hermes*, LXIX (1934), 64-67, 74; Friedrich Marx, *Zur Geschichte der Barmherzigkeit im Abendlande* (Bonn, 1917); M. Ott, "Die Humanitätslehren heidnischer Philosophie um die Zeit Christi," *Theol. Quartalschrift*, LII (1870) , 355-402; Rudolf Pfeiffer, "Humanitas Erasmiana," *Studien der Bibliothek Warburg*, XXII (1931); Max Pohlenz, τὸ πρέπον, *Nachrichten von der Gesell. der Wiss. zu Göttingen*, philol.-hist. Kl. LXXXIX, 1 (1933), 53-92, and "Antikes Führertum, Cicero De Officiis und das Lebensideal des Panaitios," *Neue Wege zur Antike* II, 3 (Berlin, 1934); R. Reitzenstein, *Werden und Wesen der Humanität im Altertum* (Strassburg, 1907); Wilhelm Soltau, "Humanität und Christentum in ihren Beziehungen zur Sklaverei," *Jahr. für das Klass. Altertum*, XXI (1908), 335-350.

[26] *Ep.* 95. 33.

Shameful it is that men, the mildest breed, should delight in mutual bloodshed . . . whereas animals devoid of reason are at peace. Man who is sacred to man is even killed for sport."[27]

The emperors were wise enough to realize that peace and humanity are not of themselves a sufficient basis for the unity of mankind. There must be some deeper spiritual bond and none is deeper than religion. The form adopted was the deification of the ruler, for which there was both a tradition and a spontaneous demand among the peoples of the East, grateful for the Roman peace. With enthusiasm the cult was adopted throughout the Roman world save by the Jews, who in time obtained tacit exemption. Christianity arising out of Judaism continued the same intransigeance, and, when denied the same privileges, carried on the fight not merely until Christians were exempt but until emperors ceased to be gods. In place of the emperor cult as the cement of the empire stepped the Christian religion.

How well suited was Christianity to serve as the bond of the world? Back of Christianity lay Judaism, the most intransigeant of religions and espoused by the most truculent people of the ancient world. The Jews and Christians had their contributions to make to the unity of mankind, but along lines different from those of the Greeks and Romans. The concrete achievement of the Jews was the demonstration that a people without political autonomy and without a fixed abode could for seven centuries preserve itself as a nation. But this could only be by resistance to assimilation. Here was ample proof that the unity of mankind must be achieved by some other method than the obliteration of diversity. Yet the very particularism of the Jews was derived from loyalty to the loftiest of all unities, the unity of God. Monotheism is the legacy of Israel. It was implicit in the religion of Moses when Israel at Sinai made a covenant with the god of the storm-cloud, bound to no locality and to no people. Unconstrained, he chose Israel to be his people and might reject them if they failed to remember his precepts to do them. In defeat Israel was able, therefore, to draw not the obvious inference that her god was weak or nonexistent but rather that he was a righteous god, chastening his chosen through the Assyrian,

[27] *Ep.* 99.

the rod of his anger. In that case he must also be the god of the Assyrian and of all the world.[28] Such monotheism by no means carried with it the unity of mankind. All men indeed are the children and the subjects of God, but some are his chosen, however recalcitrant, and others are rejected though serviceable as instruments. Universalism on such a basis could be attained only through an extension of the covenant. Yahweh had brought the Philistines from Caphtor and the Syrians from Kir just as he had brought Israel from Egypt.[29] "Blessed be Egypt, my people, and Assyria, the work of mine hands, and Israel mine inheritance."[30]

Israel entertained an ideal of universal peace. As with the Greeks and Romans, there were primitivist strains. The age of peace would be the restoration of that idyllic garden where prior to the fall the lion and the lamb lay down together. The initial concept of peace among the Hebrews differed, however, from that of the Greeks and Romans. The Hebrew peace, *shalom,* was always positive and material, almost a synonym for prosperity, invariably religious, never a goddess but a gift of God, who should usher in the age when swords would be beaten into plowshares.[31]

Universalism and particularism were constantly jostling each other in the course of Jewish history. Jeremiah could envisage a universal spiritual covenant. Ruth herself exalted the Moabites and Jonah took pity on the people of Nineveh. But Esther was vindictive and Ezra and Nehemiah endeavored to save Judaism from submersion by a program of exclusiveness in religion and in blood. The Maccabean struggle was largely over this issue. It was

---

[28] Bruno Balscheit, "Alter und Aufkommen des Monotheismus in der Israelitischen Religion," *Beihefte zur Zeitschrift für die alttestamentliche Wissenschaft,* LXIX (1938).

[29] Amos 9:7.

[30] Is. 19:24-25. Compare the article ΔιαΘήκη in Kittel, *Theol. Wörterbuch;* Hugo Gressmann, "Der Ursprung der israelitisch-jüdischen Eschatologie," *Forschungen zur Religion und Literatur des Alten und Neuentestaments,* VI (1905); Matthaeus Hoepers, "Der neue Bund bei den Propheten," *Freiburger Theol. Studien,* XXXIX (1933).

[31] Article Εἰρήνη-Shalom in Kittel, *Theol. Wörterbuch;* Johann Hempel, "Die israelitischen Anschauungen von Segen und Fluch," *Zeitschrift der deutschen Morgandländischen Gesell.,* LXXIX (1925), 20-110. On *Shalom* in proper names, *see* Martin Noth, "Die israelitischen Personennamen," *Beiträge zur Wissenschaft vom Alten und Neuen Testament,* III, 10 (1928).

essentially a civil war and began when a Jewish purist slew a Jewish apostate. The apostate did not think of himself as abandoning Judaism. He adhered to Yahweh while suffering him to become a god among the gods, sending presents to Melkart of Tyre. The purist did not ban all fusion, but Yahweh must be the only god and fusion must take the form of accretion to his characteristics. Particularism triumphed.[32]

In the meantime a dualism was projected into the heavenly places. There is indeed only one god but there are malign spiritual powers, the evil angels, the mighty Lucifer, who "exalted his throne above the stars of God."[33] The demonic powers stir up conflict in heaven and on earth. Their overthrow is possible only through a divine cataclysm in which God will smite the ungodly and establish his kingdom. The unity of mankind requires a preliminary purge and acceptance by the survivors of the rule of God. The only possible concrete embodiment of such a rule would be a theocracy on Mount Zion.[34]

Christianity arising from Judaism in its most particularist period shattered the bonds and made of Judaism not the preservative of a remnant but a religion embracing the world. Though Jesus limited his mission to the house of Israel, yet at the judgment he would divide men, not as Jews and Gentiles on the basis of blood, but as sheep and goats according to their works. The Apostle Paul went further. No man of his generation had a larger series of concentric circles of loyalty. He was of the tribe of Benjamin, of the sect of the Pharisees, of the city of Tarsus, of the empire of Rome and of the new Israel of God. For him there was no longer Jew or Greek.

Christianity gave a new quality to love, humanity and peace. Christian love is not the Greek *eros* whose end is self-fulfillment, but rather *agape,* the utterly self-giving love of that God who gave his only begotten Son for the redemption of the world. The concept of humanity in Christian hands is at once impoverished and en-

[32] Elias Bickerman, *Der Gott der Makkabäer* (Berlin, 1937), and *Die Makkabäer* (Berlin, 1935).

[33] *Is.* 14. 12-17.

[34] Martin Dibellius, "Die Christianisierung einer hellenistischen Formel," *Neue Jahr. für das Klass. Altertum,* XXXV (1915), 224-236.

riched. It was dissociated from culture and equated with charity. *Philanthropia* became philanthropy. The reason may have been simply that in the poverty-stricken Orient almsgiving was the only appropriate expression of humanity.[35] Certainly the dignity of man was not thereby diminished. The Christian Origen was the vindicator of the nobility of man against the aspersions of the pagan Celsus.[36] Peace unquestionably was transformed by Christianity. The materialistic connotations of the Hebrew *shalom* were dropped while the positive and religious characteristics were retained. Peace was not simply as with the Greeks the absence of war, but the antithesis of contention. Positively peace is a reconciling and redeeming power, the companion of life and joy.[37]

Yet Christianity, like Judaism, was fraught with the possibilities of division. That Paul who repudiated the separation of Jew and Gentile introduced the cleavage of elect and non-elect because of which Jacob and Esau strove while yet in the womb of Rebecca. And Paul carried over from Judaism the warfare in the heavenly places. One can understand how Christianity could become at once the most cohesive and most divisive force in history, and paradoxically often most cohesive in society when most divisive within itself.

Christianity was born in the manger of classical civilization as the heir of the cosmopolitanism of Stoicism and the outward peace of Rome. The fusion of all these was to become Christendom, but in the first three centuries Christianity was to be in overt conflict with certain aspects of the others. In the period before Constantine the two great unifiers of mankind, the Roman Empire and the Christian Church, were at odds. To the empire Christianity appeared as unassimilable as Judaism but easier to crush. Particularly in the third century the neo-barbarian emperors from the Danubian provinces regarded the new cult as enervating, as an expression of and an encouragement to the vices of peace. Christians looked with mingled feelings upon the empire. They ap-

[35] Hendrik Bookelstein, "Humanitas bei Lactantius," *Pisiculi, Antike und Christentum,* Ergänzungsband 1 (1939).

[36] Origen, *Contra Celsum* IV. 83.

[37] Consult also the articles "peace" in the *Dictionary of the Apostolic Church* and the *Dictionary of Christ and the Gospels.*

preciated the physical oneness of the world which facilitated the dissemination of their religion. They valued the peace and order of the *Pax Romana* and did not relish the prospect of its collapse. They were torn between prayers for the speedy coming of the Lord and for the postponement of the preliminary cataclysm. They looked upon themselves as strangers in the world, having no city of habitation but at the same time as the soul of the world, the cement of society, the power which restrains the impending chaos.[38]

With Constantine the contest ended in an alliance. The emperor ceased to be a god and became instead a lay bishop. The Church passed from a position of toleration to establishment. Christian writers like Eusebius and, in general, the theologians of the East saw in the union of these two powers the guarantee of unity, harmony, and peace for mankind. The one empire with the one emperor properly belonged to the religion of the one God and the one Lord. Polytheism had been the natural religion for a congeries of city-states inspired by demons to perpetual conflict. Monotheism is the religion conformable to a universal sway in which swords are beaten into plowshares.[39] Constantine himself embraced Christianity in the hope that it would prove the cement of the empire, and great was his disillusionment when this new religion embroiled the empire in ecclesiastical dispute and in turn coalesced with divisions already existent in the social structure and lent to them a theological cast. In the West a quarrel over Church discipline—the Donatist controversy—served to inflame the

[38] Cecil John Cadoux, *The Early Church and the World* (Edinburgh, 1925); Robert Frick, "Die Geschichte des Reich-Gottes-Gedanken in der alten Kirche," *Beihefte zur Zeitschrift für die neuentestamentliche Wissenschaft* VI (1928); Charles Guignebert, *Tertullien, étude sur ses sentiments à l'égard de l'empire et de la société civile* (Paris, 1901); Wilhelm Mangold, *De ecclesia primaeva pro Caesaribus ac magistratibus Romanis preces fundente dissertatio* (Bonn, 1881) ; Guglielmo Massart, *Società e stato nel cristianesimo primitivo, La concezione di Origene* (Padova, 1932); Karl J. Neumann, *Hippolytus von Rom in seiner Stellung zu Staat und Welt* (Leipzig, 1902); Luigi Salvatorelli, "Il pensiero del Cristianesimo antico intorno allo stato," *Bilychnis*, XVI (1920), 264-279, 333-352.

[39] Eusebius, *Or. ad Const.* XVI. 3-8, *Gr.-chr. Schriftsteller*, VII, 249-250. Erich Peterson, *Der Monotheismus als politisches Problem* (Leipzig, 1935) .

smouldering Punic resentment against a Romanized Carthage,[40]
while in the East theological dissension in the Arian controversy
threw whole populations into ferment.[41] The emperor would have
been still more deeply disheartened could he have lived to witness
the contribution of Christianity to the dissolution of the East
where the peoples, never really fused by Hellenism, distintegrated
along ancient racial lines into Copt, Syrian, Armenian and Greek,
but under theological captions. The Christian West, however, like
the classical, was to exhibit greater cohesion. The Donatist schism
was the only one of importance. Arianism never obtained a genuine hold, and when the Nicene theology became dominant in the
empire and Arianism was taken up by the barbarians, St. Ambrose
could feel that Rome had become identified not only with Christianity but with orthodoxy.[42]

Then came the barbarians. The West was overrun. Government broke down. In the midst of this debacle, Christianity was to
exhibit its greatest power of cohesion. At the outset of the new
period, St. Augustine essayed a reappraisal of the relations of
Christianity to society. In so doing he drew together all the threads
of the classical and Christian traditions and thereby did more than
any other to forge the concept of Christendom. Naive identifica-
tion of Christianity and Rome he could by no means accept.
Neither for him was the deepest cleavage that between Roman and
barbarian, nor even that between Christian and pagan, orthodox
and heretical. The great gulf for Augustine, as for Paul, was that
which separates the elect from the non-elect. This difference runs
through all history and leads to a perpetual conflict. Yet history is
more than a tug of war. It is also a decline and an ascent. The fall
of society began when Cain killed Abel and continued through the
murder of Remus by Romulus and the demolition of Carthage by
Rome—Augustine is the first to combine these themes of Roman
degeneracy into a scheme of progressive decline. The upturn came

[40] R. Pierce Beaver, "The Donatist Circumcellions," *Church History*, IV,
2 (1935), 123-133.
[41] Eusebius, *HE*, II. 65-71.
[42] Hans Freiherr von Campenhausen, "Ambrosius von Mailand als Kir-
chenpolitiker," *Arbeiten zur Kirchengeschichte*, XII (Berlin, 1929).

not with Augustus and the founding of the empire, which was only
a necessary evil due to the failure of small states to live at peace.
The first improvement came with the conversion of Constantine,
for great states apart from justice are but robbery on a large scale
and justice is possible only in a Christian state. Peace, however,
will never be completely possible on earth even in a Christian
state, but only in heaven. To equate the *Pax Romana* with the
beating of swords into plowshares is sheer nonsense. Yet man's lust
for domination can be restrained through the coercive measures
exercised by the state in accord with the principles of natural law
and the Gospel. At this point all of the classical, Jewish and
Christian strains are drawn together: justice, the law of nature,
humanity, concord, peace in the cosmos, among the animals and
among men. Yet none of these is ever perfectly realized because of
the discord between faith and unbelief, the *civitas dei* and *civitas
terrena*. The approximation to a synthesis could be accomplished
in practice only when the forces of disorder were restrained
through a state directed by the Church. In other words, the method
must be the one foreshadowed in Judaism of a theocracy.[43]

The medieval Church was eventually to take that way, but
centuries had first to elapse in which the Church proved to be the
great unifier of the West. Truly Constantine had his reward. The
Church performed the marriage for the northern and southern
peoples and could do so more easily because each presented already
a relatively unified culture. But of political unity there was none.
When the *Pax Romana* collapsed, the West, which from this point
on will be our sole concern, presented a welter of separate prin-
cipalities. The Church then assumed the role of her former partner, the empire, and from the outset held together the old Roman
population and gradually won the barbarians from Arianism to
orthodoxy or from paganism to Christianity. Centralizing tendencies in government as represented by Pippin and Charlemagne

---

[43] Harald Fuchs, "Augustin und der antike Friedensgedanke," *Neue philo-
logische Untersuchungen*, III (Berlin, 1926); Heinrich Scholz, *Glaube und Un-
glaube in der Weltgeschichte* (Leipzig, 1911); Margarete Huebner, *Untersuchungen über das Naturrecht in der altchristlichen Literatur* (Bonn, 1918).

received ecclesiastical sanction.[44] The result even in the early Middle Ages was the achievement of something approaching a universal culture. Latin became everywhere the tongue of the learned, and among the common folk the *langue d'oïl* spread until the Normans took it to England, Spain, Sicily and the Holy Land.[45]

But, despite the abortive empire of Charlemagne, in no sense did the West ever enjoy political unification, and the peoples were very conscious of their differences. The Celts had no dealings with the Saxons. The Norman conquest injected still further division into England. In Germany the Frisians, the Saxons and the Bavarians were separate entities. South of the Rhine the Normans and Bretons, the Aquitanians, the Provençals, the Basques and the Spaniards had diversities marked enough. Besides, in Spain there were the Arabs who had in common with the rest of Europe only the classical and not the Christian tradition.[46] Nor were these peoples at peace. Feudalism was a system devised in the interests of security, but security was never attained. Not even the faith proved a common bond, for in Spain the Christian and Moslem fought the Moslem and Christian. The Church then girded her loins in a new effort at unification and peace. Two institutions in particular were fostered, the Peace of God and the Truce of God. The former increased the number of non-combatants and endeavored to insure their immunity. The second limited the time for fighting until scarcely more than one quarter of the year remained as an open season.[47] When the rules of the Peace and Truce of God were not observed, churchmen to enforce the peace raised armies which became themselves so unruly that the cities were constrained to raise other armies to put them down. Then the popes thought of that ancient device for promoting peace at

[44] Hans von Schubert, *Geschichte der christlichen Kirche im Frühmittelalter* (Tübingen, 1921).

[45] Ernest Barker, "Unity in the Middle Ages," in *The Unity of Western Civilization*, ed. F. S. Marvin (Oxford, 1915).

[46] Richard Wallach, "Das abendländische Gemeinschaftsbewusstsein im Mittelalter," *Beiträge zur Kulturgeschichte des Mittelalters und der Renaissance*, XXXIX (Leipzig, 1928).

[47] Ludwig Huberti, *Studien zur Rechtsgeschichte der Gottesfrieden und Landfrieden*, I (Ansbach, 1892), 429.

home by provoking war abroad. The crusades began with a plea for the old Greek concord applied to Europe.[48]

No doubt the crusades did manage to promote a sense of Christendom against the Turk. Before the movement was spent, in the thirteenth century came that period of Europe's history in which the Israelitish theocratic ideal was most fully realized. The West had become more genuinely unified in thought and act than ever before since the collapse of the *Pax Romana*. The pope was the overlord, claiming jurisdiction wherever sin was involved, and where is it not? The courts of the Church and the canon law provided a universal legal machinery. No secular monarch was so widely and so well obeyed as was Pope Innocent III.[49] In the realm of thought Aquinas gathered up the strands from classical, Christian, Jewish and Arabic sources and constructed a pattern of society ruled by the pope and the emperor in accord with justice, reason and the law of nature.

But we must not wax too lyrical over the thirteenth century and suffer ourselves to be deluded into regarding it as a golden age, by returning to which we shall achieve our felicity. It was scarcely so peaceful as the age of the Antonines. Pope Innocent III managed only to keep the lid from blowing off the cauldron of Europe, not to prevent the brew from spilling over. The fourth crusade, instead of recovering Jerusalem, captured Constantinople and further embittered the relations of Greek and Latin Christians. The crusading ideal itself was transferred to Europe to envenom the conflicts of European states. The very age of unity witnessed the revival of a long dormant sectarianism in the Albigenses, Waldenses, Fraticelli and their ilk. The Church then endeavored to enforce unity by extermination or segregation. The Jew was sent to the Ghetto. Yet the Inquisition, devised to insure unity, became a tool of the rising national state before which, at the turn of the fourteenth century, the papacy itself succumbed. Dante's dream of world peace under a universal monarch was only an

---

[48] Carl Erdmann, "Die Entstehung des Kreuzzugsgedankens," *Forschungen zur Kirchen und Geistesgeschichte*, VI (Stuttgart, 1935) ; Bede Jarrett, *Social Theories of the Middle Ages* (London, 1926) .

[49] R F. Wright, *Medieval Internationalism* (London, 1930) .

epitaph, and the intellectual synthesis of Aquinas disintegrated in the hands of Scotus and Occam.[50]

The age of the Renaissance in the fourteenth and fifteenth centuries was marked by divergent tendencies. On the one hand the unity of Christendom was disrupted by the rise of a new principle of cohesion operating only within limited areas, namely nationalism. In that day it was a step toward unification. In France, for example, such peoples as the Aquitanians, Provençals, Normans, Bretons, Burgundians and the French proper were welded into a single nation.[51] Unmolested travel favored the exchange of goods and ideas and the building up of a common vernacular. Nationalism up to a point marked a distinct advance over the particularism of feudalism. But it collided with and weakened the universalism of the empire and of the Church, which itself became nationalized.

To offset the divisive tendencies of the new nationalism the humanists endeavored to revive the ancient classical picture of the unity of mankind. Petrarch resuscitated *humanitas* as an ideal of the man both cultivated and humane. Erasmus was the spokesman of the state as a moral organism within and without. The new nations should be the components of a single Christendom bound with adamantine chains in that harmony which holds not only men but also the stars and the beasts in the unity of the spirit and the bond of peace. Erasmus represented that cosmopolitan outlook which after the demise of Christendom has remained to us as "European culture."[52] It is very largely a secular culture and for

[50] Rudolf Stadelmann, "Vom Geist des ausgehenden Mittelalters," *Deutsche Vierteljahrschrift für Literaturwissenschaft und Geistesgeschichte*, XV (1929) ; H. Finke, "Weltimperialismus und national Regungen im späteren Mittelalter," *Freiburger Wiss. Gesell.* IV (1916); Hans Prutz, "Die Friedensidee im Mittelalter," *Sitzungsberichte der kön. Bay. Ak. der Wiss.*, philos.-philol.-hist. Kl. (1915) .

[51] Bernhard Schmeidler, "Die Bedeutung des späteren Mittelalters für die deutsche und europäische Geschichte," *Hist. Vierteljahrschrift*, XXIX (1934-1935) , 93-108.

[52] Hedwig Hintze, "Der nationale und der humanitäre Gedanke im Zeitalter der Renaissance," *Euphorion*, XXX (1929) , 112-137; Pierre Mesnard, *L'essor de la philosophie politique au XVIe siècle* (Paris, 1936) ; Rudolf Pfeiffer, "Humanitas Erasmiana," *Studien der Bibliothek Warburg*, XXII (1931) ; Inés Thürlemann, *Erasmus von Rotterdam und Joannes Ludovicus Vives als Pacifizten* (Freiburg, Schweiz, 1932) .

that reason is ceasing even to be culture and is powerless to unite. The process of secularism had its inception in the Renaissance when even a pope could seek an alliance with the Turk. Into the midst of such a Church fell a flare from Wittenberg.

The Protestant Reformation has frequently been represented as the great disrupter and Luther as the render of the seamless robe. In a sense unquestionably he was, and here appears the paradox that Christianity is never more cohesive than when it is divisive. Christian unity is based not so much upon an expanding sense of kinship among men as upon loyalty to the single truth of God. And when differing concepts of that truth divide, still the common assumptions may unite. Protestantism arrested secularism not only in those areas which broke with the Church of Rome but even within Catholicism itself. The Catholic Church is never so alive as when confronted by a vigorous competitor.

Outwardly, of course, Christendom was unintentionally partitioned. Luther meant to reform the Church as a whole.[53] Instead he provoked a proliferation of sects and a disruption of outward unity in which Protestants themselves were not to acquiesce for a century.[54] At the same time they took to themselves the existing divisions of society and thereby intensified the strains. In Germany they buttressed themselves by an alliance with feudal particularism against the universalism of the empire, in Poland and France with the ancient nobility against the centralizing tendencies of the crown, in England the reverse, but in Hungary they welcomed the Turks against the less tolerant Hapsburgs. The seamless robe indeed was rent. At the same time Protestantism exhibited a cohesion of its own even in the political sphere. Calvinism, for example, served as a bond between French Switzerland, France, Hungary, the Low Countries, Scotland and England, and the political unification of the two latter was made possible only by

[53] Kurt Matthes, "Das Corpus Christianum bei Luther," *Studien zur Geschichte der Wirtschaft und Geisteskultur*, V (1929) ; Friedrich Meinecke, "Luther über christliches Gemeinwesen und Christlichen Staat," *Hist. Zeitschrift*, CXXI (1920) .

[54] Franklin L. Baumer, "The Church of England and the Common Corps of Christendom," *Journal of Modern History* XVI, 1 (March, 1944) .—"England, the Turk and the Common Corps of Christendom," *American Historical Review* L. 1 (October, 1944) ; John T. McNeill, *Unitive Protestantism* (New York, 1930).

the adherence of Scotland to the reform.[55] Yet to say all this on one side or the other is to leave unmentioned the point of greatest significance. Protestantism revived Christianity. Protestantism made religion a dominant concern of men even in politics for another century and a half. Luther stripped the peel and saved the core of Christendom.

The same thing happened twice over in the course of English history in the seventeenth and in the eighteenth centuries through the Puritan Revolution and the Methodist revival. Puritanism saw another flowering of sects, Presbyterian, Congregational, Baptist, Quaker, Ranter, Seeker, Familist, Fifth Monarchy, etc., down even to individuals like John Smythe who believed that no one was competent to baptize him save himself. Surely here was the knell of Christendom. Nevertheless, when before had England ever been so truly and so consciously a Christian nation as during the Puritan Revolution? If today in Parliament, in labor unions, in assemblies of social scientists, an appeal to Christian norms is not irrelevant, to the Puritan Revolution goes largely the credit.

Yet not wholly. The eighteenth century saw another split in the outer structure—the emergence of another sect and at the same time another welding of the nation in the Christian mould through the Methodist revival. John Wesley kindled the total religious life of England, and above all he won the working classes for the faith. That is why the labor movement in England did not embrace dialectical materialism. The workers and the employers alike talked in the vernacular of the Gospels.

Unquestionably, however, Christian divisions after the sixteenth century did present difficulties with regard to common programs of action. As a basis for international relations not only the canon law of the Catholics but even the Bible of the Protestants appeared too controversial. For that reason an attempt was made to establish the unity of mankind upon the classical, divorced from the Christian ingredients of Christendom. Grotius formulated an international law on the basis of the natural law of Stoicism which is valid also among non-Christians, valid even if there be no God.

[55] Gerhard Ficker, *Das ausgehende Mittelalter und seine Verhältnis zur Reformation* (Leipzig, 1903).

The eighteenth century witnessed the flourishing of this tendency which cannot be called secularist in the full sense. Often the persons who espoused the divorce of certain areas of life from religion were themselves men of piety who, in the interests of unity, introduced this dichotomy. One senses that notably in the attitude of the framers of the American Constitution who excluded prayer from political deliberations.[56] The age witnessed the achievement of some measure of European unity, especially in the cultural sense. Erasmus came into his own,[57] religious persecution died down, science was cultivated across national boundaries and for the first time Russia came within the orbit of European culture. The leaders of thought occupied themselves with plans for universal peace.[58]

But the nineteenth and twentieth centuries have been marked by ever-widening fissures of national jealousies,[59] issuing in a death struggle between rival views of life. The cleavage is often described as one between Germany and the West. Differences of opinion are evident in the attempts to discover precisely wherein it consists. Some see the rift primarily as an example of the divisions of Christendom. Germany is Lutheran, marked by a supine acquiescence in political control. The West is Calvinist, intransigent and democratic. Others point to the suppression of sectarian Anabaptism in Germany in favor of a sole established church in contrast to the triumph of the sects in England and North America.[60] Another writer points to the diverse outworkings of Methodism in England and Pietism in Germany. Methodism consolidated England; Pietism engendered in Germany a high pitch of emotional enthusiasm at the very time when "the quest for the historical Jesus" was injecting doubts as to the objects of religious veneration. The enthusiasm then shifted to the nation. Despite social equality

---

[56] Otto Gierke, *Natural Law and the Theory of Society 1500 to 1800*, tr. Ernest Barker, 2 vols. (Cambridge, 1934).

[57] Werner Kaegi, "Erasmus im achtzehnten Jahrhundert," *Gedenkschrift zum 400. Todestage des Erasmus vom Rotterdam* (Basel, 1936), 205-227.

[58] Jacob ter Meulen, *Der Gedanke der International Organization in seiner Entwicklung 1300-1800*, 3 vols. (Hague, 1917-1940).

[59] Friedrich Meinecke, *Weltbürgertum und Nationalstaat* (Munich, 1922).

[60] Eduard Heimann, "The Great Gulf Between Germany and the West," *Christendom* V, 3 (1940), and the ensuing discussion.

in the Pietist cells the masses were not enlisted and drifted into antireligious Marxist Socialism. Germany has known nothing comparable to the British labor movement manned often by Methodist lay preachers.[61] These interpreters thus see the difference in terms of Christian divisions.

But this is not the deepest difference, affirmed Ernst Troeltsch. The great gulf between Germany and the West lies in this, that she has rejected the classical tradition of natural law as the basis for the unity of mankind. The Romantic Movement in Germany swept out the law of nature, valid for all men and accessible to all through the light of universal reason, and erected in its place an irrational dynamism welling up in peoples endowed with vital energy and empowering them to forge their own morality.[62] This is the true secularism, the true paganism, which has demolished alike the Christian and the classical unity.

Yes, but this is not exclusively a German disease, and the gulf is not simply between Germany and the West, declares Gerhard Ritter. And the rift did not begin with the Romantic Movement but rather in the period of the Renaissance. The secularist attitude was that of Machiavelli. The Christian-classical view in the same period was espoused by Thomas More. In the course of the succeeding centuries small and isolated nations have talked in terms of political moralism and universal right, such as the Dutch and the English. By no accident was Thomas More an Englishman and Grotius a Hollander. On the other hand the great states on the Continent have been readier to trample on all scruples for the sake of security. Now one, now another, has been the exponent of Machiavellianism. Under Napoleon it was France; under Bismarck, it was Germany.[63]

The cleavage is as old and as deep as that which Augustine discovered between the *civitas Dei* and the *civitas terrena*. It is a conflict capable of multiple manifestations, of the church against

[61] Kappel S. Pinson, *Pietism as a Factor in the Rise of German Nationalism* (New York, 1934) .

[62] Ernst Troeltsch, "The Ideas of Natural Law and Humanity in World Politics," tr. Ernest Barker in appendix to Vol. I of Otto Gierke, *Natural Law* (Cambridge, 1934).

[63] Gerhard Ritter, *Machtstaat und Utopie* (Munich, 1940) .

the state or the state against the church, of Germany against the West or of the West against the East. It is a conflict which lies within the breast of every man. In order to unite, Christianity must first divide. He who came to bring peace cast fire upon the earth. With the ideals of a secular paganism there can be no truce. But that power which is so divisive is of all the most cohesive. Our hope lies in the classical-Christian tradition of the unity of mankind. And no institution in these crumbling days has exhibited such constancy in resistance to tyranny, no institution has preserved its own international structure and mentality so faithfully, as has the Christian church.[64]

[64] Henry P. Van Dusen, *What is the Church Doing?* (New York, 1943).

2. A Critique of *A History of the Ecumenical Movement*

One of the outstanding productions of the period between the first and second Assemblies of the World Council of Churches is this History of the Ecumenical Movement. The work has been done just at the right moment, since at many points it has been possible to draw on the recollections of the pioneers, who brought the modern ecumenical movement into existence in 1910, and after many years of service are handing over their tasks to a younger generation. Memory tends to be short, and each new generation tends to start afresh, as though nothing had ever happened before in the ecumenical world.

This admirable and comprehensive history is a symposium. The simplest way to present a review is to take up each contribution separately and to provide first a digest and then a comment.

Introduction by Stephen Charles Neill

The first brief introductory section sketches the history of unity and division from the early period of the Church until the Reformation. A clear and adequate account is given of the divisions in the early Church: the Montanists, the Novatianists before Constantine, the Donatists and the Arians during his reign and the subsequent emergence of the Eastern Dissidents. The story then turns to the West and describes the origins of the Cathari, Waldenses, Hussites and Wyclifites. Account is taken of the various attempts at reunion, particularly between the Eastern and the Western churches. The conclusion is that complete unity has never

First published as a book review in *The Ecumenical Review* VI (July, 1954). The book, *A History of the Ecumenical Movement 1517-1948*, was edited by Ruth Rouse and Stephen Charles Neill, S.P.C.K. (London, 1954).

been a reality and that the ideal of unity has always been entertained.

Certain observations and reflections might perhaps have been fruitfully introduced. To begin with, divisions may be classified as to whether they arise from within the church through divergent attitudes on such subjects as creeds, discipline and liturgy. Again, they may arise from without in case the church becomes so identified with the contemporary culture as to be herself rent by the cleavages in the social structure. There may then come to be churches of the rich; churches of the poor; churches of the black or of the white, brown or yellow; churches of the East; churches of the West; Semitic versus Greek; Greek versus Roman; Latin versus Teuton and so on. Such a distinction is not unimportant for the question of unity. If the rift arises from within, it may be derived from the very vitality of Christianity which inspires intense conviction. If it comes from without, it may be due to the feebleness of Christianity which has not been able to surmount the divisions in the culture. The remedy in each case will obviously have to be different.

Another point worthy of reflection is that Christianity seems to be a unifying force within a culture when the state is weak and a disruptive force if the state is strong. At any rate, under Constantine and his successors the Church proved to be a divisive element within the empire, which came to be embroiled in ecclesiastical divisions; but when government broke down in the West, the Church did more than any other institution to create a unified culture, namely Christendom. During that period for 800 years the Church herself was without divisions.

Another very interesting question is whether historically there may not be a rhythm of division and reunion. The first four Christian centuries were marked by many divisions. From the beginning of the fifth to the middle of the twelfth century in the West, there were no divisions to speak of; but in the late twelfth century sects proliferated up to and through the period of the Reformation. The seventeenth century marked the peak, at any rate in England, of sectarianism. Then came the recession and the rise of the ecumenical spirit. One would not wish to infer a cycle theory of history, but one does observe a certain ebb and flow.

Chapter I: The Ecumenical Idea and Efforts to Realize it,
1517 to 1618 by John T. McNeill

Protestantism was so divisive in part because it emerged at
the time when Europe was already split along national lines.
Reforms arose independently in separate political units and then
were unable to achieve unity. National churches were founded in
Sweden, Denmark-Norway, England and Scotland. Then arose
sectarian movements within Protestantism such as Anabaptism.
At the same time Reformation writings constantly affirmed the
reality of the one holy catholic Church. The Protestants accepted
the ecumenical creeds, described the Church visible as catholic,
cherished conciliarism and deplored schism wherever the Word
and the scriptural sacraments were present.

Many attempts at union were made between the Roman
Catholic Church and the Protestants and between the Protestant
varieties. Erasmus worked continually for pacification and reunion
as did his followers Witzel and Cassander. The Colloquy of Ratis-
bon in 1541 was an effort to reconcile the differences. It failed. So
also did the Augsburg Interim, and there followed the Peace of
Augsburg with a territorial division. In France the Colloquy of
Poissy brought together Catholics and Huguenots but without
result.

As between Protestants, Bucer was the great man of concord.
His efforts to unite the Lutherans and Zwingli at Marburg failed
in 1529, but the Wittenberg Concord was achieved in 1536. Luther
was friendly with the Bohemians and hoped that the Brethren and
the Utraquists would unite. Calvin and the Waldensians entered
into fellowship. Calvin cultivated the Wittenbergers and Zurichers
and with the latter achieved unity in the *Consensus Tigurinus* so
that there were now only two rather than three main branches of
Continental Protestantism. In England Cranmer attempted to call
a general council of Protestants. In the reign of Edward VI England became the refuge for many Continental Protestant exiles.

In Poland the Peace of Sendomir of 1570 did not unite but
brought about mutual recognition of three confessions, namely the
Lutherans, the Calvinists and the Bohemians.

Little remains to be added to this admirable survey. One

might note with Hans von Schubert that the Augsburg Confession was an achievement in unity because only one Lutheran confession was submitted rather than several.

A more far-reaching question is whether attempts at church union, for the most part abortive, constituted the most significant background for the ecumenical movement. The concrete gains for unity were exceedingly slight. Reunion could make little headway until there was a greater spirit of tolerance and freedom. Hence in this period the history of the ecumenical movement must to a large degree coincide with the history of the struggle for religious liberty. The sixteenth century made definite gains in that area. Legal recognition within restricted areas was achieved by the Zwinglians in Switzerland, the Lutherans in Germany, the Calvinists in France, and by the Lutherans, Calvinists and Anabaptists in Holland; the English settlement was imbued with the spirit of latitudinarianism.

Chapter II: Ecumenical Activity on the Continent of Europe in the Seventeenth and Eighteenth Centuries by Martin Schmidt

The record of ecumenical attempts during the seventeenth and eighteenth centuries on the continent of Europe is "the history of a yearning but also of a promise." Two great strains of thought were operative—humanism and mysticism. The first stemmed from Erasmus and his disciple Acontius, who minimized dogma and exalted deportment. Acontius in particular popularized the distinction between the essentials and the non-essentials for salvation. The former he held were few; the latter were many. In its general tradition are to be placed such protagonists of unity as Casaubon, Calixtus, the Socinians, Grotius and Dury.

Mysticism or "spiritualism," as the Germans call it, looked for the essential in Christianity not to dogma, polity or politics but rather to piety. In this stream we find Schwenkfeld, Arndt, Boehme, Gottfried Arnold, and later on the Pietists Spener, Francke, Zinzendorf, Hochman von Hochenau and Tersteegen.

These two strains are capable of coalescing, and one finds them both in a man like Meiderlin, who coined the saying so dear to the champions of unity "in essentials unity, in non-essentials liberty, in all things charity." Leibnitz was comprehensive of all of these tendencies.

Alongside of these two main themes one finds also, especially among the Reformed, a stress on the political desirability of unity, so for example in Philippe de Mornay.

The groundwork was laid in this period for a practical argument for unity in the interest of missionary effectiveness. Pietism first made Protestantism extensively missionary.

This period saw also the rise of a new form of religious organization highly conducive to the collaboration and ultimately the reunion of the churches. This was the religious society built around some particular idea or objective and inviting from all communions those in sympathy with the particular aim. In 1780 the German Christian Fellowship was founded in Basle. It was interconfessional and international. It gave birth to the Basle Mission House and the Basle Missionary Society and stimulated in Britain the formation of the Bible Society and the Religious Tract Society.

One point in this chapter might, I think, have been explicated more fully, and that is the distinction between the essentials and the non-essentials. This principle is both inclusive and exclusive. It lets down the bars on the non-essentials but may all the more raise them as to the essentials. In particular, the theory of Acontius operated to exclude the Catholics and the Socinians and to include all other varieties of Protestantism. The reason was that Acontius defined the essentials in terms of those beliefs declared by Scripture to be necessary. There are, said he, only two, namely "The just shall live by faith"—this excluded the Catholics who relied on works—and "Believe on the Lord Jesus Christ and thou shalt be saved." This was later interpreted as excluding the Socinians.

One further point of interest is that the distinction between the essentials and the non-essentials could be used to restrict liberty and enforce conformity. The argument was that liberty should be accorded on all those points which are requisite for salvation, but that in the area of the non-essentials, uniformity should be demanded since eternal salvation would not be thereby imperilled.

Such was the position of Anglicans like Laud and Jeremy Taylor. The Puritans found themselves then under the necessity of attacking the whole distinction between the essentials and the non-essentials, since an idea which originated in the interests of liberty was being used as an instrument of restriction. Nevertheless, the idea in the main is one which has contributed alike to liberty and church union.

Chapter III: Ecumenical Movements in Great Britain in the Seventeenth and the Eighteenth Centuries by Norman Sykes

This is the period of the Puritan Revolution which marked actually the apex of sectarian tendencies in England. The first and most formidable division was that between the Presbyterians and the Anglicans, doubly so after the union of the two kingdoms because thereafter one political entity had two established churches. The Presbyterians addressed themselves to the crown with a request in the Millinary Petition for the redress of grievances, but the king did not so much satisfy "their scruples as propound his pleasure." The attempt of Charles I and Laud to impose upon Scotland the Anglican Prayer Book precipitated the Civil War. Then Presbyterianism asserted itself in England with the desire to be dominant, but there was the necessity of accommodation to the newly risen Independents and the Baptists. Cromwell sought to comprehend all three. After the Restoration Charles II tried to comprehend the Episcopalians and the Presbyterians, but the latter rejected his demands and after 1662 found themselves among the Dissenters. Further attempts at comprehension failed and instead indulgence was granted to the sects in the Act of Toleration in 1689. The Presbyterians then joined with the Independents in the Heads of Agreement, but their "Happy Union was only of brief duration."

During this period a number of men were active proponents of unity: Baxter, Dury, Basire, Jablonski and Archbishop Wake and in the eighteenth century John Wesley. One reason for the paucity of achievement was the necessity of enlisting the state. A very notable accomplishment, however, was the S.P.C.K., which, though Anglican, collaborated with the Lutherans and the Reformed on the Continent and in missionary endeavours.

The "remarkable experiment in comprehension" of Oliver Cromwell might be even more stressed. What it meant was the abandonment of the national church in favor of a national religion. The closest association of church and state was preserved; yet not one church served as the basis but rather three: the Presbyterian, the Independent and the Baptist. One might note also in this period the rise of an idea which is the antithesis of the ecumenical unless the ecumenical can surmount separateness in organization. One finds among the Baptists an abandonment of the ideal of a single church in favor of ecclesiastical pluralism, on the ground that monopoly is intolerable and competition is wholesome. Also one finds among the Independents and notably Milton the contention that variety is the law of life. The question then comes to be whether variety can best be achieved by a multiplicity of sects, each espousing a valid yet different emphasis, or whether it would be better in a single church to find a way to incorporate variety.

Chapter IV: The Orthodox Churches and the Ecumenical Movement Prior to 1910 by Georges Florovsky

The division of East and West was one of geography and language. Political factors strongly entered. The Byzantine Empire declined and disappeared, and the Byzantine church verged on a supine archaism, whereas the West grew politically strong and the Western church looked upon its own variety of Christianity as normal. Nevertheless the conviction was never lost that the Orthodox churches, alike of Constantinople and Moscow, belonged to the Church universal and, in the debates between Catholics and Protestants as to which was the heir of the primitive Church, appeal was made to the Orthodox as arbiters. Again common hostility to Rome often drew together the Orthodox in the East and the Protestants in the West.

This chapter describes the overtures between the Hussites and the Orthodox at the time of the Council of Basel in the fifteenth century. In the sixteenth century the Lutherans approached the Patriarch of Constantinople and sent him a copy of the Augsburg Confession in Greek. "There seems to be little doubt that the translation was in reality made by Melanchthon himself."

In Poland the Orthodox were subject to pleas alike from the Lutherans and from the Roman Catholic Church. Many of them went to Rome and formed a Uniate Church in 1596. To offset this move the Ecumenical Patriarch visited Moscow and accorded to the Russian Church the status of a new patriarchate in 1589. Coincidently in Poland Calvinists, Lutherans and Bohemian Brethren negotiated with the Orthodox. The attempts of Rome to woo the Easterners by offering especially attractive educational facilities in Rome led to the counter move of sending students from the East to the Protestant universities of Germany. Interchanges of opinion on the part of the Lutherans, the Anglicans and the Roman Catholics with the East continued throughout the seventeenth century. The tragic career of Cyril Loukaris, the Ecumenical Patriarch who travelled widely in the West, is a notable illustration.

In the period of Peter the Great, Russia was most open to Western influence. He imitated the national churches of the West and in the schools Orthodoxy was Lutheranised. The eighteenth century saw overtures to the Church of Russia from the Sorbonne on the one hand and from the Non-juring Bishops in England on the other.

In the nineteenth century the Russian Bible Society was willing to collaborate with the British and Foreign Bible Society. The greatest Russian theologian of the period, Philaret, was interested in unity but only on the basis of complete doctrinal agreement. The Oxford Movement in the Anglican Church tried, not too successfully, to convince the Russians that it is possible to be both Catholic and Anglican. Archbishop Tait of Canterbury secured the consent of the Ecumenical Patriarch that Anglicans dying in the East might be buried in Orthodox cemeteries. Unity was thus achieved for the dead. The old Catholics negotiated with the Orthodox churches of the East.

The rejection of Anglican orders by Rome evoked sympathy from the East, and the Ecumenical Patriarch was convinced "that all charity should be extended to the Anglicans." The chapter closes with an account of the views of Soloviev, who believed that the spiritual insight of the Orthodox East, the authority of Rome and the intellectual honesty of Protestantism are actually comprehended in a unity which transcends history.

One is impressed in this chapter by the continual failure and the persistent resumption of conversations between the West and the East. One notes also the role of disunion in the promotion of union. A common enemy makes friends. Hostility to Rome drew together the opponents of Rome. One wonders whether an increasing onslaught from secularism and militant atheism will be necessary in our day to bring about a complete union of the churches.

Chapter V: Christian Unity in Nineteenth-Century America by Don Herbert Yoder

The United States affords the supreme example of the sectarian principle. There are 250 varieties. Even the major denominations are split into such subdivisions as Two-Seed-in-the-Spirit Predestinarian Baptists. The main reason is that all of the European varieties have been transferred to America, and the achievement of complete religious liberty and the separation of church and state have facilitated further divisions, often through sectional and racial schisms. Protestants and Catholics, thrown together on an equal footing, have experienced increasing friction as Catholic strength has been increased by immigration. Relations between Protestants and the Eastern Churches have been more cordial.

Yet from the outset there have been many examples of union and cooperation projected and accomplished. In New England the First Great Awakening was both unitive and divisive. The Congregational churches were split into the Old and New Lights, but the New Lights were brought into closer relations with other revivalist bodies such as the Methodists and the German Pietists. In Pennsylvania Zinzendorf endeavoured to unite all the sects in a cooperative alliance. Unhappily he failed.

The frontier exhibited a battle of the sects with the Baptists ready to corral and immerse Methodist strays, and the mounted Methodists to rope and brand Calvinist calves. Yet the Congregationalists and Presbyterians formed the Plan of Union for joint endeavour (1801-1852) , and the resulting churches were facetiously called Presbygational.

One of the greatest steps toward unity was the development of a technique already well tried in England of an international society founded to achieve particular objectives, some of these specifically religious as in the case of the Missionary, Bible and Sunday School societies and some directed to social ends such as the achievement of peace, temperance and the abolition of slavery.

Then arose a group whose chief objective was the union of all Christians; the Disciples of Christ supposed that by taking their stand on Scripture and Scripture only they would be able to bring together all Christians through what really amounted to secession from the other churches. The outcome was a new denomination. Its witness to unity has been persistent and not without impact.

Certain family reunions have been achieved. The Cumberland and the Northern Presbyterians came together in 1906. The Methodists North and South were rejoined in 1939. The Congregationalists and a related body called "Christians" were united in 1931. The most conspicuous drawing together of the churches has not been by way of organic union but by way of collaboration in common endeavour, notably through the organization of the Federal Council of Churches.

The most striking lesson of the American scene is the demonstration that unity can exist in conjunction with diversity. There is to a very large degree a common Protestant mind. Unhappily it seldom receives a unanimous expression. Nevertheless, the Federal and the new National Councils have been able to muster and make vocal a very extensive Christian witness. Moreover, the reference to 250 varieties is misleading. There may be that number of separate denominations; indeed one would not be surprised if there were more. But there are not so many varieties. The congregational groups form a family, namely the Congregationalists, Baptists and Disciples. The Presbyterians lie in between the congregational and episcopal groups. The so-called peace churches belong together: the Quakers, Mennonites, Schwenckfelders and the Brethren. And then one would need a category for all of the new holiness cults. Four or five classes would comprehend them all.

Chapter VI: Approaches of the Churches Towards Each Other in the Nineteenth Century by Henry Renaud Turner Brandreth

The nineteenth century has been marked by a recovery of the sense of the Church. One result is the formation of six world denominational fellowships: 1. The Lambeth Conference, dating from 1869, unites all Anglicans throughout the world. 2. The American Presbyterian bodies and one in Scotland formed the Alliance of Reformed Churches in 1875. 3. The General Conference of Methodists was established in 1876. 4. The Old Catholics formed the Union of Utrecht in 1889. 5. The International Congregational Council first met in 1891. 6. The Baptist World Alliance was formed in 1905.

In the meantime in Germany, since Pietism and the Enlightenment had both weakened dogma, the drive was for union less along doctrinal lines than on a national basis. Schleiermacher's irenic spirit moved in this direction.

In England among the Anglicans the Evangelicals were ready to commune with all who sincerely follow the Scriptures. Broad Churchmen wished the Church to be so broad as to comprehend the Dissenters. The High Church party envisaged reunion with Rome by distinguishing the Rome of the official definitions, with which unity was possible, and the Rome of popular piety which would have to be corrected. The assertion of Papal infallibility by the Vatican Council in 1870 was a great blow to these hopes. Friendly relations with the Orthodox were cultivated by John Mason Neale and other Anglicans. Birbeck kept the Anglican and the Russian Churches in touch.

Free Churchmen initiated no proposals for union but responded to invitations for conferences. In Scotland the Presbyterian varieties were reduced to two.

In Germany the king of Prussia in 1817 united the Lutheran and Reformed churches. The Jerusalem bishopric was an attempt at collaboration between the Lutherans and the Anglicans in the Holy Land.

In Austria the Reformed and the Lutherans agreed to act together in all dealings with the state, otherwise to be separate.

The old Catholics cultivated mainly Eastern relations.

In Canada all of the Methodists became one in 1884 and all of the Presbyterians in 1875.

Conversations were continuous among many separated groups.

This survey of the nineteenth century conveys the impression that sectarianism was on the ebb, and the ecumenical movement was on the flow. Few new denominations arose: the Plymouth Brethren, the Old Catholics and a few others, but not many. A few secessionist movements resulted from unions but again only a very few. There was, however, a very considerable personal defection from the churches on the part of individuals who under the impact of the new science rejected Christian teaching and under the stress of mounting secularization abandoned Christian standards. One may even wonder whether the impetus to church union may not have sprung from the sense of weakness and a desire by union to arrest the trend and reassert the influence of the church against an increasingly indifferent, if not hostile, world.

Chapter VII: Voluntary Movements and the Changing Ecumenical Climate by Ruth Rouse

This essay, also, is devoted to the nineteenth century and deals with the influence of voluntary movements.

The great drive for the reunion of the churches, the author insists, does not stem from panic occasioned by defections but rather from the zeal of the evangelical awakening concerned to preach Christ rather than to propagate confessions. Protestant missionaries were willing to collaborate with Roman Catholic missionaries. The German Christian Fellowship at Basel actually for some years had a Roman Catholic priest as its secretary.

The Awakening stimulated social reform, and social reform in turn was not confessional; take, for example, the Inner Mission in Germany under Wichern or the campaign against the slave trade in Britain led by the Anglican Wilberforce with the hearty cooperation of the Dissenters. At the same time the Awakening occasioned schisms.

Two forms of evangelical alliance were proposed. One was a

union of individual Christians belonging to different churches; the other was a cooperation between denominations looking towards "incorporation afterwards." The Evangelical Alliance of 1846 was organized in accord with the first principle. Its strength lay in its international character and its support of prayer, missions, education and religious liberty. Its weakness lay in its lack of leadership and programme.

The first half of the century was marked, then, by unparalleled missionary activity, organization of an international, interconfessional society and in a deepening sense of togetherness. The second half of the century saw certain setbacks to the ecumenical movement in reactions against rationalistic Christianity in Germany, the Netherlands and the United States and in the tension within the Anglican Church between the Evangelicals and the High Church party. But these cleavages were offset by the inauguration of two great Christian youth movements, the Y.M.C.A. and the Y.W.C.A., on an interdenominational basis. Again no voluntary group was more powerful in drawing together the churches than the Student Volunteer Movement founded in 1886.

The impulse to social reform in the second half of the century as in the first brought about the cooperation of church groups.

Within the churches one discovers frequently a great indisposition to collaborate or unite; nevertheless, almost every year certain Anglicans raised the question of reunion with the Nonconformists, the continental Protestants or the Eastern churches. Christian scholars collaborated in the production of encyclopaedias and biblical translations. Conferences raised the problem of intercommunion. One of the great organizers of conferences was Henry Lunn. His Grindelwald Conference made it plain that further progress toward reunion required the presence of official delegates from the churches.

In the meantime, in 1895 the Student Christian Movements coalesced into the World Student Christian Federation. The pioneering role of the Student Christian Movement in the ecumenical movement is well exemplified in the career of John R. Mott. The movement united young people, particularly those interested in missions. Conferences to that end presupposed and intensified an interdenominational mood.

Unions for prayer had a similar effect. One was organized in Scotland in 1740 and influenced Jonathan Edwards in America. The Association for the Promotion of the Unity of Christendom was founded in order to pray for unity and included Anglicans, Roman Catholics and Greek Orthodox. The Octave of Prayer for unity observed from January 18 to 25 was started by an Anglican and warmly sponsored by a Roman Catholic, the Abbé Paul Couturier.

This chapter gives one a little more of the feeling of ups and downs than does the preceding, but with a prevailing trend toward unity. Evangelicalism and missionary influence are so stressed as to create the impression that the drive came from within the Christian Church rather than originating in response to rifts and pressures from without.

Chapter VIII: Ecumenical Bearings of the Missionary Movement and the International Missionary Council by Kenneth Scott Latourette

"The ecumenical movement was in large part the outgrowth of the missionary movement," and this in turn was the product of the great revivals. Missionaries often started out with intense confessional loyalties but were pulled together by the challenge of the common task. Moreover, the impatience of the new converts over imported divisions stimulated an effort at their elimination. The practical problems of the enterprise called for joint planning.

The World Missionary Conference meeting in Edinburgh in 1910 was seen at the time and more clearly afterwards to have been a major occurrence. At this conference two men emerged who thereafter played a decisive role, namely John R. Mott and Joseph H. Oldham. The gathering was primarily a consultative assembly of missionary societies operating among non-Christian peoples. The aim of missions was defined as planting in each non-Christian nation the "one, undivided Church of Christ." From Edinburgh came the impulse which issued in the World Conference on Faith and Order.

The Edinburgh Conference was prevailingly Anglo-American with only seventeen delegates from the Younger Churches.

Yet it was among them rather than in the West that ecumenical developments were to advance most rapidly.

World War I occasioned a setback and a temporary exclusion of the Germans from the missionary endeavour. In 1921 the International Missionary Council was summoned with delegates from fourteen countries. The Council became the central planning agency for the large majority of the Protestant missions.

The statement that the younger churches fostered ecumenical movements requires some qualifications. In South Africa the divisions were more numerous than in the lands of the older churches, and China exhibited sectarian tendencies. Nevertheless, to an amazing degree planning was achieved across ecclesiastical barriers. China is taken as an example, and a fairly detailed account is given of interdenominational cooperation. Briefer accounts are given of other lands.

The younger churches, at first isolated from each other, have in missionary conferences come to know each other. In the process they have been made aware of their dependence on and independence of the West, of their similarities and dissimilarities with each other, with a growing resolve to surmount alike the divisions of confessionalism and the barriers of race and country.

By way of reflection on this chapter one may agree with the point often made that divisions of the West make no sense when transferred to the East or the South. The question is then raised whether because we should be united abroad we should also be united at home. Might there not be some point in perpetuating in a local setting some cherished tradition which is indigenous, real and hallowed in a Western community? Plainly it will not do to transport New York to New Guinea or New Jersey to Japan; but one need not therefore infer that everything distinctive and local must be eradicated from Western Christianity; but this is only another way of saying a united church must find some method of conserving variety.

Chapter IX: The World Conference on Faith and Order by Tissington Tatlow

Plans for the World Conference on Faith and Order were launched in 1910 and were on the point of realization when World War I interrupted. After the war the plan was resumed. Persistent planning eventuated in the First World Conference at Lausanne in 1927. The major Protestant bodies were represented together with the Old Catholics, the Anglicans and the Orthodox. A single celebration of the Lord's Supper proved to be impossible; yet gains were made in the direction of Bishop Brent's ideal, "Unity in diversity."

Ten years later the Second World Conference assembled at Edinburgh in 1937. Archbishop Temple of York did much to foster that spirit which affirmed a unity transcending the agreement of minds. These gatherings provided deep spiritual experiences. They made the way of conference seem natural and emphasized the wrongness of division. At the same time they revealed the non-theological factors impeding reunion.

Chapter X: Plans of Union and Reunion 1910 to 1948 by Stephen Charles Neill

An account is here given of the difficulties encountered and overcome in some of the notable unions of recent times, e.g. of the Presbyterians of Scotland and of the Methodists in America. These unions were not so difficult because they were interconfessional. More complicated was the union in Canada of the Presbyterians, Methodists and Congregationalists. When one reads of all the problems involved in the doctrine, worship and polity and of the complications with the state, one marvels that anything came of it at all.

The next sections deal with unions in China, Japan and France. Trans-confessional fellowship has been achieved in Germany. The "Evangelical Church" in Germany is simply a loose association. The Bonn Agreement of 1931 has made possible intercommunion between the Old Catholics, Anglicans and Polish Catholics. Episcopal and non-episcopal churches have been united in

South India. The groups involved were the Presbyterians, Methodists, Anglicans and Congregationalists.

An account is then given of plans pending either for corporate union or closer fellowship in Ceylon and Australia.

An epilogue to the chapter points out how diversified are the areas on which unity must be achieved, namely doctrine, polity and worship. The genuineness of the variant views is recognized, and the contention that competition may be wholesome is not scouted. No organic union in any case is desirable or possible without a prior union of spirit, and short of organic union, federal union has advantages, and cooperation is highly to be prized. Concluding observations point out that unions cannot be hurried, that it were better to wait than to alienate a conscientious minority. The encouraging observation is made that no union once accomplished has been dissolved.

Then comes a chart of mergers all over the world involving full organic unity achieved between 1910 and 1952, a most impressive list. Another list comprises examples of limited intercommunion. Still another list displays the negotiations in progress, conversations under way and plans abandoned.

Chapter XI: Movements for International Friendship and Life and Work 1910 to 1925 by Nils Karlström
Chapter XII: Movements for International Friendship and Life and Work 1925 to 1948 by Nils Ehrenström

An account of the collaborative efforts on the part of the churches, as expressed through the World Alliance for International Friendship through the Churches, and the Universal Christian Council on Life and Work, in the areas of economic and industrial problems, social and moral reforms, international relations and education.

Chapter XIII: Other Aspects of The Ecumenical Movement 1910 to 1948 by Ruth Rouse

The chapter is devoted to the contribution of world Christian lay movements, namely the Y.M.C.A., Y.W.C.A., the Student Christian Movement and the World Student Christian Federation.

Then world denominational fellowships are surveyed—namely the Alliance of Reformed Churches, the World Methodist Council and the Friends World Committee for Consultation and many more— and finally movements for formal ecclesiastical cooperation such as the Federal Council of Churches of Christ in America and other similar bodies throughout the world.

Chapter XIV: The Eastern Churches and the Ecumenical Movement in the Twentieth Century by Nicholas Zernov

Orthodox cooperation with the ecumenical movement has led to no reunions but to a better understanding.

Chapter XV: The Roman Catholic Church and the Ecumenical Movement 1910 to 1948 by Oliver Stratford Tomkins

There is no modification in Rome's traditional claims. Rome has looked with interest on the ecumenical gatherings, and there may have been a growth in charity.

Chapter XVI: The Genesis of the World Council of Churches by Willem Adolf Visser 't Hooft

The strong ecumenical affirmations of the World Council of Churches have actually contributed to the strengthening of confessional consciousness in many churches. "The question for the future is whether this new confessional emphasis will lead to a deadlock in the ecumenical discussions or whether it will lead to an encounter on a deeper and therefore more fruitful level."

Conclusion

Bishop Neill, in concluding, points out that a new fellowship has come into being which a generation ago would have seemed incredible. This is a good omen for the future. Yet this fellowship is limited. It is too urban, too much confined to church leaders and perhaps too preoccupied with itself. We are not to forget that our chief objective is that the world may believe. To that end church union is a means.

This book as a whole is a thorough and thrilling account of a great enterprise. After reading the whole, the question arises as to what have been the main factors making for the astonishing degree of unity achieved in our time. The book stresses above all else the influence of the evangelical revivals. Undoubtedly this emphasis is correct. The rivals did indeed separate the twice-born from the once-born, but they united the twice-born across all divisions of confessions, caste, race and country. They stimulated missions with the intent not to propagate a denominational creed but to communicate a spirit and a life. Missionaries collaborated, and the irrelevance of Western differences to other cultures occasioned simplification and unification of the missionary message.

Another movement which also has made a contribution is the Enlightenment, and its role is less recognized in this book. The Enlightenment, like Pietism, was international. It, too, was anti-dogmatic. The stress was on the ethical, and the ethical is universal. The Enlightenment points not to a world for Christ movement but to a world parliament of religions. Tolerance extends not only to Christian varieties but to non-Christian religions, and the programme is directed toward Christianizing those religions from within rather than to making converts. For Christians the conclusion may be not reunion but merely mutual respect and tolerance.

A third factor not adequately recognized is the impact of secularism and the need for a united front against it.

These qualifications are mentioned not so much by way of criticism as to suggest discussion. The book, while contributing a vast store of information, raises all along the line questions for further probing.

3. Bossuet and Leibnitz and the Reunion of the Churches

One of the great chapters in the history of attempts at the reunion of Christendom centered in a correspondence extending over a period of twenty-four years between Bossuet, the most outstanding ecclesiastic of France in the late seventeenth century, and Leibnitz, the most comprehensively learned layman among the Lutherans. Back of these conversations lay a record of earlier failure and a peculiar urgency for a new attempt.

Fully a century and a half had elapsed since the collapse of the last great previous effort at an understanding between Catholics and Protestants at the Council of Regensburg in 1542. John Calvin had attended on the Protestant side and Cardinal Contarini on the Catholic. The latter was of a much more conciliatory temper than the former, but unfortunately he did not represent his communion. His concessions were repudiated and the papal chair was speedily occupied by Calvin's counterpart, the implacable Caraffa, who as Pope Paul IV introduced the rigor alike in morals and dogma characteristic of the Counter-Reformation. The sequel was the Council of Trent.

And there the matter rested until the Thirty Years War tore open old wounds and inflicted new ones, embittering the feeling not only between the Catholics and Protestants, but also between the Lutherans and Calvinists. The land was ravaged, villages sacked, universities and churches destroyed. Men recoiled and were ready to seek almost any way for peace and order. Some princes returned to Rome. Among them was John Frederick, the elector of Hanover, the namesake of that very prince who more than any other had assisted Luther in the establishment of the Reformation. But John Frederick did not return to Rome in order

First published in *The Chronicle*, XLIII, 5 (February, 1943).

to exterminate Protestantism. Rather he sought to gather about him a group of mediating theologians of both confessions. Among this group Leibnitz found his place. John Frederick was succeeded by a similarly liberal Lutheran whose wife Sophia, the mother of George I of England, was a Calvinist. She had a sister in France, a Catholic, the abbess of Maubuisson. The Catholic sister was unremitting in her efforts to convert the Protestant. Each sister sought help. The abbess turned to Bossuet, the electress to Leibnitz, and the convent of Maubuisson became the forwarding office for their letters.

Before ever the correspondence started, however, Hanover had been the center of a lively movement for reunion and the negotiations were under way before the great protagonists locked horns. A Lutheran theologian at Hanover named Molanus had made as generous an offer to Rome as Protestants ever have or ever could be expected to make. The proposal was that both parties should refrain from reciprocal condemnation until the meeting of a new and truly representative council in which the Protestant superintendents should participate as bishops. To the decisions of this council Protestants should submit. Leibnitz was thoroughly in accord with the offer. He had no objection on principle—at least not at that time—to the idea of submission, for the acceptance of the Augsburg confession implied submission to the diet by which it was promulgated.

The Catholics in turn were very generously disposed and their representative appears to have conceded that Catholics

... would yield in giving the chalice to the laity; saint worship and good works were to be explained in such terms as would not detract from the honor due to God and to the merits of Christ's death; Protestants were to retain their practices which tend to edification; their ministers were to be at liberty to marry, even a second time; the clergy of each party were to preach and catechise in turn under the names of "Old Catholics" and "New Catholics"; the Eucharist was to be received occasionally at each other's hands in token of intercommunion; the Council of Trent and its anathemas were to be in abeyance until the meeting of a new General Council; the Protestants were to appear and to vote by their superintendents; the Pope would release all Protestants from the name of "heretics" by a formal Bull, and they in turn would declare that they did not regard him as Antichrist, but as the second Patriach of Christendom.

These overtures were not unauthorized and Pope Innocent XI, when some of the cardinals were inclined to demur on the ground that such concessions detracted from the authority of the Council of Trent, replied that no more had been granted than to the Greeks in the matter of the chalice and clerical marriage at the Council of Florence. Yet nothing came of the negotiations. Fault lay probably on both sides. The only section of Germany to receive the Roman advances with any cordiality was Hanover, and as for Rome, the liberal Innocent XI was succeeded by a series of reactionaries.

While these approaches were pending the correspondence was conducted between Leibnitz and Bossuet. The atmosphere and attitudes of the participants appeared highly favorable. Leibnitz was more than conciliatory. He had had an almost Catholic period in which he had endeavored to present the teaching of Rome to Protestants in terms so plausible that the authenticity of his manuscript when first discovered was called into question. Bossuet in turn was the most persuasive converter of Protestants to Rome by his sympathetic approach. Instead of bludgeoning, he had made an appeal to reason by pointing out the chaos of the variations of Protestantism.

Nevertheless the interchanges of the twenty-four years led only to a deeper appreciation of the wideness of the gulf and made of Leibnitz not a convert to Rome but a precursor of the rationalists. The stone of stumbling was the Council of Trent. There Bossuet took his stand. The Protestants must accept the pronouncements of the council. "The Roman church," he declared, "though it may grant concessions according to time and circumstances in matters which are unessential and in matters of discipline, will never yield any particle of divine doctrine, nor especially that which has been defined by the Council of Trent." Leibnitz replied that the Church of Rome had perfectly good precedent for permitting the work of one council to be set aside by another. Had not the Council of Basel reversed the Council of Constance, in that the rule of communion in one kind only was relaxed in favor of the Bohemians? Pope Eugenius III consented to the concordat and Leo X long after declared his approval. If, then, Rome was thus ready to set aside the decrees of an ecumenical council in order to conciliate the Bohemians, why might not the same complaisance be manifested in order to reclaim the Germans?

But Bossuet dug in his toes. "An ecumenical council," he held, "is infallible because Jesus Christ entrusted the custodianship of revelation to the apostles and to their successors, the bishops and pastors, who when gathered in assembly speak with the authority of the Holy Ghost. Those who will not agree to these principles must never hope for Reunion with us because they will never agree, except superficially, to the doctrine of the infallibility of the Church, which is the only sound principle for the Reunion of Christendom."

But was the Council of Trent an ecumenical Council? rejoined Leibnitz. Certain doctors of Italy and Spain "reproach the French for deviating from certain articles of the Council and especially from that concerning the essentials of a valid marriage. This is a matter of doctrine and not merely of discipline." Moreover, where does infallibility reside? Some find it in the Pope, some in a Council without the Pope. Here Leibnitz was resorting to the same tactics as Bossuet himself, who had sought to discredit Protestantism by pointing out its variations. Leibnitz retorted that there are variations in Catholicism. Some accept Trent in its entirety, some only in part; and while all agree as to infallibility, some have a papal and some a conciliar theory.

To demand more as the condition of reunion than is required of those already on the inside is manifestly unfair. Incidentally this is an offense of which not only the Roman but sometimes the Anglican Church has been guilty in its overtures for reunion. One is reminded of the dictum that the church is like a bottle, with plenty of room on the inside but narrow at the neck. The amplitude of the inside is certainly more marked in the Anglican than in the Roman communion, but both make a serious blunder if they suppose that the way to reunion lies through a bottleneck.

Leibnitz grew bolder, dropped sparring, and took the initiative in attack. At one point he claimed Trent was not infallible and not acceptable, and that was in admitting the Old Testament Apocrypha to the canon. The point may well appear trivial, but debates about infallibility frequently center on trivialities, because to infallibility a little mistake is quite as damaging as a large one. Leibnitz' contention was that the Council of Trent had reversed the judgment of the early Church. If that were true, whichever position were right, infallibility stood to lose. For either the early Church must have been mistaken or else the Council of Trent. The debate then ran off into a learned discussion of the Biblical canon in which Leibnitz revealed himself as a more competent historical scholar than his adversary.

Bossuet was weary and ill and broke off the correspondence. It had been conducted with courtesy. He had never been so blunt as one of his friends who told Leibnitz that he would never make headway unless he were ready to say with the prodigal son, "I have sinned and am not worthy to be called thy son." In that case, Mother Church would kill the fatted calf on behalf of the Protestants. But if Bossuet was not quite so offensive, his attitude did not differ one whit from that of his less tactful associate.

All of this is very discouraging with regard to any possibility of reunion. If the most sincere efforts broke down in a day when all appeared so propitious, is there any hope that another attempt would be more successful? Conceivably it might, for there were obstacles to reunion at that time which lay behind, even though they did not come to the fore, in the correspondence. Bossuet was a sort of ecclesiastical prime minister to Louis XIV, who revoked the Edict of Nantes. A churchman who, along with all of his persuasiveness, could condone the dragonnades was scarcely in the position of the father in the parable, eagerly scanning the horizon for the prodigal's return. Then, too, Bossuet was a Frenchman, for whom coming to terms with the overtures of a German Lutheran did not comport too well with his nationalism. In other words, the atmosphere then was after all not quite so favorable as it at first sight appears. Perhaps a new attempt could be made under more propitious auspices.

But Rome would do well to ponder the conclusion of that admirable work on Leibnitz on which the present paper is based. The book is by G. J. Jordon and is entitled *The Reunion of the Churches. A Study of G. W. Leibnitz and His Great Attempt.* His summary reads:

The ardent spirit of Leibnitz and the generous terms which he offered in the name of Hanover were met by the traditional hard obscurantism of Rome. Never can Rome have more reasonable terms; the increasing tendency of modern times to face religious questions with tolerance and reason cannot offer anything more unprejudiced. This correspondence reveals Rome's besetting sin, and must stand at the head of all negotiations for modern attempts at Reunion, as a warning that, until Rome takes herself to task, the most liberal proposals of Protestantism will be flouted and rejected.

In the light of the second Vatican Council one may add that Rome now is taking herself to task.

II. Church Unity and the Denominations

4. Unity, Utrecht and the Unitarians

Great strides are being made toward the union of all the Christian groups separate from Rome. Edinburgh and Oxford have paved the way and Utrecht has drafted a constitution. The Greek Catholics and the Lutherans, the Anglicans and the Nonconformists, even the Quakers have had a part.

The council at Utrecht wondered what should be required by way of belief. Some desired the inclusion of the Apostles' or the Nicene Creed. In the end this only was exacted: "Acceptance of our Lord Jesus Christ as God and Savior." The Unitarians and the Universalists protest that not only they are thereby excluded, but likewise the majority of Congregationalists and the liberals in the other denominations. The president of the Unitarian Association of America contends that "public morality and social reform" are central in Christianity and if anything belongs to the periphery it is the creeds and the theological dogmas. Jesus was not a learned theologian, but he was aflame for social righteousness. This was what he meant by the kingdom, and the kingdom, the president says, should come first.

The patron saint of those who thus decry theology has always been the penitent thief. On what a minimum of theology was he admitted into paradise! Without baptism, without the Lord's Supper, totally innocent of infra- and supra-lapsarianism, con- and tran-substantiation, pre- and post-millenarianism. Right! But was the penitent thief after all without a creed? He believed that the man on the cross was a king who would surmount death and who, in his heavenly kingdom, could do something for those who trusted in him. This is a stupendous faith. The disciples themselves at that moment did not believe so much.

First published in *The Christian Century*, LV (October, 1938). Reprinted by permission.

Social reform involves a creed. Dorothy Thompson's recent plea for European refugees assumes a faith in humanity—that men are worth helping, that one man is as much worth helping as another regardless of race, that an appeal to fair-mindedness and generosity will meet with response. And to the creed of Dorothy Thompson might easily be appended an impressive list of anathemas. If social reform and humanitarianism cannot dispense with an implicit creed how much less can Christianity, which came into the world as a religion with a message transcending Judaism and Stoicism? Utrecht might well have formulated a statement of faith. Christianity makes affirmations about God and man, about life and goodness, affirmations which were never more in need of proclamation than today when the Christian view is so brutally flouted.

I venture to suggest some of the affirmations which might have been made. The formulation is individual and could be improved in conference, but the subject matter I offer without hesitancy because it is drawn from the historic Christian stand.

The first is the affirmation of the essential goodness of life. God made the world and saw that it was good. Here is the core of the Christian doctrine of the creation as set forth in the first article of the Apostles' Creed, "I believe in God the Father Almighty, maker of heaven and earth." Those who deny this statement are those who deny the goodness of life. For them God is not the creator, because God is good and the world bad. For them the aim of life should be to escape from life, to stop the weary wheel of existence and sink into nirvana. Such a creed cuts the nerve of all social reform, which rests on the faith that life although corrupt is basically good and that its goodness can be recovered. All utopias and all reformations share this faith. The Unitarians who would shelve creeds cannot shelve this one. They are the first to subscribe to the first article of the first historic creed.

Christianity believes that God makes himself known to man through man more than through nature. Here is the core of the doctrine of the incarnation. This term is derived from *in carne,* in flesh. God is revealed through flesh better than through stones and stars. Nature displays only the power and majesty of God, not his pity and compassion. The sea yawns and engulfs a populous island. The earth cracks and flames and swallows up a city. No pity here! Nature cannot prove that life follows death. The ancient religions, contemporary with Christianity, sought in nature the proof of immortality, supposing that the gods died in winter and rose in spring. But there is no proof here, only a colorful symbol. No seed, if really dead, ever bursts in the spring. Christianity says that we must look to the Word of God in humanity to discover compassion and resurrection.

Christianity affirms that the way to life is through death, the way to joy through sorrow, the way to fullness of life through sacrifice. This is the doctrine of the cross. Eternal life lies beyond tragedy. Here is the most distinctive, the most offensive and the most ineradicable note in Christianity. Those who deny the cross have cut adrift from the Christian tradition. Christianity with starker realism than any other religion has looked with unaverted face upon the ugliest tragedy of history and has seen there the emergence of triumph and eternal life.

This life is the light of men, and it carries the power of transfiguration. Conversion is a Christian affirmation and another stumbling block. Celsus called Christianity an association of robbers, because robbers were admittedly accepted into the Christian fellowship and Celsus could not conceive of their changing. Christians pointed to the life of the churches as living proof that they had been changed. Here indeed was found the most conclusive proof of the resurrection, for how could a dead Christ effect such transformations?

Christianity demands loyalty to Christ as Lord. That was the first affirmation about Jesus. Especially now that lordship needs to be reaffirmed, when many lords are demanding unlimited allegiance. A friend informed me that when a Japanese Christian proposed to substitute for the Trinity a quaternity of Father, Son, Holy Spirit and the Emperor, he was rebuked for thus demeaning His Majesty.

Here are five essential affirmations: that life is good, that God is better revealed in flesh than in nature, that the good and eternal life emerges from tragedy, that human character can be altered, that Christ is Lord. These affirmations seem to me essential. Those who cannot make them, but yet love the Lord, should be asked to linger in the court of the Gentiles.

Utrecht might have said something like this. What it did say is altogether unacceptable, because meaningless. We are to believe that Jesus Christ is God. What does that mean? That he is the ruler of the universe acting in the role of the Son, as sometimes he acts in the role of the Father or of the Spirit? The formula might mean that—in which case Jesus would not be a man in any proper sense of the term at all. This was the view of the Sabellians. Again the words might mean that Jesus is God in the sense that he has only a divine nature and not a human nature. This was the view of the Monophysites. Or it might mean that Jesus is God in the only sense in which there is any God, namely in the sense that he is the highest formulation of human ideals. If this meaning be put upon the words the extreme humanist could subscribe.

Again if the formula be translated into Greek—and we are not to suppose that an ecumenical statement will be confined to English—then God becomes a more ambiguous expression. *Theos* can mean "deity" or merely "divine." In the latter sense the Arians applied the term to Christ. Here, then, is a statement about the godhead of Christ which might be accepted by Sabellians, Monophysites, Arians and humanists. If our conviction is that unity should be attained by a formula which each can interpret in his own way, then the creed of Utrecht is a masterpiece. The aim should rather be, I believe, to think as clearly and speak as precisely as we know how and to attain flexibility by humility and tolerance rather than by deliberate or unconscious ambiguity.

The creed of Nicaea is superior to that of Utrecht because its description of Christ, if properly translated, is both clear and meaningful. The plea of the editor of *The Christian Century* that we "emancipate ourselves from issues that are purely verbalistic by discovering a kinship of meaning despite the opposition implied in words" might well start with Nicaea, and with the most offensive word of its creed, *homoöusios*. The term has been unhappily translated "consubstantial." A better rendering would be "of one being." The Son is of one being with the Father. The import of the formula is the exclusion of the merely accidental. How can

Christ reveal the Father if he be nothing more than a chance spray unrelated to the sea? Nicaea was trying to safeguard the revelation of God in flesh by making more explicit the New Testament declaration that God was in Christ reconciling the world unto himself. The accidental, the merely moral is excluded. Christ participated in the being of God and for that reason Christ is not an isolated episode in history, but the key to cosmic reality.

Christ is not thereby segregated from humanity, for we also participate in the being of God and salvation consists in a fuller participation in that being. The Greek theologians, from Ignatius through Irenaeus, Athanasius and John of Damascus to the Russian thinkers of our own day, assert that Christ became what we are in order that we might become what he is. We are to grow into godhead. Our lives are to be transfigured. This transfiguration is not magic, though the body is involved as well as the spirit. The Greeks had a perception of the value of religion to the body. The whole man is to be transfigured. Moral change is involved. To become God and to become a son of God are synonymous phrases. The transfiguration is sometimes described as entering into eternal life, which is a quality of life to be enjoyed now and hereafter.

The preeminence of Christ for such a view is something like that of Columbus over all subsequent voyagers to America. Because of what Columbus did we are able to traverse the same course in about one-twelfth of the time and with only a day or two of discomfort. Greater things than he we are able to do. But who would compare the spiritual significance of our journeyings across the sea with that of the cruise of one who had to seize an idea, persuade a king and queen, quell a rebellious crew and watch the interminable waves, never sure himself that his idea was right until it was confirmed by the sight of land?

The Unitarians would probably subscribe to such a view. At any rate Michael Servetus, the Antitrinitarian martyr, accepted the Greek conception of salvation and for precisely that reason Calvin thought him an impious heretic. Intoxicated with the idea of divine transcendence Calvin considered the deification of humanity a vilification of deity. Servetus answered that he wished not to degrade Christ to the level of men, but to elevate men to the level of Christ. Servetus was closer at this point to Athanasius than was Calvin, but neither knew it. The Unitarians might awake to find themselves in the stream of Greek mysticism.

In the meantime, those of us who stand in the Trinitarian tradition should recall in our approach to the Unitarians that we have sins to expiate. Our spiritual ancestor, John Calvin, burned Servetus because he would confess only Christ the Son of the Eternal God, not Christ the Eternal Son. The penal legislation of England, from the Restoration almost to the present day, was directed against Roman Catholics and Unitarians, just the groups left out by Utrecht. We have sinned against the spirit of Christ, and that is more serious than to err with regard to his person. Let us indeed preserve the ecumenical tradition, but not the code of Justinian with its death penalty for denial of the Trinity.

5. Friends in Relation to the Churches

The theme of the relationship of the Friends to the other churches may have been proposed to me because I am at the same time an ordained minister of the Congregational Church and an affiliated member of the Society of Friends. Yet for this reason alone, it would not have been suggested were it not that Friends are concerned as to their place in a world community of Christians and particularly so since the formation of the World Council of Churches. The British Friends at the outset declined to join because the council was defined as "a fellowship of churches which accept our Lord Jesus Christ as God and Savior." The objection was perhaps less to the content of the statement than to the demand because Friends have always been averse to creedal affirmations. On this side of the water, however, qualms have been largely allayed by the assurance of the World Council that the statement is not a creed. All save the Fundamentalist Friends in Canada and the United States have been satisfied with this elucidation. I must say that I find it most unconvincing. A creed is a statement of faith. This is a statement of faith. A creed is used both to include and to exclude. This formula is used both to include and to exclude. What then is it, if not a creed? Also, in my judgment it is a very bad creed, because ambiguous. Friends would have done well to protest in the interests of clarification.[1] At the same time, one cannot but rejoice that so many of the Friends are participating in the life of the World Council.

Friends are concerned, also, for their wider relations to all of the churches whether within or beyond the council. The theme of

Delivered as the Ward Lecture, Guilford College, North Carolina, November 12, 1954.

[1] The difficulties are well stated in *The Vocation of Friends in the Modern World*, Second Study Booklet (Friends' House, London, 1951), p. 58.

ecumenical relations has been discussed by members of the Society. Percy Bartlett has a pamphlet entitled *Quakers and the Christian Church* (London, 1942), and Edward Grubb in his *Quaker Thought and History* (New York, 1925) has a chapter entitled "Christian Reunion." Henry Cadbury has given an address upon this topic.[2]

A perusal of the discussions brings to light the curious anomaly that, whereas the original separation of the Friends from other Christians is defended as wholesome, every subsequent defection from the Society itself is deplored as tragic. Such a view, one would suppose, could be defended only on the assumption that the Friends exhibit the one true form of Christianity. Hence the coming out of the true from the false would be a gain, and any deviation from the true would be a loss.

But this is not the position which Friends commonly take today. Those very authors who defend the original separation and lament the subsequent divisions do not do so because in their judgment early Quakerism was the perfect variety of Christianity. Modern Quakers are rather disposed to proclaim their emancipation from now one and now another element in their religious heritage.

Grubb, for example, regrets the indifference of the founders of the Society to theology. This anti-intellectualism was responsible in his judgment for some of the later division. With reference to the Hicksite schism he says, "I believe the whole disastrous episode might have been avoided if the minds of Friends on both sides of the controversy had not been starved. Nothing strikes the modern student more than the crudity of ideas and the ignorance of religious truth that were shown by the combatants on both sides."[3]

Charles M. Woodman in his book *Quakers Find a Way* has a diametrically opposite explanation of the schism. It was due pre-

[2] Compare William H. Thorpe, "Friends' Place and Contribution within the Christian Church," in *The Society of Friends, the Church and the State 1955*," *The Friends Advance of the Five Years Meeting of Friends* (Richmond, (Friends' Book Centre, London, 1952) ; "Christian World Fellowship 1954-1955," *The Friends Advance of the Five Years Meeting of Friends* (Richmond, Indiana) .

[3] Grubb, *op. cit.*, p. 43.

cisely to preoccupation with dogma. Had Hicks and Grellet "recognized that Quakerism is essentially a spiritual experience and that intellectual statements of such experiences are at best feeble and inadequate presentations of what really lies too deep for words, the greatest tragedy Quakerism ever faced might well have been avoided."[4] Woodman sees this not altogether as a corruption of original Quakerism, for the mischief was present at the outset. The initial movement was constricted by Calvinism and prevented thereby from enjoying the fullness of mystical experience. When George Fox in The Letter to the Governor of the Barbadoes expressed belief in the substitutionary efficacy of Christ's death, the founder was "guilty of backsliding." The early Quakers, says Woodman, were wrong in regarding the Bible as all of one level and as dictated by God and as inerrant. The taboo on music, he claims, forfeited "a priceless Divine possession."[5]

Modern historians of Quakerism are more and more inclined to recognize that the early movement was a phase of Puritanism, sharing alike in its magnificence and in some of its foibles and offering us therefore in this generation an example but not a rigid pattern. With the Puritans the Quakers shared in the battle for religious liberty. Witness the superb deportment of William Penn on trial. Friends were Puritans in their sturdy resistance to tyranny. Friends were not remote from Puritans in some of the emphases which are often regarded as distinctive. Friends said that the outward word of the Bible must be interpreted by the light within. Puritans said by the illumination of the Holy Spirit. Friends were often subject to intense emotional enthusiasm, Puritans likewise. Friends sought to reduce Christianity to its absolute essentials. So also did the Puritans, though they did not strip so much away. Some of the less attractive features of Puritanism appeared also among the Friends, aversion to music as titillating and distracting in worship, if not indeed a mark of the vainglory of the world. Quaker invective against stage plays—Barclay's scorn of acting as dissimulation and Penn's scorn for the "languishing voices" in the

[4] Woodman, *Quakers Find a Way* (Indianapolis and New York, 1950), p. 100.

[5] *Ibid.*, p. 160.

theater savor of the strictures of that Puritan William Prynne in his *Scourge of Stage Players.*[6]

Some of the points made by early Friends were conditioned by the circumstances of the times, and we may properly inquire whether the circumstances of our day necessitate the same solutions. The Friends were Puritans. Yet they differed from other Puritans. Characteristic of the Puritan movement was a breakdown into a number of sects each very hostile and recriminatory toward the others. Today we all regret the acrimony of the dispute between George Fox and Roger Williams. Fox wrote of him as "A New-England-fire-brand quenched," and Williams replied with "George Fox digg'd out of his burrowes." Each was saying something important for his time. Yet perhaps not in all respects for our time. The Quakers, discovering in their day so much contention with regard to polity, vestments and sacraments said in effect, "These are not essential. We can have a true church without any of them. We will show you that not only may the church dispense with a bishop but also with a minister. No robes are necessary, no altars, no candles, no storied cathedrals, no sacraments even. God can be worshipped in simplicity, in silence, in unpremeditated speech, and all of your supposed aids from without are but encumbrances." Friends gave a marvelous example of a Christianity revitalized by simplification, but whether Christianity need remain forever so simplified is open to question. Throughout Christian history one finds an oscillation in this regard. When complexity is disturbing, there is a move toward simplicity, and when simplicity proves to be an impoverishment, there is a trend toward complexity. And each may serve its own day.

Modern Friends, then, are less and less disposed to regard the earliest Quakerism as the only valid form of Christianity, let alone as sacrosanct in all of its details. The beginnings are examined with a critical and selective spirit.

Yet assuming that some elements in the first Quakerism were universally valid—as indeed they were—how are they to be conserved—as a pattern to be repeated without deviation or as a theme to be developed with variations? What is entailed in preservation?

[6] Ezra Kempton Maxfield, "Friendly Testimony Regarding Stage Plays," *Bulletin of Friends Historical Association,* XIV (1925).

Do we mean stagnation or continuity within growth? As a matter of fact, there can be no life without growth and no growth without change. If Quakerism should become encrusted, unadaptable, rigid, then it would already have ceased to be itself. The genius of the movement cannot be preserved simply by continuing ancient modes of behavior.

Already the decision has been reached that plain dress is not essential for the plain testimony. In the matter of speech a curious reversal has taken place. In the beginning the reason for the use of the "thee" and "thou" was social equalitarianism. The English language at that time, like French, German, Italian and other tongues today, had two modes of address, the polite and the familiar. "Thee" and "thou" were used toward intimates, children, servants; Protestants who felt better acquainted with God than did the Catholics used this form, also, in prayer. The less intimate and always the more exalted in social rank were to be called "you." George Fox believed that, since in the eyes of God there is no respect of persons, all should be addressed in the same manner, and he employed toward all the familiar form. Today his point has been won. All are treated alike, though the form is reversed. "Thee" and "thou" have become obsolete save in prayer, where they express reverence rather than intimacy. The form "you" has become universal. Among the Quakers the plain speech has come to be a badge of intimacy within the Society rather than a protest against social snobbery without. Friends may, if they will, keep the plain speech as a quaint and endearing custom, but it does not mean what once it did. And to shift from this to other ways of stressing social equality would be much more truly a continuation of the spirit of the founders than to adhere to a formal custom bereft now of its original significance.

The continuing separation of the Friends from other bodies is not, then, to be justified on the ground that Friends in the first place represented an absolutely unique and absolutely satisfactory form of Christianity, and in any case the spirit of original Quakerism does not preclude change. If perhaps separation was requisite in the beginning, it is not for that reason of necessity to be continued in perpetuity.

Another reason, however, is adduced for the division of denominations. It is not because any one represents the whole truth, rather the reverse. Each represents only a partial truth, yet a truth and a very important truth, commonly neglected by other Christian bodies. The witness to the totality of Christian life and experience, in view of the limitations of human nature, is possible only through varieties of religious experience and varieties of church structure and form. This theory of diversity was first enunciated during the Puritan Revolution. John Milton declared that the variation of the burgeoning spring is more in accord with God's plan than the uniformity of congealed winter. Oliver Cromwell pointed out that the Old Testament mentions a number of trees: The plantain, sycamore, olive, palm and cedar, all different and yet all giving shade. So also in religion there should be variety. By this token schism was justified if some valid aspect of the faith had been overlooked, and continued schism was justified in order to provide a witness and concrete expression of the several strands. Percy Bartlett on these grounds defends the original and the continuing separateness of Friends. The distinctive note to which they should bear witness in his judgment is the service of worship, consisting of silence and unplanned speech. Nothing like it is to be found elsewhere, and a moment of silence in a liturgical service is not comparable. There must be first the discipline of settling and waiting upon the Spirit. Henry Cadbury in his recent address lays stress on three distinctive points. The first is the responsibility of all members of the Society for its worship and for its affairs. The second is the equality of women, and the third is the peace testimony. Friends have something to offer, something to stand for and something to stand by. And they must not suffer these valid Christian notes to be muted by any mergers. This is not to decry other bodies. The validity of their witness also is recognized. Thus the sects can accord each other respect without forming a single organization.

This view of denominationalism has a certain plausibility, but does it not mean an acquiescence in the partial? If each group has something of the truth but not the whole truth, then to stay by one's own and leave other valid emphases to the rest is to be content with an impoverishment. Again does not this theory add up to the view that Christians should be grouped according to temperament? We commonly feel that it is quite unChristian to group ourselves according to wealth, social status, race and ethnic origins. Is it any less deplorable if one church is committed to preserving the intellectual side of Christianity and draws to itself the theologians, whereas another appeals to the aesthetic and invites the musicians and the artists, while a third is socially concerned and devotes itself to philanthropy and so on? Such specialization reminds one of the case of a pioneer of medical missions, Peter Parker, who in the early nineteenth century went out to Canton with the intention of restricting himself to the diseases of the eye. He soon found multitudes suffering in every portion of their anatomies, and was speedily driven to become a general practitioner.

In the light of these considerations let us now examine the divisions which have occurred within the Society of Friends. A reevaluation of these schisms may throw some light on the relationship of Friends to the churches, for it is difficult to see on what basis Friends can so unanimously condemn the rifts within the Society and justify the separation from without.

The divisions of Friends have resulted because of greater and lesser degrees of accommodation to the religious environment. Some Friends were more responsive to current attitudes than others, and in consequence divisions occurred. If we assume that any accommodation was corruption, then our judgment with regard to these separations is prepared in advance, but we have already noted that change may be a better preservative than stagnation. We should therefore examine each case with openness of mind.

In the eighteenth century Deism was a rational form of Christianity which invaded the Society of Friends and led some to searching inquiries. No schism resulted, but individuals were disowned. The Deists were leveling strictures against the morality of the Old Testament. Peter Annet, for example, in his tract *David, the Man After God's Own Heart* was very satirical with regard to David's bloodshed and adultery. One marvels that Friends had not been earlier disturbed over the wars of the Old Testament. Toward the end of the eighteenth century some elders maintained that the Hebrew wars for the extirpation of the Canaanites could not be regarded as due to the express command of God. For a God of love could not have been in former times a God of vengeance. This was, of course, to deny the veracity of statements in the Old Testament. Among those disowned for such views was a woman, Hannah Barnard. She was charged with "promoting a disbelief of some of the Scriptures of the Old Testament; particularly those which assert that the Almighty commanded the Israelites to make war upon other nations." "I found myself reduced," said she, "to the alternative of either believing that the Almighty's nature and will were changeable like those of a finite man or that it never was his positive will and pleasure for his rational creatures to destroy one another's lives in any age of the world."[7] Few among Friends today would fail to agree with her. Yet she was disowned. The bearing which this may have upon our situation is this, that if for a conviction and a right conviction Friends are disowned by other bodies, they cannot for the sake of unity renounce their conviction.

What Rufus Jones called the greatest tragedy in Quaker history occurred in the 1820's, the Hicksite schism. Grubb, as we have already noticed, attributed it to intellectual starvation, whereas Woodman blamed the concern for theology. Rufus Jones says the division was due rather to an abandonment of a zig zag course.[8] Up to this time Quakerism had tacked between the authority of the Spirit and the authority of the Scripture, but now the vessel adopted a straight course, and those who would not have it so boarded another ship in an opposite direction. To use another figure, the synthesis was dissolved between private illumination and Biblical revelation. Hicks is commonly supposed to represent the influence of Unitarianism upon Quakerism. His affinities appear to me to lie rather with the Transcendentalist Movement. The light within played for Hicks a role similar to the oversoul of Emerson. Hicks did not, however, adopt Emerson's theory of God immanent in nature. Rather he exaggerated the early Quaker disparagement of all outward helps, and whereas the first generation had rejected the sacraments on that account, he went so far as

[7] Rufus M. Jones, *The Later Periods of Quakerism,* I (London, 1921), 302-303.
[8] *Ibid.,* pp. 457-458.

to include the historical Jesus as himself only an outward help. Our reliance should be rather on the Christ within, who is but another name for the inward light. Thus the historical core of Christianity was destroyed, and the unique revelation of God in Christ became only an anticipation of that which takes place in every human soul.

Stephen Grellet, on the other hand, was influenced by the Evangelical Revival, with its emphasis upon salvation solely through the expiatory death and redeeming work of the historical Christ.[9] Biblical and theological interests were revived. So sharp an accentuation of the two aspects of the Quaker testimony, hitherto held in conjunction, produced the schism.

Under the circumstances one cannot see any other legitimate outcome than division. It is all very well to say that these men should have appreciated their deeper unity. Such a statement must not be taken so far as to imply that they should have been indifferent to truth. If they did have profoundly divergent conclusions with regard to the very source of religious revelation, then their ways for the time being had to part. At the same time, the division was deplorable because each was partially right and each was partially wrong. The calamity was that the healthy tension between historical revelation and inward illumination had broken down, and we may rejoice today in the reunion, not because men have ceased to care about the truth but because the partial has been corrected by the whole.

The Hicksite split is somewhat differently interpreted by Elbert Russell, who sees the basic ground in the falling apart of the city and the country Friends about Philadelphia. The farmer folk resented the centralization of authority in the hands of urban elders and supported Hicks less on account of theology than because of his insurgence.[10] If this be so, then Friends like other branches of the Church became so identified with their culture as to be ruptured by rifts already present in the social structure. Whenever the Church fails to maintain her unity against the rents

[9] Edward Grubb, "The Evangelical Movement and Its Impact on the Society of Friends," *The Friends Quarterly Examiner* (January, 1924).

[10] Elbert Russell, "The Separation after a Century," *Friends Intelligencer* (1928).

of the world, there is reason to lament. This division, now happily healed, should prompt inquiry as to whether Friends today are separated from other Christians on sociological grounds. Friends are commonly in the upper strata. They do not attract either the indigent or the ignorant. But these the Gospel does not reject.

Finally the Wilburites reacted against the Evangelical theology of Grellet in the name of the ancient Quaker pattern. But the old zig zag could not be restored immediately after the separation had occurred. The present need was for a re-examination of the entire problem of revelation. Friends needed a theologian rather than a return to the vague formulations of the founders.

The question of the sacraments has occasioned not a major schism but some disowning among Friends. The original reason for rejecting the sacraments was of a piece with the repudiation of music and of art. All of these were considered creaturely. Since God is a spirit, he must be worshipped in spirit with no sensory medium appealing to the ear, the eye or the mouth. Baptism was declared to be only of the spirit. The command of Christ in Matthew 28 to baptize all nations was interpreted by the older exegetes among the Friends as referring not to water baptism, since water was not mentioned, but only to spiritual regeneration. Some later Friends took advantage of Biblical criticism to deny the authenticity of these words.[11] Yet, as a matter of fact, there can be absolutely no question that in the New Testament and continuously thereafter the disciples did baptize with water, and they did celebrate the Lord's Supper with real bread and real wine. Moved by these considerations, David Updegraff, an Ohio Friend, in the 1880's revived these ordinances. He was disowned by eight meetings, and the Ohio Yearly Meeting in 1885 made the pronouncement: "We believe that the baptism which appertains to the present dispensation is that of Christ, who baptizes his people with the Holy Ghost, and that the true communion is a spiritual partaking of the body and blood of Christ by faith. Therefore, no one should be received, acknowledged or retained in the position of minister or elder among us, who continues to participate in or

[11] James H. Moon, *Why Friends (Quakers) Do Not Baptize with Water* (1909).

advocate the necessity of the outward right of baptism ... or the Supper."[12] Surely, ran the argument, the Society of Friends cannot have misunderstood its teachers for two hundred years. Updegraff replied that if George Fox was right in contending that the Church of his day had misunderstood the Master for sixteen hundred years, what was so preposterous in suggesting that the Friends might have misunderstood George Fox for two hundred years? Updegraff went on then to cite a number of passages from the early Quakers who did not make an absolute out of abstention from the water of baptism or the bread of the Supper but left each to follow the guidance of the inner light. So Updegraff would not impose these ordinances on others but asked only that he be accorded the liberty of his conscience. In consequence, he was disowned. Today such rigor is no longer exercised.

Yet although latitude is allowed and respect accorded to individual conviction, the Friends as a whole still refrain from any celebration of the sacraments and any use of artistic or musical symbols in the service of worship. May one who is also a Congregationalist be permitted to remind Friends that by banishing all symbolism they run the risk of introducing symbolism of a lower order. I know of two meeting houses which have no altar, no candles, no signs of the Evangelists, no crucifixes and no cross. Instead, in the front of the meeting house blazes a roaring fire. It is not there for heat. The building has already been warmed. It can be there only as an aid to the focusing of attention. The historic symbolism of the Church has been replaced by the device of primitive, pagan fire-worshippers.

Where now are these reflections leading us? We should all agree that Friends do have certain valid and distinctive testimonies to bear. The service of worship is unique. The role of the entire membership in the affairs of the Society is almost unique. The equality of women is only approximated in other denominations, and the peace testimony, though borne also by the Mennonites and the Brethren, is certainly not so clearly and exclusively advocated by other religious groups. One would be extremely unhappy if

[12] David B. Updegraff, *An Address on the Ordinances* (Columbus, Ohio, 1885).

these positions of the Friends should be weakened by any organic union with other bodies. At the same time there is the possibility that Friends are bearing only a partial witness and that their own religious life could be enriched if they were able either by organic union or by borrowings to supplement their own tradition.

But here a warning must be introduced against the mere blending of forms. There must be a sense of artistic harmonies and unities in whatever combinations are effected. In the realm of music the sonata and the chorale are distinct and cannot simply be jumbled. In the realm of architecture the liturgical church has the altar in front, the pulpit and the reading desk on the sides and the central aisle leading up to the altar. In the preaching church of the Congregational tradition the pulpit is in the center, a solid block of pews in front and the aisles on the side. It will not do to place the altar at the head and then to have the pews massed in the center with side aisles. The altar requires a central aisle. Likewise the old Congregational meeting house does not lend itself to stained glass windows, and the very simple meeting houses of the Quakers may lose their chaste appeal if they are subjected to any excessive adornment.

There is the possibility, however, that different types of worship can be practised by the same individuals at different times. My wife and I commonly attend first Friends meeting and then a Congregational service. There is no reason why the other churches could not introduce the practice of a genuine Friends' unplanned meeting on some week-night occasion, and there is equally no reason why the Friends, if they wished, should not celebrate the sacrament of the Lord's Supper not as a part of the ordinary meeting but on some separate occasion.

Many of the Friends have a very deep feeling against such a participation. One Friend told me that in her community, since there was no Friends' meeting, she attended the Congregational church. At the celebration of the sacraments she was uneasy. She was loath to get up and leave and equally loath to take part. Now plainly, if she could not participate in a reverent, devout and meaningful manner, she ought to have abstained. But if the celebration on the part of the congregation was a genuine act of worship, then she need not have found the bread and the wine to be insupportable obstacles.

Perhaps the query may come, why not then participate in footwashing? To which I would reply, indeed, why not? I have done so when among the Brethren, and I found the rite deeply moving. I do not feel any urge, however, to try to make it universal because it does not have a continuing tradition reaching back to the time of the New Testament, nor is it in any sense a universal symbol of Christendom.

Far be it from me, however, to urge Friends to reintroduce the sacraments. This must be a matter of private decision, and, if there is no preparation of spirit, to participate would be a desecration. This, however, is plain: neither water nor the lack of water, neither bread nor the lack of bread is so significant as the communion of the spirit, and where it is real, then one should count oneself privileged to be allowed to partake and, if not to partake, at any rate simply to be present.

I remember an occasion in France when I was serving with the American Friends Service Committee during World War I. We were in a village where there was no Protestant service. I went to the Catholic mass. That Sunday it was being celebrated by a French priest on behalf of German prisoners. They sang in their own rich tongue. The priest murmured inaudibly, in Latin; and, as he did so, my mind reverted to a Congregational church in the State of Washington, and again I heard my father repeating the simple words of institution, how our Lord in the night that he was betrayed took bread and broke it and gave to his disciples saying, "Take, eat, this is my body which was broken for you. This do in remembrance of me."

Let not Friends forget the vital testimony of bygone days. Let not Friends dedicate themselves to the preservation of encrusted forms. Preserve rather the valid, seek the well rounded truth, respect diversity of honest conviction, join reverently with all who are reverent, seek the unity of the spirit and pray for unity of the body. William Penn well said, "The humble, meek, merciful, just, pious and devout souls are everywhere of one religion; and when death has taken off the mask, they will know one another, though the divers liveries they wear here may make them strangers." And Isaac Pennington declared: "This is the true ground of love and unity, not that such a man walks and does just as I do, but that I feel the same spirit and life in him."[13]

[13] Cited in Edward Grubb, *Quaker Thought and History* (New York, 1925), p. 146.

6. The Congregationalists

I. The Essence of Congregationalism

The problem of a merger of the Congregational Christian Churches with other bodies, whether of the same or of variant polity, goes back to the question of the essence of Congregationalism. The problem is partly legal because the courts rule that in case a union meets with dissent, and the dissenters are closer to the essence of the tradition, they retain the property. It is, of course, more than a legal problem because Congregationalists feel a responsibility to conserve the valid core.

Some assume that to define the essence of Congregationalism is all very simple, since essence may be construed in terms of origins. In a measure this is true, yet not in any wooden fashion, because a religious body, if it be alive, must grow and change like a human being.

One must remember likewise that every denomination in the period of its origins was affected by the peculiar circumstances of that particular time, and quite conceivably those circumstances are not worthy to be perpetuated. The Lutheran body, for example, began in a period of intense doctrinal agitation. For that reason the Lutherans have consistently emphasized doctrinal rectitude. The Congregationalists arose when polity and liturgy were in controversy. They have consequently been comparatively indifferent to doctrine and have stressed rather the organization of the church as of paramount concern. One would hope that neither would feel that its essence lay in a continuance of that which was conditioned merely by the circumstances of its origin.

Congregationalism had its rise during the Puritan Revolution in England. In this period liberty was the cry in every area of life—liberty in the sense of the removal of restrictions; liberty of trade, liberty in government and liberty in religion.

First published in *The Christian Century* with the title "Is Congregationalism Sectarian?" (February, 1954).

This demand did not center on doctrine, and the reason was that the Anglican church was latitudinarian as to doctrine. A distinction was made between the essentials and the non-essentials. In the area of the essentials, for which one might be damned, freedom was allowed to each to believe as he liked. But in the sphere of the non-essentials, to which polity and liturgy were assigned, uniformity was required in order that all Englishmen might worship God in the same manner with seemliness and decorum. This demand for uniformity was stoutly resisted by the Independents, later called Congregationalists. They would have local congregations determine their own affairs.

These circumstances explain why for some the very essence of Congregationalism is to be found in an indifference to creeds and an insistence on congregational polity and a simple liturgy. One may rightly query whether such an insistence may not be simply the perpetuation of a mood conditioned by the circumstances of that particular century.

The essence of a religious body cannot be defined solely in terms of its beginnings. One needs to take into account the entire course of its history. Those elements which have been persistent and have determined major courses of action come close to being of the essence. Let us then briefly sketch the main characteristics of Congregationalism throughout its history, both in the Old World and in the New.

In the beginning Congregationalists were actuated by certain principles in framing their view of the church. The first principle was anti-Romanism. The Congregationalists desired to strip from the Church of England all the "rags of anti-Christ." For that reason they rejected the Christian year and the liturgical type of architecture. The norm for reconstruction was the Bible and especially the New Testament, which was deemed to afford the true polity. The Old Testament afforded the model of the commonwealth in which the saints should rule. United by covenant in congregations they constituted the governing bodies in the church and state.

At once arose the problem of the relation of these Congregational churches to the Church of England. Of late we have been reminded that the Congregationalists consisted of Separatists and non-Separatists. The former esteemed the Church of England so corrupt that communion with her was impossible. The latter would commune if permitted. Now the contention is that all the Congregationalists who came to New England were non-Separatists, and that therefore the door is open to an organic reunion; namely, a merger with the Church of England.

Too much is being made of the point. To be sure the non-Separatists left the door open for communion, but that does not necessarily entail the organic unity of denominations. We must remember that if these men were non-Separatists, they were at the same time nonconformists. They took a position as to polity and liturgy which made it inevitable that the Church of England would refuse them communion, and they were not willing to compromise in order to be received at the Lord's Table in the national church. Practically speaking, therefore, their position entailed schism.

More to the point is this, that they were not sticklers for their polity in its entirety, provided they could secure the essence, which was conceived to lie in the autonomy of congregations whose will was not to be overridden by a synod or bishop. This did not mean, however, that bishops or synods as such had necessarily to be abolished. Some Congregationalists in fact sought to congregationalize the Church of England under the forms of episcopacy by planting congregationally minded ministers in the parishes; similarly, under the Presbyterian regnancy there were Congregational groups which functioned under presbyteries. This would indicate that Congregationalism has not been unalterably opposed to organic union with either Episcopal or Presbyterian bodies.

A point of still greater consequence is that early Congregationalism was not separatist with reference to the state and society. The Baptists were. Roger Williams set forth their political philosophy when he insisted that the regenerate are few, that they and they alone should constitute the church, but the state should include all inhabitants; and therefore the church and the state must go their separate ways. The corollary was that the Christian as a Christian should eschew political responsibilities and the church should not aspire to Christianize society.

The Congregationalists were never of this mind. They tried

to set up holy commonwealths in which church and state in union sought to fashion the life of the communities. This difference may well explain why Congregationalism has had vastly less success in union with the Baptists than with the Presbyterians, the Episcopalians and the Methodists, none of them congregational in polity. The question is indeed thereby raised whether polity is of the essence of Congregationalism.

In the New World the Congregationalists established at first theocracies, miniatures of a national church, in particular localities such as Plymouth, Boston, Salem, New Haven, Hartford. Church and state were united, but not church, state and community. The saints constituted the church and the state; only those who had had a heartfelt experience of regeneration could be members of the church, and only members of the church could vote. Those who qualified were a minority. At Plymouth after 23 years, the colony numbered 634 males, and of that number only 233 enjoyed the franchise. At New Haven one-tenth constituted church and state. The rest were called "inhabitants." Of them it was required that they should accept the rule of the religious oligarchy. They were not excluded from its ranks by any considerations of property or social prestige. If they could meet the religious test, they could qualify. Otherwise they must acquiesce or else not seek to dwell within the confines of New England. The measure of positive constraint employed was slight, because for the most part the inhabitants were persuaded of the rightness of the rule of the saints.

The polity was congregational. Wherever a group existed sufficiently large to form a fellowship by covenant, a congregation enjoying autonomy was established. Yet there was connectionalism. In the matter of ordination and dismissal the consent of neighboring churches was desired and sometimes adjudication was invited. Councils were called for specific purposes and might sit perhaps for several years until their commission was discharged. Ministers were ordained only for service in a particular congregation and for the duration of that service, not for life. John Cotton, while on shipboard, declined to baptize his own child on the ground that at that moment, not being in charge of a church, he was not an ordained minister. On resignation from a parish the minister became a layman, and on taking another parish he was again ordained.

Creeds were not emphasized but were taken for granted. The "Cambridge Platform" simply assumed subscription to the Westminster Confession. Common consent in this area obviated controversy, and therefore warded off rigidity. Creeds were never enforced narrowly but were used "for substance of doctrine." To say, however, that they were used only as testimonies and never as tests is going quite too far. If that had been true, by what token would the Unitarians have been rejected?

The liturgy was extremely plain. Church music was confined to Psalm- and hymn-singing and without even the giving of pitch. Seldom did those who began on different notes end on the same. The Christian year was rejected. The Pilgrims deliberately worked on Christmas Day to show their contempt for Christ-mass, that is, the Roman Catholic mass, "the devil with the sting in his tail." Easter was likewise repudiated. (Harriet Beecher Stowe tells of a Puritan minister near Boston who married an Episcopalian wife from the metropolis. When she undertook to take two of the boys of the parish to Boston for the celebration of Easter, their parents believed that she was taking them to see the "whore of the Apocalypse." "Who's she?" inquired one of the boys of the other, and the better informed replied, "She is the one who burned John Rogers.") Church architecture was defiantly anti-Roman. In Jonathan Edwards' church in Northampton the pulpit was set on the side in the middle of the nave with a door opposite, to get as far away as possible from the Catholic type.

Now what has happened to all this? Plainly the outward structure of the theocracy is gone. Church and state are separate. By various stages the holy commonwealth disintegrated. In time the strangers became restive under the rule of the saints—and more particularly the sons of the saints, who could not qualify as successors to their parents—and desired participation in the political and religious life of the community. One solution was to lower the requirements for membership in the church. Another was to convert the entire population that they might all qualify. This was the attempt of Jonathan Edwards in the first Great Awakening. What it did instead was to split the churches into the New Lights and the Old, and thereby weaken the hold of the theocracies.

In the meantime the colonies grew less rigorous in the exclusion of dissenters. In came Baptists, Quakers, Episcopalians, not to mention infidels, and they all made common cause to unseat the Congregationalists. In the early decades of the nineteenth century, section by section the union of church and state was abrogated. The separation was friendly, and the two institutions continued to support and influence each other. This is a part of the Puritan legacy. But formally they are distinct. At this point the Baptists have won.

As to polity, the most crucial change is the abandonment of the belief that polity can be determined out of the New Testament. Historical scholarship has demonstrated diversity on this score within the New Testament itself: in one place a charismatic ministry, in another the beginnings of a system of bishops and deacons; in one quarter the term "apostle" restricted to the Twelve and to Paul, in another a designation for any traveling evangelist; and so on. Diversity, change, and growth in the direction of centralization mark the New Testament period.

The most noticeable change in congregational polity was the emergence in 1861 of a permanent national council. Much debate ensued and still continues as to its relation to the churches. The controversy is quite recent, however, because in early times the council was assumed to be the creature and the agent of the churches, brought into being by them and with authority to act on their behalf, though not to impose decisions without express consent.

The council was at one time definitely commissioned to explore and to consummate unions with other evangelical bodies. In 1918 the Presbyterians proposed a union of all evangelical denominations in the United States. In response a conference of such churches was called in 1920, and a plan of organic union was projected and then referred to the constituent churches. The national council of the Congregational body conducted a plebiscite and summarized the results as revealing "an unequivocal approval by our churches of the idea of some practicable form of union between denominations naturally competitive which will put an end as quickly as possible to the scandalous rivalry still discernible in our cities, in home missionary districts, and on foreign fields." Only one other denomination registered a similar approval and in consequence the plan never materialized. Yet one might plausibly argue that the council continued to operate under this mandate and was still so doing when in 1931 the union was effected between the Congregational and the Christian churches.

But when the merger with the Evangelical and Reformed Church was contested and taken to the courts, leaders of the Congregational Christian Churches sought to allay the fears of objectors that the autonomy of local churches would be jeopardized by pleading that the council was acting only for itself and was in fact an autonomous body. The judge then inquired whether the General Council could merge either with the Roman Catholic Church or with the Union of American Hebrew Congregations. The answer was that acting for itself the council could do so; the churches need not be consulted and would not be in any way affected. But the plan of union called for a merger of the churches. The judge therefore ruled with unimpeachable logic that, since according to the testimony of the witnesses the council could act only for itself, it therefore had no authority to carry through the plan of union."

This theory of the autonomy of the council is quite without support in previous theory, and Douglas Horton in his book *Congregationalism, A Study in Church Polity* says (p. 32): "No council can remain Congregational Christian a moment after the Congregational Christian churches upon which it depends have withdrawn their recognition." That being the case, the council is definitely not autonomous.

Yet a distinction is drawn between a council consisting of instructed and of uninstructed delegates. The contention is that the General Council is not under specific instruction, and if, then, it makes a pronouncement it cannot pretend to be speaking for the churches but only for itself. There is validity in this point. Any representative body, if called upon for a quick decision precluding an appeal to the constituency, can declare only what it believes in a general way to be the mind of its members and should make plain that it is not registering a poll of opinion. In a matter of such consequence as a union with another body, however, delegates ought to be instructed, and no church should be included without its express consent. But if that consent is given and if the council is commissioned to act on behalf of the local church, one cannot see how even the earliest Congregational polity is thereby violated.

Another historical change in the area of polity was of only temporary duration. Congregationalism in Connecticut was Presbyterian from 1708 to 1784. Some would hold that during these years Congregationalism was not Congregationalism. Plainly it was not entirely congregational. Yet it was the church that received and transmitted Congregationalism from the earlier to the later time. Can one rightly say that during the span of deviation these churches had lost the connection? The same question might, of course, be raised in a doctrinal sphere. The Unitarian churches in Massachusetts claim to be the successors of the Pilgrims, while the Congregational churches contest the claim. What makes the Congregational plea dubious is that during the present century many occupants of Congregational pulpits have been unitarian in theology and have not been disowned. What then is essential to make a church Congregational? I do not mean to imply that there are no norms but only to indicate that they do not lend themselves readily to precise formulation.

When it comes to creeds, their content obviously has changed. We have passed from the Westminster Confession, the Savoy Declaration, the Burial Hill and the Kansas City statements to that of the United Church. Incidentally, there are those who make much of the point that no one of these statements was called a creed; but the same might be said of the greatest creeds of Christendom. Philip Schaff in his *Creeds of Christendom* speaks of the Apostolic *Symbol,* the Nicene *Symbol,* the Augsburg *Confession,* the Heidelberg *Catechism.* Surely we need not quibble over a word. We Congregationalists have had written statements of faith from the beginning down to 1931, when out of deference to the Christian Church we gave up the practice. Now that we have reverted to a written statement through our union with the Evangelical and Reformed Church, we have merely revived the custom which prevailed throughout the longer part of our history.

Again, the point is emphasized that joining a Congregational church is not by the subscription to a creed but by the taking of a covenant. True, but the covenant has often contained a creed; witness the covenant of a church in Maine in 1772:

> We do, therefore, seriously and solemnly, and with one heart and hand, own and adore the only living and true God, the Lord Jehovah, the Father, Son and Holy Ghost, to be our God.
> We believe the Sacred Scriptures to be the Word of God, and the only perfect rule of our faith and practice.
> We own and confess ourselves sinners, and unworthy of God's mercy; and we would penitently ask forgiveness of God, who alone can forgive sin.
> We believe in Jesus Christ as the only Mediator between God and man, by whom alone we can obtain pardon and salvation, even eternal life.

What is this if it be not a creed?

The greatest change, perhaps, is in the manner in which creeds are understood. From the outset there was no rigidity of interpretation, and the common formula was "for substance of doctrine." Horace Bushnell went further when he said that he regarded creeds as symbols which defy precise formulation. He would subscribe to a creed only if he could do so to several at the same time, thereby making it plain that he did not adhere to any one in a narrow fashion. Egbert Smyth went still further when he announced boldly that creeds are only tentative and are in need of constant revision.

In liturgy the changes are glaring. Christmas came back in the 1850's. In the same period music and organs began to invade the churches. As late as 1771 Ezra Stiles at Yale reported with consternation that an organ taken from a concert hall in Boston and formerly used to promote "festivity, merriment, effeminacy, luxury and midnight reveling" had been transferred to an Episcopal church in Providence. But in 1852 Horace Bushnell gave a superb address on religious music before the Beethoven Society at Yale. Even Lent has come back, and in architecture the pulpit is very frequently displaced by the altar.

What then is essential Congregationalism? The union of church and state is gone. Coercion for religion is gone. Polity has

shifted. Creeds have changed. Ritualism has invaded and sacramentalism also. Are we still the church of our fathers? Since we
have already changed so much and still believe that we are Congregationalists, how much farther can we change without deviating
from our genuine pattern?

Such queries are to be addressed not simply to civil courts
but to ourselves. We must inquire what is our essence. Some would
answer that it is to be found in the autonomy of local congregations. But just what is sacrosanct about autonomy? And why did
our fathers consider it to be important? Some today say that the
autonomy of the local church is derived from the New Testament
doctrine that all men are equal in the eyes of God. But is that the
New Testament doctrine? The New Testament says indeed that
God is no respecter of persons—that is to say, he has no regard for
human distinctions—but it does not say all men are equal, for in
that case what of the doctrine of predestination? Neither does the
New Testament abrogate ranks within civil society or within the
church. In the congregation there are those who are counted
pillars. And if the teaching of the New Testament did imply an
absolute equality of all men in the eyes of God would not the
inference be the autonomy of every individual rather than of the
congregation?

I would venture to suggest that the valid core of this notion
of congregational autonomy lies in two points. The first is lay
participation in the life of the church. This requires that the congregation not only be in charge of its own affairs but also that it be
relatively small. William Ames held that the congregation should
not be allowed to grow beyond the point where all the members
could commune together at the same time. One might add that it
should not be suffered to reach the point where the hen can no
longer gather the chickens under her wings—that is to say, the
minister no longer give personal attention to his flock. Local
exigencies may require the violation of these principles, but at any
rate that is the ideal.

The other point is that majorities should not ride roughshod
over minorities. This means not merely that the wishes of congregations should not be flouted, but that within the congregation
the dissenter should be treated with respect and consideration. By

the same token, minorities should not wantonly impede the will of majorities. And on many an issue personal predilections should be yielded for the sake of harmony.

There are several other persistent notes in Congregationalism which appear to me to be even more important than polity. One is the concept of the holy commonwealth, the divine society, to be striven for here on earth. This is the deepest root of the social gospel. It explains why Congregationalists at one time favored the union of church and state and have always encouraged a friendly collaboration. It may also explain why, as noted above, Congregationalists have actually had more success in unions with Presbyterians, Methodists and Episcopalians than with bodies of congregational polity such as the Baptists.

Another note is breadth of spirit and a readiness to treat many matters as non-essential and therefore open to variety. Congregationalists will practice either infant baptism or adult baptism provided that in each case the rite be infused with a proper meaning and that a preference be not invested with an exclusive claim.

Finally we may do well to realize that the conflict at present going on within Congregationalism is only a part of a conflict which is rending our entire culture; namely, the conflict between the claims of centralization and individualism. An interesting example of it occurred when a proposal was introduced in the United Nations for a reform of the calendar. The business interests were in favor of a plan whereby every month would have the same number of days and every day would fall on the same date in every year. This was to be achieved by having the year end on a Sunday and commence on a Sunday. Thus two Sundays would fall together with no intervening week.

To this the orthodox Christians objected that thereby the days would be eliminated in which God created the world; the orthodox Jews that a Sabbath would be gone; the orthodox Mohammedans that a sacred Friday would be eliminated. The Dutch complained of the loss of the queen's birthday and the French protested that such standardization would take the poetry out of life. Here, then, were religion, patriotism and poetry resisting the uniformity demanded by business.

Much of the emotional fervor of those who resisted the merger with the Evangelical and Reformed Church was derived from the fear that any centralization was but the first step down the road to totalitarianism. Fears of totalitarianism are only too well grounded, and one of the greatest problems of our time is to find a way, as the centralization demanded by world expansion goes on, to conserve that freedom which enables men to breathe and move and live. Yet to suppose that a union with the Evangelical and Reformed Church would be a step toward totalitarianism is most unconvincing to those who are personally acquainted with the leaders of that denomination. And one who like myself labors in a theological seminary comprising some thirty denominations feels that the temper of them all, whatever their polity, is opposed to every Leviathan that would stifle the freedom of man. We are making too much of the diversities remaining within our Protestantism, because as a matter of fact, whatever our denomination, our version of Christianity and our outlook set us over against the totalitarian tendencies of Catholicism and secularism alike in our age.

II. *Congregationalism: The Middle Way*

The previous article has dealt with the question of the degree to which Congregationalism can diverge from its initial pattern without deviation from its essential character. Another question is whether Congregationalism is in a position to foster union among other bodies by standing in the middle and reaching out to the right and to the left. We have already noted that as a matter of fact every body with any degree of coherence is a *via media*. We have also observed that to be in the middle does not necessarily enable one to unite the ends, because a gesture to the one may alienate the other. The significant point is not, after all, the median position but the character of the extremes between which the mediator stands.

First published in *Christendom*, V (Summer, 1940). The article as here reprinted has been considerably reduced because much of its content has been covered in No. 9, "The Sectarian Theory of the Church," and in No. 6, Part I, "The Essence of Congregationalism."

The Anglicans make much of their median position between Protestantism and Catholicism, but one may wonder whether it is so significant, because it arose out of the attempt to nationalize a portion of Roman Catholicism by setting up in England a national church otherwise little different at the outset from Rome. To be sure, Calvin's theology later invaded the Church of England, but this church has never been vitally affected by the sectarian tradition which took hold in England during the Puritan revolution. Congregationalism was at the center of this emphasis and Congregationalism is much more fundamentally a *via media,* because it combines elements of the church and of the sect types.

In Congregationalism this appears in the combination of a regenerate membership and the practice of infant baptism. The first separates the church from the community; the second unites them in case all babies in a given area are baptized. Of course in early Congregationalism this was not the practice. Only the children of believers were to be baptized. At the same time, baptizing babies at all introduces another level of church affiliation and makes easier other ventures in the direction of comprehensiveness with respect to the community, such as the union of church and state. This is itself a mark of the church type and came to pass in New England Congregationalism.

The combination of sect and church types was of course not peculiar to Congregationalism. Calvin had tried to combine the types. To meet the Anabaptist criticism he demanded a church distinguishable from the world by purity of life; yet he did not pretend that the tares could be altogether weeded out. He thought of the church in terms of the predestined whom God has chosen and man cannot recognize. Nevertheless good works are the best psychological means by which to convince ourselves that we are of the elect. He desired that the entire community should belong to the church, yet that the church should comprise only the saints. He was able to realize his ideal only by making Geneva a select community. Catholics and Libertines were expelled and refugees in huge numbers received. Not just the church but the whole town became a city set upon a hill. In Scotland the entire country was included in the establishment of Presbyterianism, but only the worthy were admitted by token to communion.

In New England likewise the community was selective and Winthrop stoutly objected to the reception of new comers who would not subscribe to the covenant of the church and the compact of the state. Church and state were allied. Only church members could vote in the body politic, but only those who gave moral and emotional evidence of a state of grace were admitted to church membership, and only the children of members were granted baptism. The two concepts of the church now began to rend each other. So few could produce the credentials that the church threatened to dwindle to a fragment of the community. Hence the children of those who could produce only the moral but not the emotional marks of grace were admitted to baptism. Jonathan Edwards endeavored to recover the ideal by converting the whole community. He failed, and the solution was the separation of church and state. So ended the last serious attempt to realize the ideal of the Catholic Church of the Middle Ages of a Christian society under the guidance of the church.

The problem has agitated all Christendom, but nowhere has the strain been so acute as in American Congregationalism, and nowhere is the residue so evident. English Congregationalism was driven both by principle and circumstance into a separation from the establishment. Concern for England as a whole then found its expression chiefly in the role of Nonconformists in political life. Within the Church of England the problem was made acute again in the eighteenth century by John Wesley, who was essentially a Calvinist in his desire to make the church at once holy and Catholic. He aspired to do for the whole of England what Calvin had done for Geneva, but he was forced into separatism by his insistence on holiness. In Scotland Presbyterianism remained an established church but discipline declined. Here strain was resolved by a drift in the direction of the church comprehensive.

American Congregationalism, though disestablished and relatively diminished in numbers as a result of the influx of Catholic immigrants, has retained nevertheless an acute sense of responsibility for the moral tone of the entire community. The community in the meantime has expanded from the Bay Colony to the whole of the United States. At the same time the Congregational concern for the realization of the kingdom on earth has invaded other religious groups, even those which began as holy communities despondent of the world at large. The social gospel enlisted all American Protestantism and the United States became the sphere of the divine society. Prohibition was an attempt to impose an ethic on the country as a whole. In the Great War, the entire land was conceived as a gathered people, an elect nation with a mission for the world.

Disillusionment of course followed, and such pretensions now sound arrogant and naive. Nevertheless America has not yet altogether lost the faith, compounded of Calvinism and the spirit of the frontier, that the Kingdom of God in some measure at least can be realized on earth. And here lies the great difference between American and Continental Protestantism, with England of late veering to the Continent. Lutheranism was never hopeful with regard to the world at large, nor of the possibility of erecting the Kingdom of God anywhere on earth. The Christian, according to Luther—because he is in the world and out of love for those who are not yet emancipated from the world—must participate in civil institutions including war, but only with heaviness of heart, never dreaming by such means to do more than restrain sin. American Christianity, with its Calvinist faith that God would realize his purpose in history, has oscillated between crusades and pacifism, as now the one technique and now the other seemed more effective for the realization of the Kingdom. This attitude is still vigorous among us and our present pacifism might easily flare into a crusade. [This was written in 1940.] British Congregationalism, however, has turned Lutheran and now fights with no *deus vult,* with no hope of planting Jerusalem in England's green and pleasant land, nor even of creating in Germany a promise-keeping government —only in the hope of restraining outrageous villainy. This difference in social attitude which now divides Europe from America and British from American Congregationalism may well prove a more serious obstacle to ecumenical Christianity than the older forms of division.

Such an analysis may well leave us wondering where we are. Whatever may be the effect on church unity, the sectarian ideal of holiness and the "church" ideal of comprehensiveness are both valid. There is intrinsic validity in the middle way between the church as a gathered group with an emphasis on holiness and the church as a comprehensive society like the ark of Noah including the clean and the unclean. In spite of all the scorn which is heaped today upon those who make any pretensions to righteousness, the note of holiness cannot be relinquished. The truth remains that the pattern of the Christian life ought to offer a quality discernibly different from that prevailing in society. We cannot pretend that it does; and even to claim that it should lays us open to the charge of self-righteousness and hypocrisy for which British and American Christians have been so commonly lampooned by Continentals. Nevertheless despite the risks, holiness is one of the marks of the church. The Congregational insistence on an actual and not an imputed righteousness is an ideal not to be lightly abandoned, however much one may recognize one's unworthiness and the un-predictable operation of grace in those who are apparently un-worthy. Here Congregationalists are one with the Baptists, Quak-ers, Mennonites, Dunkards, Brethren and Methodists.

But comprehensiveness is an indispensable note too. The Gospel of John records that 153 fish were caught in the net when Peter went fishing at the behest of the risen Lord. The number puzzled the commentators until the discovery was made that the ancients supposed 153 to be the total number of the varieties of fish. The net took them all in. Even so is Christianity concerned for society and willing to take the risk of bad fish along with the good and of tares with the wheat. Probably this is why Congrega-tionalists have held at once to the gathered church and to infant baptism. The gathered church ought to receive only adults, but like the Catholic, Lutheran, Anglican and Presbyterian churches, Congregationalists have been unwilling to sever themselves from the sense of the solidarity of life in which God operates in ways unfathomable by man.

Does the middle way place its adherents in an advantageous position for accomplishing the unity of the church? Not necessari-ly, as we have seen, but the Congregational middle way has this advantage, that it combines concepts of the Church which tran-scend historic circumstances. The antinomy of the church Catholic and the church holy began in the very days of the Apostles and never ceased to trouble the new Israel of God. Congregationalism ought to be in a position to understand both extremes and possibly to essay a role of reconciliation; perhaps, too, it may offer something of an example of balance in that syncretism which is rendering the present state of Protestantism so chaotic. In sloughing off old casings and incorporating elements of strength from other bodies Congregationalism has displayed the quality of organic life while avoiding usually those indiscriminate borrowings which wreck the symmetry and simplicity of the inherited way.

7. The Disciples: Alexander Campbell and Church Unity

Alexander Campbell has the singular distinction of being the only Christian reformer whose achievement was the denial of his intention. He sought to unite all of the evangelical churches and instead founded one more. To a degree a similar anomaly is discoverable also in Martin Luther, who set out to reform Christendom and ended by rending Christendom. Or again in John Wesley, who endeavored to revive the Church of England and headed a secession from the Church of England. Nevertheless, in the case of these latter two, the discrepancy is not so glaring. Luther did reform, even though he divided, and Wesley did revive, even though he seceded. But Alexander Campbell sought to unite and increased division.

The outcome cannot altogether be regarded as a malign trick of a capricious fate. There was something of the same anomaly in the man's deportment, because he sprayed Christian divisions with vitriol. He was an artist in denunciation, ridicule and satire, and reveled in debate, whether with Owen the Infidel, Purcell the Roman Catholic Bishop or Rice the Infant Baptist. Public disputations in those days were a great popular diversion, the equivalent among the saints of the race track and the prize ring, and Alexander Campbell was a heavyweight champion. The story is told that Bishop Vardeman, having been selected to moderate a debate in which Campbell was to defend immersion, was traveling in a gig to Washington over a muddy road when he overtook a man on foot and remarked to the traveler that he must have very important business to be trudging to Washington through such weather. The man answered that he was going to hear Campbell debate. Vardeman, suspecting that the man might be on the opposite side, sought

First published in *The Sage of Bethany,* ed. Perry E. Gresham (St. Louis, 1960).

to twit him by suggesting that Campbell might whip his champion. The man answered that if this were the Mr. Campbell whom he had heard on a previous occasion, then "all creation cannot whip Mr. Campbell."[1]

He was adept at satire, which is an admirable weapon in debate but not often an instrument of conciliation. Here is an example of his counsel to preachers:

> Let your sermon be full of "the enticing words of man's wisdom," and let it be beautified with just divisions, with tropes and with metaphors, and with hyperbole, and apostrophe, and with interrogation, and with acclamation, and with syllogisms, and with sophisms. . . .
>
> And take good heed to your attitudes and your gestures, knowing when to bend and when to erect. . . .
>
> Let your voice at times be smooth as the stream of the valley, and soft as the breeze that waves not the bough on its banks; and at times let it swell like the wave of the ocean, or like the whirlwind on the mountain top.
>
> Then shall you charm the ears of your hearers and their hearts shall be softened, and their minds shall be astounded, and their souls shall incline to you; and the men shall incline to you, and likewise the women; yea, to your sayings and to your persons shall they be inclined.
>
> And be you mindful not to offend the people; rebuke you not their sins. . . .
>
> If a brother shall raise up the banner of war against brother, and christians against christians, rebuke them not. . . .
>
> If any man go into a foreign land and seize upon his fellow man, and put irons on his feet and irons on his hands, and bring him across the great deep into bondage; nay, if he tear asunder the dearest ties of nature, the tenderest leagues of the human heart; if he tear the wife from the husband, and force the struggling infant from its mother's bleeding breast, rebuke him not!
>
> And although he sell them in foreign slavery to toil beneath the lash all their days, tell him not that his doings are of Antichrist; for lo! he is rich and gives to the church.[2]

The first part of this declamation might not have stung, since but few would have applied the strictures to themselves, but the castigations on the slave trade and war might easily have provoked resentment.

---

[1] Memoirs of Alexander Campbell, ed., Robert Richardson (2 vols., Philadelphia, 1868-1870), II, 73.

[2] *The Christian Baptist,* II, 167-168.

This passage is an example of his style. It does not, of course, apply to divisions among Christians. But here is another excerpt which strikes directly at the Baptists, the very group with whom for a time he was in closest affiliation. He is parodying an account of an ordination as given in the Latter Day Luminary. Here is Campbell's rendering:

> On Wednesday, the 11th of June, A.D. 44, the Rev. Saulus Paulus and the Rev. Joses Barnabas were set apart as missionaries to the Gentiles dispended throughout the world, by a committee of the board of managers of the Baptist General Convention, met in the city of Antioch. An interesting sermon was delivered on the occasion by the Rev. Simon Niger, from Isaiah xliii, 4. "The isles shall wait for his law." Rev. Lucius of Cyrene led in offering up the consecrating prayer. Rev. Manaen gave Mr. Paulus and his companion (Mr. Barnabas) an appropriate charge; and the Rev. John Mark gave them the right hand of fellowship. . . . The Rev. Lucius of Cyrene offered up the concluding prayer. The services were performed in the Rev. Mr. Simeon Niger's meeting-house. The day was fine, and the assemblage was very large, and proved, by their fixed and silent attention to the services, how much they felt for the world that lieth in wickedness; and by a collection of $86.25 cents, they showed a willingness to aid the Rev. Mr. Paulus and the Rev. Mr. Barnabas in carrying the gospel to the heathen.
>
> Mr. Paulus is a young man, and a native of the city of Tarsus; he received his classical and theological education in the theological seminary in Jerusalem. He appeared before the committee a man of good sense, of ardent piety, and understandingly led by the spirit of God to the work in which he has now engaged.[3]

This passage, to be sure, comes from Campbell's earliest and most acrimonious period. A number of points are pilloried. One is the use of titles for ministers. Reverends and Right Reverends were unknown in the days of Peter and Paul. Will Satan, Campbell demanded, be routed by an army of D.D.'s? (Incidentally, four of the Disciples at Yale have earned the degree of Ph.D. by writing about Alexander Campbell.[4]) Another point was that missionaries

---

[3] *Ibid.*, I, 1823, edition of 1856, p. 17.

[4] Robert Frederick West, *Alexander Campbell and Natural Religion* (New Haven, 1948) ; Denton R. Lindley, *The Structure of the Church in the Thought of Alexander Campbell,* 1947, unpublished; Harold L. Lunger, *The Political Ethics of Alexander Campbell* (St. Louis, 1954) ; Granville T. Walker, *Preaching in the Thought of Alexander Campbell* (St. Louis, 1954) .

should not be paid, that church gatherings should not be in fixed meetinghouses, that ministerial candidates should not receive special training nor should they be conscious of a call from God. Rather, they should be chosen by the congregation on the basis of previous qualifications. Some of these strictures were later to be modified. But the point is that the Baptists could scarcely relish his sally any more than his jibe that they had dehorned the beast and produced a hornless ox, still able to maul if not to gore.

As for the Presbyterians, he picked up a notice in one of their journals which lamented "vacant churches deprived of the means of grace." "Oh, Peter! Oh, Paul," Campbell ejaculated, "churches vacant!" How could they be vacant as long as they had members, and how could they be deprived of the means of grace so long as the congregation could appoint one of their own number to administer the Sacraments? However warranted this jibe, the tone was not precisely irenic.

Nevertheless, the failure of Alexander Campbell's efforts for the reunion of the churches is not to be attributed primarily to his attitude. He riddled and ridiculed, but he was not contentious nor cantankerous. Once he ventured to rib an Episcopal minister by branding the affair of Henry VIII and Anne Boleyn as an ugly story. The rector retorted that the Bible contained some ugly stories. Campbell laughed, and arm in arm they went in for dinner.[5] Debate and even controversy need not of necessity preclude unity.

Nor again is the work of Alexander for church unity to be written off as vain. Dean Inge once remarked that in religion nothing fails like success, and he might have said that nothing succeeds like failure. A witness is itself of value, and may bear ultimate fruit. Campbell was certainly right in deploring the divisions rampant in his day. He had come from North Ireland where the Presbyterians inherited from Scotland the divisions between the established church and the seceders. And these in turn were split into the Burghers and the Anti-Burghers. This division was crossed by that of the New and the Old Lights to form four parties: New Light Burghers, Old Light Burghers, New Light

[5] Richardson, *op. cit.*, II, 64.

Anti-Burghers, and Old Light Anti-Burghers. The point between Burghers and Anti-Burghers had reference to an oath required in Scotland but not in Ireland, let alone in Kentucky. The father of Alexander Campbell, Thomas Campbell, in 1807 came to the United States as the pastor of a Seceder Presbyterian church and when he dared to minister to all varieties of Presbyterians in the area, he was expelled.

Alexander Campbell could not conceive of Christ so divided that there could be a Baptist, Methodist, Presbyterian, Episcopal and Roman Catholic conscience. (He did not mention the Congregationalists, who did not flourish in his region.) Besides, said he, there is in Kentucky a Licking Association Baptist conscience and a Particular Baptist conscience. Under fictitious names he reported the situation in his district in 1825: "William Pedibus, the shoemaker, lost the custom of all the Presbyterians in town, because he said that Parson Trim denied free agency. And Thomas Vulcanus, the blacksmith, never shod a Methodist's horse since the time he censored Elder Vox's sermon on the possibility of falling from grace."

Campbell lived, as W. E. Garrison has pointed out, when sectarianism had accomplished its work in breaking rigid authoritarianism and tyranny, and had itself become an abuse because of its minute particularism and petty rancor. The time had come to forget or minimize ancient and often outmoded differences and to realize a genuine unity in Christ. If Campbell did found a new denomination, it was a denomination dedicated to Christian unity and has produced a number of noble advocates. A century of exhortation on their part has markedly contributed to the strength of the contemporary ecumenical movement. Another point worthy of note is that Campbell perceived the utter folly of sectarian differences on the mission field, and there it was that the church unity movement had its first inception.

Yet there is no denying that Campbell in his lifetime met with failure. This may be attributed solely to the perversity of the sects, and indeed Campbell said that union required them to "throw away nothing that they possess but error and falsehood." But then, of course, the question would arise as to what is error and what is falsehood. The failure of his scheme, however, I would suggest lay neither in his own belligerence nor in his opponent's stubbornness, but rather in his formulation of the conditions for unity. The core of his program was epitomized in a slogan already popular: "In essentials unity, in non-essentials liberty, in both charity." The term "essential" referred to that which is necessary to be believed or done as a condition for salvation, and unity meant that on these points no latitude was permissible. All those admitted to the church must agree and conform as to essentials. On matters not requisite for salvation, on which one would not be damned either way, diversity could be allowed, and toward those without as well as toward those within a kindly spirit should be entertained.

This slogan had behind it a long history.[6] St. Augustine had long since recognized a distinction between points of greater and lesser importance and quoted with relish the retort to one who asked what God was doing before he created the world; namely, that he was making hell for those who asked too many questions. On the eve of the Reformation the Brethren of the Common Life employed the idea in order to disparage theological speculation. Their patron saint was the Penitent Thief who was saved with so little theology. He believed only that Christ could get him to Paradise. Erasmus of Rotterdam in this tradition recommended deferring to the judgment day the discussion of thorny and in-soluble riddles, such as the distinction between the generation of the Son and procession of the Holy Ghost, or as to how God could be both three and one. That alone, said Erasmus, can be essential for salvation which can be universally understood and the em-phasis should be placed on the fruits of the spirit rather than on the tenets of the head. Sebastian Castellio, in the great controversy over the execution of Servetus for heresy, ventured to classify among the non-essentials the belief in the Trinity and predestina-tion, as well as an opinion as to whether Christ was ubiquitous as Luther held, or seated at the right hand of God the Father as Zwingli and Calvin contended. But the man who gave the idea its most influential formulation was Jacob Acontius in a book en-titled *The Wiles of Satan*. He there affirmed that alone to be

[6] Walter Koehler, "Die Geistesahnen des Acontius," *Festschrift für Karl Müller* (Tübingen, 1922), 198-208.

essential to salvation which is so designated in Scripture and he could discover only two points. One is, "The just shall live by faith." Therefore they are excluded who live by works and this rules out the Catholics. The other text is, "Believe on the Lord Jesus Christ and you shall be saved." This would exclude the Sabellians and, one would have thought, also the Socinians, though Acontius did not draw this conclusion. He broke a lance for Anabaptists who adopted a Gnostic attitude as to the flesh of Christ, not on the ground that they were right but that the point was not essential for salvation.

One observes that the principle of unity in essentials and liberty in non-essentials is exclusive as well as inclusive. Only those who unite on essentials can be admitted and only they may enjoy liberty as to non-essentials. The outworking of the principle is strikingly illustrated in the scheme of Oliver Cromwell who, in line with the idea of Acontius, excluded the Catholics and the Unitarians. He included in the following order of preference the Congregationalists, Baptists, and Presbyterians with the Anglicans and Quakers on the fringe subject to restriction primarily on political grounds because the Anglicans adhered to the crown and the Quakers would not fight against the king.

Alexander Campbell had the same basic plan and he defined the essentials in the same manner. With Acontius he held that the points necessary for salvation can be only those so stipulated in the New Testament. This is our sole source of the knowledge of God. This is, as it were, the charter of the church. We are to "open the New Testament as if mortal man had never seen it before," casting aside all preconceived notions, all sophisticated subtleties, all creeds which are merely inferences from the Bible and therefore the inventions of men. If we thus open the Book we shall find two conditions for salvation. Said Campbell:

THE BELIEF OF ONE FACT . . . *is all that is requisite, as far as faith goes, to salvation. The belief of this* ONE FACT, *and submission to* ONE INSTITUTION *expressive of it, is all that is required of Heaven to admission into the church.* . . . The one fact is expressed in a single proposition—*that Jesus the Nazarene is the Messiah* . . . the *one institution* is baptism into the name of the Father, and of the Son, and the Holy Spirit.[7]

7 *The Christian System*, p. 101.

Observe that there is an article of belief. Campbell did not object to a creed, for any article of faith is a creed. Neither did he object to the use of a creed as a test. His objection was to any creed which goes beyond the Bible. In addition to belief he postulated one demand as to practice, namely, baptism.

If Campbell had stopped here he might have had a basis on which a very large degree of union could have been possible. The Universalists would not have been excluded. Campbell considered them mistaken though no worse than those who think that hell holds infants not a span long. Both have "mounted their winged horse and soared beyond the regions of revelation." He defended the right of a Universalist named Raines to Christian fellowship because he advanced Universalism as a private opinion and not as a part of the gospel. Such tolerance was considered to have been vindicated when Raines later renounced his error.

The demands formulated by Campbell would not have excluded the Unitarians. Many of them would have confessed that Jesus was the Messiah. They might have balked at baptism in the name of the Father, the Son, and the Holy Ghost, though these terms could have been defined in a New Testament rather than in a Nicene sense. Campbell affirmed that he would not reject a man because he was a Unitarian, if he would confess that Jesus of Nazareth is the Messiah, the Son of God. On the other hand, the Socinians, whom he defined as those who called Jesus the son of Joseph, he described not as Christians but as "drivelling philosophers." And he went on to say, "From my heart I pity these Socinians . . . and would not, the Bible being in my hand, rush into the presence of the Judge of quick and dead with their sentiments, for twice the value of the universe."[8]

The conditions as stipulated above are certainly broad. But then Campbell began by definition and addition to narrow the range. Baptism, said he, meant only adult baptism. In the New Testament he could find no reference to infant baptism, therefore it could not have been practiced and therefore it is not to be observed by us. With one stroke he cut off the possibility of union with all of the churches except the Baptists, unless, of course, the

[8] *The Christian Baptist,* p. 51.

others were to abandon their own tenets. As for those who did not, said he:

Infants, idiots, deaf and dumb persons, innocent Pagans ... with all the pious Pedobaptists, we commend to the mercy of God. But such of them as willfully *despise* this salvation, and who, having the opportunity to be immersed for the remission of their sins, willfully *despise* or refuse, we have as little hope for them as they have for all who refuse salvation *on their own terms of the gospel.*[9]

Next he arrived at the conclusion that the term "baptize" in the New Testament could mean only immersion. He found no record of sprinkling; therefore there was no sprinkling. And if immersion was the universal mode, then the New Testament verse should be translated "Repent and be immersed." Immersion is necessary to salvation because only in this way are we in actual possession of the remission of our sins. The non-immersed may indeed be happy in the peace of God because they are not aware that they are lost, but none can enjoy a rational hope save those immersed for the remission of sins. On the other hand, both as to adult baptism and immersion as absolute conditions for salvation or even church union there was some wavering.

At another time he said, "There is no occasion for making immersion on a profession of faith absolutely essential to a Christian." Again he declared that there are pedobaptist congregations "of whose Christianity,... I think as highly, as of most Baptist congregations, and with whom I could wish to be on the very same terms of Christian communion on which I stand with the whole Baptist society."

His tendency was, however, to grow more and more restrictive. There were two principles operative in his procedure. One was to return to the simplicity of the New Testament faith and require no more. The other was to restore the practice of the Early Christian community and to suffer no less. A further assumption was that the practice of the New Testament churches must have been uniform. Campbell noted in the Book of Acts (20:7) the verse which begins, "On the first day of the week when the dis-

[9] *The Christian System*, p. 203.

ciples [at Troas] came together for the breaking of the loaf."
[Campbell's translation]. The purpose of the assembly, then, was
to celebrate the Lord's Supper. What was done on that first day
must have been done on every first day, and what was done at
Troas must have been done in every Christian community. And
what then constituted the universal practice of the early church is
binding, likewise, upon present-day Christians. Whether Campbell intended to say that the observance of this practice is necessary
for salvation is not clear. He did consider it necessary for church
membership and presumably also for Christian unity. He may
have shifted his definition of essential from that which is essential
for salvation to that which is necessary for unity. In any case, he
had introduced a further restrictive principle. In fact, he had
reached the point where he could not unite with anybody. The
insistence on adult baptism cut off all save the Baptists, and
weekly communion eliminated them. Campbell had ended up
with a new denomination.

What then of church unity? It is not entirely clear that he
desired it any more. He declared, as a matter of fact, quite early
in his career, "I have no idea of seeing, nor one wish to see, the
sects unite in one grand army. This would be dangerous to our
liberties and laws. For this the Saviour did not pray."[10] Was then
his ideal that there should be denominations, but that they should
cherish each other in a spirit of charity? Organic unity would then
be relinquished as an ideal.

He noted the possibility of fellowship at different levels. Already there were Baptists and paedobaptists who met together in
monthly meetings for prayer and praise, yet they were not willing
to take communion together. He agreed that baptism must precede
communion, and of course baptism administered in the proper
way. Still it was an anomaly to be willing to pray and praise in
unison and not to sit down at the Lord's Table. He seemed unsettled in his own mind, whether to remove the disparity by
moving forward to the Lord's Table or by going in the other
direction to cut off the joint prayer meetings.

When one surveys Campbell's life work now, it may seem

---

[10] *The Christian Baptist*, p. 140.

pathetic because he decried the haggling of the sects and yet set up such conditions for Christian unity that none could unite save those who adopted a system different from that of all the rest. It is easy enough to pick flaws and discover inconsistencies in his scheme. His assumption that New Testament practice was uniform is entirely untenable and one wonders why on his own premises he did not go on to daily communion, because we read in the Book of Acts that "the disciples continued daily in breaking bread." Campbell got around this by making a distinction between the Lord's Supper and the love feast. But for this separation there is no warrant prior to the second century. In any case, the entire effort to discover a uniform pattern in early Christian practice has been proved untenable by modern historical research.

Consequently, we cannot go back to Alexander Campbell for a specific scheme of church unity, but we can learn from him. And one thing we can learn is his willingness to learn. He changed a great deal during his lifetime. He confessed that once he had been like the Indian's tree, so straight that it leaned a little the other way. His opposition to missionary societies and to a trained ministry was abandoned after he became the leader of a new denomination. In fact, his whole program suffered change. One writer has suggested that until 1830 his effort was to unite the churches, that from 1830 until his death the plan was to draw the receptive out of the unreformed churches. A third stage came after his death when the Disciples became a denomination and took their place as colleagues with mutual respect for the others. That stage may not have been reached by Alexander Campbell, but he was on the way. He was never static. His very progress, of course, may be regarded as an abandonment of his ideal of unity. And yet that was not the case. He never ceased to lament sectarianism. Just what better scheme we can devise to overcome it, is for us to work out. We are indebted to him for a persistent harping on the scandal, not only of division, but of acrimony.

The greatest thing about the man was his spirit. Commenting on his debate with the Presbyterians, he said:

I have no object but truth, and whatever may be published against my pamphlet, in a christian and candid manner, shall receive every attention. But let them not lose their temper, nor substitute railing for argument. . . . If any are convinced, let them beware of stifling convictions. . . .

Though I am decidedly convinced of the complete independency of the apostolical churches, and of the duty of following them, I would not be understood as placing undue importance upon this point. Christians of every denomination I love; and I will never, I hope, withhold my hand, or my countenance from any who, after impartial investigation, conscientiously differ from me. I can from my heart say, "Grace be with all those who love our Lord Jesus Christ in sincerity and truth."[11]

[11] *Ibid.*, p. 75.

8. The Making of a Pluralistic Society: A Protestant View

Introductory Note

Since the year 1958, when this essay was written, a great change in the climate of Catholic-Protestant relations was initiated by Pope John XXIII, who called Protestants not heretics but "separated brethren." At the second Vatican Council Protestant observers were given the chief seats and were sometimes informally addressed as "carissimi fratres." If this spirit is continued by the late pope's successor the situation envisioned by Richard Niebuhr in the quotation cited in this article may actually come to pass.

Some measure of official recognition is almost bound to be given to the process already underway whereby Protestants and Catholics have been moving, the one clockwise and the other counter-clockwise, toward points of convergence. With respect to the liturgy the Protestants of the Puritan tradition have revived the observance of the Christian year and are giving priority to the altar above the pulpit. One even hears that sometimes more candle wax is melted on Congregational than on Catholic altars. In the meantime the Catholics are sometimes moving the altar in the form of a communion table down next to the congregation. The dialogue Mass is favored with large congregational response and hymn singing is fostered, even to the use of Protestant hymns such as Luther's "Mighty Fortress." Permission has been given to say the Mass in Chinese and Hebrew. Presumably it will not be said frequently in either, but with the principle established there may be further extensions in the use of the vernacular. At the point of church government, Protestants are moving in the direction of centralization. Witness the National Council in the United States

First published in *Religion and the State University*, ed. Erich A. Walter, copyright University of Michigan Press (Ann Arbor, 1958).

and the World Council of Churches. Coincidentally the Catholics are talking of enlarging the role of the bishops and of restricting correspondingly the scope of the popes. In theology the Protestants have largely moved away from the ultra-liberalism of the turn of the century and have resuscitated the tenets of the Reformation theology of Luther and Calvin. Catholics at the same time have accepted the methods of Biblical criticism and today there is scarcely any difference in outlook between Catholic and Protestant scholars with regard to the Old Testament and little with regard to the New. As for the attitude to the Protestant Reformation the Catholic approach to Luther has become much more understanding and the late pope was ready to assign some blame for the schism to the Catholic Church.

Nevertheless, organic unity can scarcely come to pass unless the issues delineated in this article are squarely faced, and whereas joint religious services may become more common, none of the major religious bodies would be content to have all services jointly. In any case religious pluralism is here to stay, even if Catholics and Protestants should unite, because other groups are involved. Mutual respect, fraternal collaboration and joint meetings for prayer and discussion do not need, however, to wait for organic unity and are already taking place.

.   .   .   .

Those concerned for religion on the American campus are confronted by the fact that their students are adherents of diverse faiths. In addition to the three main religions in America, each with its own subvarieties, there is a fourth, which might be called the religion of Enlightenment, a Christianity attenuated as to doctrine and accentuated as to social idealism. Thomas Jefferson was its high priest and our democracy is its daughter. These three or four varieties have learned after wars of religion to coexist. They do so because of the triumph of the philosophy of the Enlightenment. Start talking about religious differences with the common man and he will exclaim, "At bottom we are all the same. We believe in God. We believe in goodness; the rest does not matter." This is precisely the point of view, in the Renaissance, of Boccaccio, with his story of the three identical rings representing Christianity, Judaism, and Islam; a story re-employed by that great figure of the Enlightenment Ephraim Lessing as a theme for his play *Nathan the Wise*. It was the philosophy of John Locke, who averred that if he were on the road that leads to Jerusalem it was of no consequence whether he wore buskins, cut his hair short or long, ate or refrained from meat, or had as a guide one clothed in white and crowned with a miter. Such trivial points as these, said he, make implacable enemies of Christians, "who are all agreed in the substantial and truly fundamental part of religion."

This point of view is very prevalent, but it does not so far prevail as to make possible a unified religious program on the part of the three or four groups in the university. The Catholics, the Protestants (especially the Fundamentalists), and the Orthodox Jews will not admit that the points of difference are trivial. The liberal Jews and the liberal Protestants are closer to the philosophy of the Enlightenment, though they too, and notably today, would not relegate doctrine so blithely to the area of the non-essentials.

The degree to which this pluralism obstructs a program of religion in the universities depends somewhat on the reason for which the inclusion of religion is desired. One reason for introducing religion into the curriculum—and a perfectly valid reason— is that religion is a subject of universal interest with regard to which every educated man should have at least a modicum of understanding because religion has been so determinative in the formation of cultures. The number of religions is of no consequence here save to increase the amount and the complexity of the material to be studied. There may still be a question whether or not courses should be taught by adherents of the several faiths. For the most part this would be impossible on budgetary grounds, and even if it were possible to employ a Protestant, a Catholic, and a Jew as professors of religion, similar consideration could not be extended to teachers representing all the religions of the world. The most defensible technique would resemble that used for the languages whereby a philologian directs a course with the aid of native informants; thus an expert on comparative religion might supplement his offerings with lectures by members of the religions expounded.

But no one of the three main religions in our land is satisfied with only this approach. All would claim that religion is something more than anthropology or sociology or history and that one cannot really understand religion without being religious. The sincere adherent of a faith must desire ultimately, however adroit the approach, to make converts because he believes that his particular faith has the answer to life's most fundamental questions and problems.

What shall we say of this our universe which increasing knowledge discloses as ever more appallingly vast, whose extent is measured only in terms of light-years and whose duration dwarfs the life of man to less than the span of an insect? Evidence of staggering intelligence we see in its intricate structure and delicate balance, evidence of purpose in its dynamic, creative self-elaboration, and differentiation within organic wholeness. But is there here any friendliness to man? In the bleak recesses of stellar space, in the nuclear explosions of solar radiation, in the erratic and devastating course of tornadoes, in the eruption of volcanoes and in the cooling of planets, is there anything but the inexorable working of an inscrutable purpose indifferent to mankind? Have we been accorded by capricious fate a temporary haven on a sun-basking planet only that, after the mind of man has exploited every resource for survival, we shall at last succumb when our earth has become as extinct as the craters of the moon? And what of all those who have gone before and of those who are yet to come? What is the destiny of those who have labored in the morning of man, carving bisons on the walls of their caves, of those who for millenia followed unchanged the ancestral ways of the forest primeval? Of those who throughout the centuries have by searching found out some of the secrets and added to the treasure house of knowledge? Are they now and shall we shortly all be resolved into the dust from which we came without the answers we crave to those riddles? And what of the grave inequalities that life inflicts, the barbarous torments that men have suffered at the hands of men? Is there no vindication? And for those who have so sinned against their fellows, is there no forgiveness? If we must answer "No," straight down the line, what then is the meaning of life and of mortality? We may indeed say with the resolute poet brooding over the recession of faith, "Let us be true then, love, to one another." But how great a place have love and honor in a universe where man alone has evolved and cherishes such ideals? And to come to our own situation, what is the point of fostering universities and of acquiring more knowledge, perchance with the consequence of hastening man's destruction? Or should we perhaps use our science to get it over with and not wait for the great freeze to encompass a burned-out world?

If religion has the answers to such universal questions, surely no subject could be more appropriate in a university dedicated to the quest of knowledge. But now comes a difficulty that is accentuated though not created by religious pluralism. Judaism and Christianity are religions of historic revelation. They announce a way to truth which is not that of the university, because revelation is conceived by all of these religions, at least in their more naive stages, as something given in times past, a deposit to be accepted and elucidated, not to be questioned, whereas for the university truth is a quest where nothing is to be taken for granted and every hypothesis subjected to critical scrutiny. Truth as a deposit and truth as a quest, can these concepts coexist?

The notion of truth as a quest is derived from our Hellenic heritage. This was the presupposition of Socrates, of Plato, of Aristotle. The idea had a rebirth in the Renaissance when Erasmus applied it to the study of the Scripture. The classic formulation was given by that Renaissance Puritan John Milton, who declared that in theology as in arithmetic the golden rule is, "To be still searching what we know not by what we know, still closing up truth to truth as we find it." He was confident that in so doing truth would emerge. "Let truth and falsehood grapple; whoever knew truth put to the worse in a free and open encounter?" Father Murray, the editor of the Jesuit journal *America*, asks us whether we can any longer be so naive as to believe that. Now of course we have seen that the enemies of free encounter can so take advantage of free encounter as to destroy it. But the point was that among a company of seekers, all dedicated to free encounter, in which each would propound his hypothesis for the criticism of his colleagues, where each stood ready to convince or be convinced, truth would prevail. A further ingredient in this faith is that, "Truth crushed to earth will rise again." This second assertion is indeed a faith rather than a fact, and even the first does not admit of unexceptional verification. But it is the best method we have of arriving at truth, and it is the fundamental assumption of our universities.

The great religions claim that truth, though in some measure an object of a quest, in its most important phase (as it relates to the ultimate) is the subject of a deposit. Truth is given through a self-disclosure of God at definite times in the past and recorded in inspired sacred writings. The most unqualified form of this claim is made by the Roman Catholic church. Father W. H. Van de Pol says:

> Holy Scripture and the Church have always presented revelation as the making known by God of certain definite truths which before were hidden in the mind of God, but now, at the end of time, are announced and made known to all who believe. From the beginning, revelation, preaching, and faith have had a definite and unchangeable scope and content. These truths have always been proclaimed by divine authority, and it is precisely on account of this that they call for unconditional belief and unhesitating obedience on the part of man. The act of faith involves a complete surrender of man to the revelation of God, and to the authoritative teaching of the contents of this definite, final revelation.[1]

This is not to say that the revelation as given in scripture is explicit in every respect. Precisely because it is not, God has endowed the Church with the power of inerrant elucidation, and this power is focused on the pope. He is not an organ of revelation but only of explication. He is the unique recipient of that aid from the Holy Spirit which will so watch over his normal processes of reasoning that, in making deductions from the revelation already given in the areas of faith and morals, when and only when he makes a pronouncement binding upon all Catholics, will he then be infallibly preserved from error.

The Catholic church claims, then, to be the custodian of the revelation given through Christ and recorded in the Scriptures, capable of formulation in doctrinal propositions and susceptible of further elaboration by inerrant deduction.

[1] W. H. Van de Pol, D.D., *The Christian Dilemma* (New York, 1952), p. 21.

Is it possible, apart from religious diversity, to combine such a position as to the method of arriving at truth with that assumed by the modern university? It was done, of course, in the medieval university where theology was the queen of the sciences, and it was accomplished by a demarcation of sphere. Certain disciplines, such as physics, rest upon the inquiry of the human mind. Here the pagan Aristotle was regnant. Only theology proper dealt with revelation. Yet conflict arose even in the medieval university, and notably between philosophy and theology, when the philosophy in vogue came to be nominalism, which claims that reality consists of unrelated particulars, or more precisely, of particulars related only by contiguity in space and time. Difficulty arises when this view is applied to the doctrine of the Trinity, whose three persons transcend space and time. If, then, they have no relation save contiguity in space and time, the three persons in the Godhead become three unrelated absolutes, and the outcome is tritheism. The exponents of this view agreed that it did not comport with the theological teaching that the three are one. The solution was found in the doctrine if not of double truth at least of double logic.

The situation today is not vastly dissimilar. Catholic theology is compatible with natural science on the basis of a division of spheres, and many distinguished scientists are Catholic. In the area of philosophy only the Thomist's position is congruous with Catholic theology, and even in the natural sciences conflicts may arise and have arisen as in the case of Genesis versus geology and evolution. The pope has ruled that Adam was a real person from whom the human race is descended, an assumption with which no non-Catholic biologist would be ready to commence. One may wonder whether Catholicism can be genuinely at home in any university other than in a Catholic university. In any university whatever Catholic theology could be taught, but only by declaring itself to be at variance with some or at least an aspect of some of the other disciplines.

With regard to non-Catholics the case is different, and here it is that religious pluralism injects a difficulty at the most central point, the very concept of revelation. The Fundamentalist Christian and presumably the Orthodox Jew—as to Judaism I am less well informed than as to Christianity—find revelation in the Scriptures, which are taken to be entirely inerrant. Yet they do have to be interpreted, as the Roman Catholic church rightly insists, and what happens is that each Christian sect has its own scheme of interpretation. Once I sat in on an interchange between a Christadelphian and a Jehovah's Witness. They appeared to me to be of the same stripe, but they were quite unable to achieve common ground because of discrepant modes of interpretation. Fundamentalists are of course able in a university to do distinguished work in all of the disciplines not at variance with their own faith, and they may even fulfill the requirements of courses in a theology contrary to their own by mastering the body of information. A Fundamentalist can take a doctor's degree in religion in a liberal institution by being open to every fact and impervious to every idea. The purpose in so doing is to use the degree as a weapon with which to combat the point of view of the institution by which the degree was conferred. There may be some point in continuing such a situation because it does mean that in a measure a channel of possible communication is kept open. Yet one cannot but regard the case as sad if in religion the meeting of minds and hearts cannot go beyond the factual.

Those who belong to the liberal group among the non-Catholics entertain a view of revelation distinctly different from that both of the Catholics and of the conservatives in their own bodies. The term liberal is here used for those who have accepted the methods of historical criticism as applied to the sacred books and are not disposed in any case to think of revelation in terms that can be reduced to neat proposition. In this sense Karl Barth, who has lavished so much criticism on Protestant Liberalism, is himself in many respects in the liberal camp.

Three examples may serve to illustrate differing views of revelation. The first is that of Nicholas Berdyaev, a representative of the Russian Orthodox Church. He may be considered because he has been much read in American Protestant seminaries and because his point of view has its parallels in some phases of Protestant Liberalism as it did also in Catholic Modernism. "Revelation," says Berdyaev, "is not something which drops into a man's lap from outside and in which he has nothing but an entirely passive part to play." Berdyaev is the heir of that mysticism of the Eastern Church, not unknown to the Western, which finds the goal of religion in the union of man with God so that man himself is made divine. In the experience of union the distinction between faith and reason disappears because this belongs to the world of objectification. Revelation cannot be objectified. It cannot be formulated into propositions which in themselves are true or false. Revelation is a spiritual event. The truth which it communicates must be grasped integrally. Unless truth takes place in a man truth is not obtained. Revelation makes use of historical facts as symbols. "The Christian conception of the divine Incarnation ought not to mean the deification of historical facts. Christian truth cannot be made to depend upon historical facts, which cannot be fully attested nor ingenuously accepted as reality."[2]

This statement leaves one wondering as to the relation of faith and history. Is revelation the continuous self-disclosure of God in mystical experience for which the records of history provide only a garment of symbol or are we capable of receiving revelation in personal experience only because of the unique self-disclosure of God in the past? Berdyaev might respond to this question as he did to another: "There is," said he, "a question which is put by people who are wholly submerged in objectification and consequently in the spirit of authoritarianism. It is, 'Where then is there a fixed and abiding standard of truth?' And to that question I decline to give my answer."[3]

The second example is that of a Protestant layman, a Congregationalist and a natural scientist, Edmund Sinnott, who in his work *Two Roads to Truth* describes the one as the way of intellect, reason, science; the other as a way of insight, intuition, unreasoned assurance, instinctive feeling. The second way is strongly akin to aesthetic sensibility.

Beauty is a subtle, indefinable thing. Great art and poetry and music, nature's innumerable and radiant beauties—these set man's spirit singing. They warm his heart and wake within him a sense of glory and

---

[2] Nicolas Berdyaev, *Truth and Revelation* (London, 1953), pp. 47-48.
[3] *Ibid.,* p. 40.

delight, lifting him to such ecstasy that, like the religious mystic, he becomes for a little while a higher sort of being, in tune with mysterious
harmonies.[4]

The insight of the individual is incalculably indebted to the
past—to the Hebrew and Christian past—yet is not to be restricted
by the past. He continues:

Where all things thus are on the march it seems to the scientist the
height of folly to try to tie up truth within the limits of a dogma, either
philosophical or religious, and to deny the possibility of fuller understanding even of spiritual matters. Reverence for the past should never
become a strait jacket for the present. Insistence on a truth that is certain
and perfect, never to be changed, science repudiates.... Science respects
the past, but builds upon it for a greater future. Why, one asks, should we
not expect religion to have the same expansiveness, the same splendidly
growing vision of the truth, as it explores mysteries deeper than science
can ever probe?... He who told Simon to launch out into the deep would
never counsel timid conservatism in such matters or seek to pour the
truth's new wine into bottles of dogmatic certainty. "The worship of
God," says Whitehead, "is not a rule of safety—it is an adventure of the
spirit, a flight after the unattainable. The death of religion comes with
the repression of the high hope of adventure."[5]

With this view of revelation the conflict between truth as a
deposit and truth as a quest disappears. The difference lies between truth as sight and truth as insight.

The third example is afforded by Richard Niebuhr, a Protestant theologian, a liberal as to historical criticism, but with a much
deeper feeling for revelation in history than one finds in Berdyaev's questing for obliteration of objective distinctions through
union with the divine. Niebuhr understands revelation as the
disclosure of meaning in history and in life. The prophets by
revelation illumined the history of Israel and gave to the men of
their day an understanding of the memories of their people. Jesus,
born in the fullness of time, brought to life the meaning of the
convergence of the religion of the Hebrews and the philosophy of
the Greeks.

[4] Edmund W. Sinnott, *Two Roads to Truth* (New York, 1953), pp. 44-45.
[5] *Ibid.*, p. 192.

Revelation continues. . . . The work has not been completed, for the past is infinite, and thought, even with the aid of revelation, is painful, and doubt assails the human heart. But for the Christian church the whole past is potentially a single epic. In the presence of the revelatory occasion it can and must remember in tranquillity the long story of human ascent from the dust, of descent into the sloughs of brutality and sin, the nameless sufferings of untold numbers of generations, the groaning and travailing of creation until now—all that otherwise is remembered only with despair. There is no part of that past that can be ignored or regarded as beyond possibility of redemption from meaninglessness. And it is the ability of the revelation to save all the past from senselessness that is one of the marks of its revelatory character.[6]

Such revelation cannot be set forth in a set of articles true or false. One does not assent to revelation as true simply by agreeing that it is so. The discovery of meaningfulness in life and history has to be felt, not simply believed, and it will not be felt unless there is first an inner transformation. "The response to revelation is quite as much a confession of sin as a confession of faith." What revelation

. . . means for us cannot be expressed in the impersonal ways of creeds or other propositions but only in responsive acts of a personal character. We acknowledge revelation by no third person proposition, such as that there is a God, but only in the direct confession of the heart, "Thou art my God." We can state the convincement given in the revelatory moment only in a prayer saying, "Our Father." Revelation as the self-disclosure of the infinite person is realized in us only through the faith which is a personal act of commitment, of confidence and trust, not a belief about the nature of things.[7]

Such a view of revelation does not involve the discrepancy of the Catholic and Fundamentalist view as against the scientific, but it raises a much more profound question as to whether revelation can be taught at all. What will one do in a university with a course which must start with a confession of sin, and cannot the most untutored man make such a confession and receive the answer that gives meaning to his life and all that he knows of life?

[6] H. Richard Niebuhr, *The Meaning of Revelation* (New York, 1946), pp. 112-113.
[7] *Ibid.*, pp. 153-154.

What then will one do with revelation in a university? The answer is that one can study the records of religious experience, the Bible as religious experience, religious biography as experience of religion. One can discover how others were brought to these moments of insight. An artist told me that he had no feeling for El Greco, but he looked and studied and observed and exposed himself until there burst on him an awed response to the clouds brooding over Toledo. It is the same with poetry and music. They can be studied by way of exposure. They will never be known until the spirit lists to blow.

If then there are differences so deep between the three religions and between varieties within these religions, how can religion be presented in a university where all three and more are present? Reconciliation of their divergent viewpoints is at present out of the question. Father van de Pol says that Protestants and Catholics must regard each other as heretics. He does not attach to the word all of the old invidious connotations. He is not issuing a summons for an auto-da-fé. He uses heretic in its primitive sense as one who is in error. Catholics hold out to Protestants no hope of reunion save by way of submission on our part, and we find the claims of Rome altogether untenable. The doctrine of papal infallibility is a great hindrance. We realize that the pope is claimed to be infallible only when he speaks on faith and morals, only when he elucidates previous revelation, and only when he speaks officially and makes his pronouncement binding upon all Catholics. He may in an unofficial statement be guilty of heresy as was Pope Honorius. Again Leo XIII pronounced the text in I John 5 which reads, "And there are three in heaven that witness, the Father, the Spirit and Son" to be an authentic part of this epistle, though not discoverable in any manuscript prior to the fifteenth century. Thirty years later another pope reversed this judgment. But this did not invalidate the infallibility of Leo in Catholic eyes, because he was not speaking officially. The distinction appears to Protestants very tenuous. Will the Spirit which bloweth where it listeth so submit itself to that which is official? Even more repugnant to us is the claim that infallibility has no relation to the character of the pope. We can understand that a man does not need to be perfect in order to speak the truth, but that he should not only be immoral but even indifferent to religion and yet able to speak infallibly about religion taxes all credence. Leo X, for example, was a flippant pope more interested in hunting, gambling, and art than in religion. Yet the *Dictionnaire de Théologie Catholique* reckons his bull, *Exsurge Domine,* as among the infallible pronouncements.

Even more grave is the preoccupation of liberal Protestantism with demythologizing, that is to say the endeavor to extract the religious core from the Scriptures while discarding the outmoded scientific thought forms of the first century; whereas Catholicism is occupied in making more mythology, at variance, we think, both with history and with science, as for example the declaration of the Assumption of the Virgin. But this is not the place to air all of our differences. The point is that they are deep and not easily to be bridged. And they are lamentable because the very revelation which might bring balm to the world is discredited if the religions which profess to have received it are so at variance as to what it is. All of which is not to say that there are not great areas of agreement, and one is inclined to believe that the man who dishes out the hamburgers may be right in saying, "at bottom we are all the same, we believe in God, we believe in goodness, the rest does not matter." Yet it is easier for a Protestant to say this than for a Catholic, because for a Protestant what matters is not so much precise belief as interior piety and the Protestant is glad to testify that the Catholic has it. But interior piety or spirituality though esteemed by the Catholic is not sufficient without dogmatic rectitude. The gulf is still there. Happily some are striving to bridge it. Father George A. Tavard, who has written a very understanding book about Protestantism, is seeking to make Catholicism more acceptable by a revival of the Augustinianism of the late Middle Ages as exemplified in Saint Bonaventura, for whom the conflict of faith and knowledge was resolved in the vision of God. Richard Niebuhr remarks:

There will be no union of Catholics and Protestants until through the common memory of Jesus Christ the former repent of the sin of Peter and the latter of the sin of Luther, until Protestants acknowledge Thomas Aquinas as one of their fathers, the Inquisition as their own sin and Ignatius Loyola as one of their own Reformers, until Catholics have

canonized Luther and Calvin, done repentance for Protestant nationalism, and appropriated Schleiermacher and Barth as their theologians.[8]

The time for this has not yet come and until it does we shall
not be able to organize a joint department of religion in a university. The only possibility is that a department of religion should
offer courses given by Protestants, by Catholics, and by Jews working quite independently. They would be inculcating their own
faiths. But this is impossible in a state institution because of the
limitations imposed on education by the separation of church and
state. What can be done is that religious bodies at their own ex-
pense may set up faculties of theology on the university campus
and offer courses open to election by all students, for which the
university will grant credits toward its own degree. In some places
this is being done.

Yet this in itself is not enough, and no one of the faiths is
content simply to give instruction. The impression must not be
given that Catholics, because they can state revelation in propositions to be believed or rejected, are any less disposed than Protestants or Jews to say that belief must be more than intellectual
assent if it is to be a saving faith. All of the three religions are
concerned for the practice of religion alike in acts of worship and
of social concern. The latter presents no problem. Fortunately, all
three faiths experience no difficulty whatever in collaboration on
such matters as social justice, opposition to racial discrimination,
political immorality, and the like. This most important area does
not require discussion here because pluralism offers no difficulty.

But worship does, and much more so for the Catholic than
for the Protestant and the Jew. Because the Catholic feels that
right worship requires right doctrine, and a liturgy acceptable to
a non-Catholic cannot be satisfactory to a Catholic. The liberal
Protestant and the liberal Jew place much greater stress on attitudes—reverence, awe, contrition, humility, adoration—and are
willing to worship together with those who express these attitudes
in other dogmatic terms. For us the dogmas have value more as
symbols than as precise formulations of ultimate truth. That is
why when I was in France with a Quaker unit of the Red Cross

[8] *Ibid.*, p. 119.

during World War I whenever we were in a village where there was no Protestant church I went to mass. Even on Catholic assumptions I cannot see why an occasional joint service of worship could not be worked out which would contain no dogmatic assertion unacceptable to any of the three. It could not possibly contain a full statement of the faith of each of the three, but it might center on common elements. As a Protestant I should have no difficulty in sharing with a Jew in a service drawn entirely from the Old Testament. He would have more difficulty in joining with me in a service including passages from the New Testament, but they might be so chosen that a liberal Jew would not feel obligated to withdraw. As a Protestant I could share with a Catholic in a service made up of scripture passages, of prayers from Saint Chrysostom, Saint Augustine, and John Henry Newman, hymns from Saint Ambrose, Jacopone da Todi, Saint Francis Xavier, and Gilbert Chesterton, and of meditations from Saint Francis, Saint Bernard, and Saint François de Sales. And I cannot see why a Catholic could not share in a service taken from the classics of Protestant devotional literature. I once gave a talk, by the way, on such literature over a Catholic radio program. Father Tavard says that: "Luther ranks among the most delicate devotional writers with his essay on *Christian Liberty* and his very devout commentary on Mary's *Magnificat*."[9]

A Catholic chaplain of one of our state universities tells us that it cannot be and warns us not to embarrass Catholics by inviting them to do what they must refuse. A Catholic, he says, can pray with anyone save an atheist (that he thinks would be tough) [10] privately, but not officially. One would like to know, in the first place, whether this is a universal ruling. There are regional differences in such matters. The Bishop of Syracuse, for example, has forbidden Catholic students to participate in a Religious Emphasis program. But the bishops in other areas permit it. The present bishop of Connecticut has reversed the practice of his predecessors who permitted a priest in New Haven

[9] George A. Tavard, *The Catholic Approach to Protestantism* (New York, 1955).

[10] Robert J. Welsh, *Religious Education* (November-December, 1956), p. 426.

to take part on the platform in a public service of Thanksgiving with scripture, hymns, prayer, and sermon. But I am told that such joint services continue in other places. Here is a point on which we should be glad to be more precisely informed. If the bishop says "No," we should not embarrass the priest, but there is no reason why we should not address ourselves to the bishop.

Admittedly, however, joint worship could be only occasional. Christians would not be satisfied with a chapel service all the year through which did not go beyond the Old Testament, and Catholics would not be willing to be continuously reserved in references to the Blessed Virgin and to the Saints. But if we can do so there is a point in holding joint services, because God is one and truth is one, and if we are sincere in our desire to worship the one God in truth, though manifestly, since we disagree, some of us must be in error, nevertheless we cannot go astray in joining in common adoration and petition for forgiveness and illumination from the Father of Lights, with whom there is no shadow of turning.

Neither should it be impossible to discuss our differences. Some of the interfaith movements have insisted that in all joint endeavors reference to dogma should be avoided and in no case should there be debate. This means getting together by avoiding fundamentals. But let us remember that students do not leave these matters alone. In private bull sessions no knuckles are gloved and no friendships are broken. Discussion on a public platform might indeed lead to acrimony, but what could be the objection to interchanges between representatives of the three faiths among small student groups? On the same level why might there not be informal, unofficial services of worship in areas where bishops have forbidden collaboration in public worship? The chaplain mentioned above said that he could pray privately with anyone. Did he mean only with one, or might not a group of half a dozen, a cell in other words, engage together in meditation and prayer? Every avenue of collaboration at every level should be explored.

9. The Sectarian Theory
of the Church

The distinction between the church and the sect has become, since the classic work of Ernst Troeltsch, a commonplace in the parlance of religious sociologists. Yet however suggestive the distinction the two terms seldom describe actual religious bodies with precision. Church and sect may perhaps best be used to denominate varied emphases within Christianity, both valid, ideally and often actually existing side by side, sometimes coming into conflict and resulting in separate organizations.

The two may be graphically characterized by saying that the church is an ark of salvation, the sect a fellowship of the saints; the church is leaven, the sect is salt; the church offers the broken bread, the sect demands the drinking of the cup of the passion. The church is an institution administering the means of grace. The sect is a brotherhood of those who seek to live the Gospel. The emphasis in the one case is sacramental and often creedal, in the other ethical. The church tends to be large, the sect to be small, because there are many who follow Christ in the breaking of the bread but few in the drinking of the cup, as the *Imitation of Christ* well observed. The church strives to become coextensive with society because the means of grace should be made as widely available as possible and are efficacious with the minimum response on the part of the recipient. Babies at birth receive the sacrament of baptism and are regarded from that moment as belonging to the church. Infant baptism is thus a mark of the church type. The moral demands are relaxed because salvation depends not upon ethical achievement but upon the reception of the sacraments and acquiescence in the creeds. The ethical requirements for continuance in the church are not rigoristic. Discipline tends to be moder-

First published in *Christendom*, X, 3 (Summer, 1946).

ate and the ban may be more readily used to exclude those who question the faith than those who fail to realize the ethical standards. The tares to be left until the harvest are the moral offenders, not the heretics who are already on the outside and may be compelled to come in. Because the church is large and ideally coterminous with the community an affiliation of the church is natural and appropriate with other agencies of society, particularly the state. Hence the church type finds the union of church and state congenial.

The sect type calls for the exemplification of the radical ethic of the New Testament. The Christian should take no oath, refrain from going to law, abstain from participation in war and very commonly also in government. Goods should be held in common. Those who lapse from the standards are to be excluded from the society. But no one should be constrained to enter the group, whose membership must be voluntary. Babies, incapable of personal adherence, cannot be received. Baptism should be reserved to seal an adult commitment which is the condition of church membership. The sect rests on the covenant of the members with each other. It is a voluntary society. Because its ethical demands are rigoristic it must always be a minority, influencing society by example rather than by permeation. A desire for personal holiness and a fear of contamination from the world may be a note of the sectarian attitude but need not be. A self-abnegating concern to walk in the footsteps of the Master in company with like-minded disciples is usually the primary motive.

Commonly the sect arises as a protest against the church, but the situation is not incapable of reversal. During the Boer War in a Canadian church a prayer of the minister for the wounded and dying on both sides precipitated the withdrawal of an intransigent imperialistic minority in protest because the majority supported the minister's espousal of the attitudes of the Sermon on the Mount. A secession from a sect in a churchly direction is, however, seldom necessary because the sect itself so readily becomes a church and because individuals can so easily withdraw and join a church. Sometimes moreover the church itself is sufficiently rigoristic to forestall secessions on moral grounds as in the Counter-Reformation.

In many instances a secession from the church in a sectarian direction is also unnecessary because the church is able to accommodate the sectarian type within itself. One device is monasticism, which offers an opportunity for the practice of a rigoristic ethic in segregated communities but in communion with the church. Again the *ecclesiola* may enable a voluntary society to be formed within the structure of a birthright group.

The sect frequently begins as a protest against the secularization of the church and in particular against the association or too close affiliation of the church with the state. The objection may be to the coercive power of the state as incompatible with the ethic of nonresistance. Or it may be to the low quality of the citizenry made up of the entire constituency of the community. If, however, citizenship can be made sufficiently selective this objection may disappear as in New England Congregationalism where state and church were coterminous in membership with each other but not with the community. Only church members could be citizens and only those displaying the creedal and emotional signs of grace could be church members. The result was that in the New Haven colony only one-tenth of the population constituted the church and state.

The church and sect can be combined as in Genevan Calvinism, which stressed at once the sacraments as channels of grace and virtuous living as a duty to God and a means of convincing oneself of election. Discipline was rigorous both as to creed and deed. The church was a voluntary society but also coterminous with the state and community because those who for any length of time resisted the church were expelled from the town. Calvinism retained infant baptism and yet demanded adherence to the church.

The inner life of the sect presents great diversity. The ethical emphasis does not of necessity preclude the hierarchical polity, sacramental system, and elaborate liturgy to be found in many of the churches. The secession of a sect will often entail alteration only at the point which has occasioned the breach. In the early centuries, for example, the schisms of Hippolytus, Novatian, and the Donatists involved no rejection of episcopacy. Again, sects may be driven speedily to adopt certain unwelcome features of the church. A mendicant group can survive only by reason of a supporting body. If disowned by that body it must then divide and develop its own supporting constituency. This happened to the Waldenses when their expulsion from the church cut off the alms of the faithful.

Generally, however, sects tend to develop freer and simpler forms of church life. Women frequently enjoy a high place, as in Montanism and Anabaptism. Social equalitarianism is customary. Members call each other brother and sister. In the lands where a familiar and a polite mode of address are current the familiar is preferred. The Quakers even went so far as to employ the plain speech to men of high and low degree within and without the fellowship. The anomalies of organization of which the sects are capable are strikingly illustrated by the case of Faustus Socinus, who became the leader of the Polish Antitrinitarians without being admitted to their society. The condition of membership was adult baptism. Socinus was ready to accept the rite as a gesture of brotherliness but not as a requisite for salvation. He was rejected but nevertheless affiliated with the congregation and became its recognized spokesman. The atmosphere of a sect can be harmonious and obviously must be, to a large degree, in those groups which maintain a continuous life for centuries. Yet most of them have gone through periods of contentiousness and extreme censoriousness.

The sect has difficulty in perpetuating itself. It originated in a flash of indignation and zeal fanned by ridicule and often persecution. In the second generation the children may not share the passionate convictions of the fathers, particularly if the external pressures are relaxed and the group fraternizes with the surrounding society. Richard Niebuhr (*The Social Sources of Denominationalism*) has gone so far as to say that the sect must always be a first generation movement. Joachim Wach (*Sociology of Religion*) replies that such groups as the Dukhoobors, Chlysty, Dunkards, Amish, and Hutterian Brethren have perpetuated their sectarian characteristics for centuries. They have done so only by isolating themselves from the culture round about. The sect thrives best on the frontier where isolation is easily possible and the complications of modern industrialization, imperialism and militarism can be avoided. But when the modern juggernaut catches up the sect is imperiled. In the United States, for example, the so-called historic peace churches, the Friends, Brethren, and Mennonites, have recently been passing from sects into churches.

These groups present an interesting illustration of the varying degrees to which sects practice segregation in order to preserve their integrity. Of the three the Mennonites have always been the most exclusive, the Friends the least, and the Brethren have taken the middle of the way. This may well be because of the diverse circumstances of their origins. The Mennonites arose under the death penalty, the Brethren under banishment, the Friends merely under political and social disabilities. The Mennonites despaired of the world and regarded government as ordained of God only to restrain sinners and as worthy to be administered only by sinners. Christians should render only passive obedience and until recent times in the United States the Mennonites refused to hold office save in a community of their own. The Brethren were willing in Pennsylvania to go to the polls to keep the Friends in office. And the Friends have ever been ready to participate in government short of taking part in war. For that reason the Friends continually find themselves in ambiguous situations and are compelled to wrestle with "cases of conscience" which for the Mennonites and Brethren never arise.

If the sect can become a church on emergence from persecution, a church can become a sect if reduced to a minority. The Catholic Church in the early years in the United States was a sect among the sects in the sense that it was distinctly a minority and sometimes a persecuted group. Communion with the Church universal was, of course, never relinquished and many sectarian characteristics could never be acquired, but one mark of the sect, an aversion to the use of constraint in religion, became a slogan of American Catholicism. The separation of church and state was also cordially endorsed.

The sharp distinction between the types has been in a measure broken down in modern times by the rise of the "society," a group devoted to sponsoring and exemplifying a particular cause, such as pacifism, antislavery, birth control, prohibition, and the like. The radical ethic of the Gospel thus finds an outlet without subjecting the structure of the church to the strains which in former days issued in new sect formations.

New types, moreover, are emerging which satisfy the desire for intimate fellowship without exhibiting other sectarian characteristics. The more or less secular fraternal organizations serve this end. Of late years in the United States holiness groups have emerged, largely in industralized urban areas. Since their concern is less to imitate the Son than to be filled with the Spirit they are under no pressure to separate themselves from the economic and political life of the community. Their ecstatic emotionalism can find expression, whether in the camp meeting, on the frontier or in the vacant store of the metropolis. Some writers prefer to invest the word "cult" with a special sense in order to designate these groups.

We may well inquire whether sectarianism in the form of separatism has a permanent place in the life of the church. Many would feel that the ideal is to provide outlets for the sectarian spirit within the framework of the church. Until well into the seventeenth century schism of itself was regarded as perhaps necessary but always lamentable. Every group blamed some other for the crime of rending the seamless robe of Christ. For the first time in the age of English sectarianism the Baptists in particular advanced the view that competition in church life is wholesome and any enforced uniformity positively monstrous. The doctrine of *laissez faire* was transferred from economics to religion. Something may be said for it. Catholicism is never so exemplary as when and where it is confronted with a vigorous Protestant competition. The sects have made an inestimable contribution to the religious life of Britain and the United States at the points of vitality, morality, and liberty. One has only to compare the religious history of Germany to observe the loss occasioned by the suppression of the sectarian movements of the Reformation. In our own day Protestantism in Germany has received an enormous infusion of vitality through the emergence of the Confessional Church. Certainly sectarianism even to the point of separatism has a permanent place if major bodies are too insensible to the claims of Christian truth and righteousness to heed criticism.

On the other hand, separatism frequently voices petty rancor.

Seldom is schism free from personal pique. One recalls Lucilla, that factious female in the Donatist dispute, who bolted because a deacon would not suffer her to kiss in church an uncertified bone of a martyr. She is the patron saint of querulous individualists. Separatism vitiates concerted action against all the secularism of our time and vividly exemplifies the failure of Christianity to achieve the unity of the spirit.

No absolute judgment of good or bad can well be pronounced. Sectarianism and schism can never be ruled out as an ultimate recourse. Each age has its own needs and a certain rhythm is observable between divisive and unifying periods. The genius of our time is distinctly ecumenical.

III. The Church and Society

10. Ernst Troeltsch—Thirty Years Later, A Critique of *The Social Teaching of the Christian Churches*

A work which deserves an extensive analysis and review thirty years after its initial appearance must be a pioneer endeavor of abiding significance. Such is Troeltsch's *The Social Teaching of the Christian Churches.* He introduced a new method of writing church history with a view to the impact of Christianity upon civilization and particular cultures. Troeltsch, to be sure, was not absolutely original—who ever is?—for he learned much from his colleague Max Weber, with whom he lived in the same house during the period of the writing of *The Social Teaching,* and in many respects was stimulated by his friend's studies in the sociology of religion. But Troeltsch brought to the execution of the task a much deeper grounding in philosophy and theology and for that reason may properly be regarded as the inaugurator of a new method in the field of church history.

His work has already passed through several stages both of refutation and of influence. When the book appeared in Germany the author was already a controversial figure because of an essay translated into English with the title, "Protestantism and Progress," in which he contended that for Protestants the dividing line in church history is not the Reformation, which belonged essentially to the Middle Ages, but rather the Enlightenment, which first applied historical criticism rigorously even to the Biblical documents and rationalistic inquiry even to the most established and cardinal Christian doctrines. Despite all subsequent reconstruc-

First published in *Theology Today,* VIII, 1 (April, 1951). Reprinted by permission. An appraisal of Ernst Troeltsch, *The Social Teaching of the Christian Churches,* Halley Stewart Publications 1, 2 vols. (London: George Allen and Unwin, Ltd., 1949).

tion, the modern Protestant has never since been able to stand on
the same ground as his forebears of the sixteenth century. *The
Social Teaching of the Christian Churches* on its first appearance
did little to augment the controversy, until it was attacked by Karl
Holl, who contended that Troeltsch, on the basis of a slender
acquaintance with the sources, had indulged in grandiose generalizations and that in particular he was mistaken in relegating
Luther to the Middle Ages instead of seeing in him the precursor
of modern times. With the controversy at its height Troeltsch died
and none was left to defend him in his own manner. In any case a
new generation rose on the Continent with a lance of its own to
break on quite another score. The objection was to Troeltsch's
endeavor all along the line to relate Christianity to culture. Such
an attempt savored of relativism with regard to Christianity itself,
whereas neo-orthodoxy was concerned to emphasize the absolute
quality of the Christian revelation over against secularism with
ensuing chaos and tyranny. In consequence on the Continent,
Troeltsch fell into comparative neglect.

Coincidently in the United States his influence mounted.
Twenty-five years ago he was little known. When Willem Adolf
Visser 't Hooft in 1928 brought out a book on *The Background
of the Social Gospel in America,* he remarked that Americans were
not interested in history and if Rauschenbusch were asked as to the
sources of the social gospel, he would answer that of course the
source was the Gospel; whereas Visser 't Hooft discovered three
more proximate historical roots, namely, the Calvinist ideal of the
Kingdom of God, the pietist revivalism as exhibited in Methodism,
and the humanitarianism of the Enlightenment as exhibited in the
Unitarian movement. Americans, he suggested, who desired to
understand the genius of their own culture, would do well to study
and apply the methods of Ernst Troeltsch.

The giver of this advice perhaps at that time did not know
that some Americans were already deeply imbibing from Troeltsch.
Reinhold Niebuhr's *Does Civilization Need Religion?* (1927) and
Richard Niebuhr's *The Social Sources of Denominationalism*
(1929) were both applications of the Troeltschian method. Then
came the translation of Troeltsch by Olive Wyon in 1931, of which
the present work is a new printing. Since Troeltsch's detractors,

notably Holl, did not enjoy the benefit of an English translation, the field in the Anglo-Saxon world has been his, and in the interim his influence has so mounted that in many quarters he is treated as a veritable gospel, and his conclusions are accepted with an uncritical devotion wholly alien to his own spirit.

The procedure of Troeltsch consisted in an effort to reconstruct the characteristic marks of Christianity in particular epochs and cultures, and then to compare the one manifestation with the other. He made no pretense of an extensive acquaintance with the sources. His procedure was rather to take the best dozen or so books for each period and out of these to construct a picture of the dominant characteristics. The method has its obvious limitations. Any work so executed is bound to be subject to the fire of specialists. Yet there is scarcely any other way in which a sweeping synthesis can be achieved. This only must be borne in mind: that conclusions reached in such a fashion must ever be regarded as tentative, and a work like that of Troeltsch should be canonized rather for its methodology than for its positive conclusions. At the same time a reviewer must not carp at details but should center attention rather upon the main thesis and only thereafter indicate less significant defects of fact or interpretation.

The Early Church

Troeltsch takes as his first chronological period the Church in the Roman Empire. Within this span he draws no sharp line of demarcation between the age of persecution and the age of imperial favor. His main point is that Christianity in the beginning was concerned above all else with man's relationship to God and was not committed like Stoicism to the amelioration of social ills. Yet Christianity effected a much more drastic transformation of society than Stoicism, not by any direct attack but rather by a transformation in values. This was possible because Christianity neither renounced nor accepted the world. Creation in accord with the Jewish tradition was regarded as good, and the material world was rather to be mastered by heroism than repudiated through asceticism. Yet although the creation was good, corruption had entered with the Fall and in consequence there was need for redemption and purification. This the Christian Gospel effected in that the old Adam was supplanted by the new. The regeneration experienced through Christ profoundly affected the demeanor of the Christian fellowship, and that fellowship in turn made its impact upon the world. Nevertheless, the Church in the Roman Empire never envisaged the possibility of a Christian society. Church and world, though living together, yet should be distinct. The Christian could not be unequally yoked with unbelievers and never contemplated that all men would become believers. Moreover, while leveling all social distinctions in the eyes of God, Christianity substituted a new and more drastic distinction between the elect and the non-elect, and this very distinction stood in the way of the concept of an entire society consisting of Christians. Such a concept arose only in the Middle Ages and, since it was not anticipated in the imperial period, can be ascribed only to the peculiar circumstances subsequently prevailing in the West.

Such is the main thesis of the first section. A number of considerations point to qualification of the statements. Some of them are noted by Troeltsch himself but are not sufficiently weighted. He observes that the Eastern Roman Empire did have a Middle Ages of its own marked by a belief in a Christian civilization, with this difference from the Christendom of the West, that in the East the leadership was taken by the state rather than, as in the West, by the Church. But if this be true, the peculiar circumstances in the West can be held responsible only for the rise of the papal theocracy and not for the concept of a Christian culture.

A more serious defect in Troeltsch's treatment arises from the very exigencies of his method. In order to compare one period with another he centered on that which was average in each period and neglected the minority opinion which was to grow into the position of the majority in the next age. For the early section Troeltsch fastened on Paul as the crucial figure and delineated for the most part only his views of the relationship of the Church and the world. That may be why even Augustine received no separate and extended treatment. If only the Pauline strain be noticed, then the generalization is sound that the early Church did not contemplate a unified Christian culture. But even in the early period there were other strains alongside of the Pauline.

Paul as a matter of fact stands in the middle of the road between the Book of Revelation, with its intense hostility to the Roman Empire, and the Lukan writings, which regarded Rome not simply as the power which restrains but also as a positive patron of Christianity. The Gospel of Luke alone recorded the synchronism of the birth of Christ and the fifteenth year of Tiberius, and the Book of Acts frequently emphasized the friendliness of Roman magistrates. In the following century the fragment of Melito of Sardis even went so far as to suggest that the Roman Empire and Christianity were two conjoint works of God for the accomplishment of his historical purpose. This line, which was distinctly rare in the ante-Nicene period, received after Constantine a most extensive development. And here one may feel that Troeltsch ought more sharply to have distinguished the age of persecution from the age of imperial favor. After Constantine some of the Eastern theologians came very close indeed to envisaging the possibility of a Christian civilization.

The leader among them was Eusebius of Caesarea, who argued that the religion of one God, one Lord, and one baptism called for a political entity similarly one in its worldwide scope and one in its rulership. Alongside of the one religion and the one Church should be one empire and one emperor. This whole theme subsequent to Troeltsch has been developed by Erik Peterson in his book *Der Monotheismus als politisches Problem* (1935). Eusebius was not an isolated voice and his view was echoed repeatedly in the East. The line runs directly from him to the Caesaropapism of the eastern Middle Ages.

In the West the development was unquestionably different. There the Church was to take the lead. But this idea was also not without its foreshadowing, notably in the writings of St. Augustine. Troeltsch of course recognized Augustine's hints at theocracy but pointed out very properly that centuries elapsed before they came to fruition, and inferred in consequence that the ideas cannot have been determinative. Here one may concede that new circumstances were indeed requisite for the implementation of the ideas, yet without the ideas one does not see why the collapse of the earlier unities in the West should have eventuated in a Christian civilization under the direction of the Church. Probably one reason why

Troeltsch did not assign a greater significance to the influence of Augustine was the tendency to interpret each pivotal figure in terms of that which preceded. Augustine was regarded as the epitome of antiquity, as Luther was portrayed in terms of the Middle Ages, whereas Troeltsch's critic, Holl, was disposed rather to understand Augustine in terms of the Middle Ages and Luther in terms of the modern period. As a matter of fact, each of these figures was like a ring through which varicolored threads are drawn and twisted into a new pattern. And Augustine is highly significant for the development in the West, because he introduced a conception very different from that of Eusebius and the eastern theologians. He did not with them see any conjoint work of God in the founding of the Roman Empire at the time of the birth of Christ. Rather he was able to think of the Empire as tolerable only after the conversion of Constantine and the emergence of rulers like him and like Theodosius, who were ready to follow the leadership of the Church. In other words, in the comparison of Eusebius and Augustine one finds already foreshadowed the most characteristic differences between the Christian Middle Ages of the East and of the West.

Troeltsch says in a footnote that a knowledge of Russian church history would be helpful in testing his generalizations, and at that point he was distinctly right. The subsequent studies of Fedotov, Vernadsky, and Miliukov reveal that the idea of a Christian civilization took root in Russia from Byzantium, but the pattern of Caesaropapism was not for a long time transferred for the simple reason that no empire existed. At the courts of the Russian princes, churchmen were the directing spirits because they alone were competent. No papal theocracy developed, however, because the Russian Church was long dependent upon the patriarch of Constantinople. The particular solutions of the problem were thus necessarily varied and determined by circumstance, but the ideal of a Christian culture was operative alike in the West and in the East (and in Russia), and its roots run back to strains discoverable even in the ante-Nicene period.

But Troeltsch does discover at the very outset the adumbration of an idea destined to exert an enormous role in providing a bridge between Christianity and culture. This was the idea of natural law, a morality eternal, valid, universally recognizable, derived from the order of creation rather than of redemption, hence operative in non-Christian as well as Christian cultures. This natural law is not anti-Christian but only a sub-Christian morality. The Church could therefore appropriate it and build thereon. The actual content of this law, according to Troeltsch, was differentiated by a distinction of the state of man before and after the Fall. The Stoics had posited a golden age without war, without slavery, and without property, and then an age of iron in which these three institutions had come to prevail. Christians appropriated this view and readily equated the golden age of the Stoics with the Garden of Eden and the natural law with the decalogue.

Troeltsch's picture at this point is accurate for the mature doctrine at the time when it was appropriated by the Church Fathers, but many of the details will not bear examination. I have not been able to discover, as Troeltsch does, any clear differentiation in Seneca between the absolute and the relative natural law. The distinction appears to me first to be obvious in Ulpian, but this does not matter much so far as the Church Fathers are concerned. What is more to the point is that Christians before Constantine made use of the concept of natural law, not as a bridge to the affiliation with society but rather, as Troeltsch's own quotations reveal, in order to justify political disobedience through the refusal of emperor worship. Not until after Constantine do we find natural law used to baptize the current institutions of society such as slavery, property, and war. And the line even here is not sharp between the various periods. For example, on the matter of the absolute and the relative natural law we find that Ambrose endorsed the absolute with regard to property, but only the relative in the case of slavery and war. Thus very tentatively were the accommodations achieved.

The Middle Ages

The second section of Troeltsch's work deals with the Middle Ages and is divided into two unequal portions. The first and the larger takes up the papal theocracy and the high Middle Ages; the second and smaller treats of the sects of the late Middle Ages. The former poses the initial question, why Thomas Aquinas should have assumed the existence of a Christian society, since that assumption was far from obvious. Even though the East did in a sense have a Christian Empire, the interpenetration of Christianity and culture was never intimate. The Empire undertook to be the representative of religion, and the Church was relegated to worship in the parish and contemplation in the monastery. But in the West it was different, and the difference can be explained only on the basis of a different set of circumstances. To begin with, the barbarian invasions occasioned a reversion to an agricultural economy on a barter basis. Man thus dealt directly with man instead of through the impersonal agency of money. A system developed in which every man was geared into a scheme of ascending relations marked by fidelity, responsibility, charity, and benevolent patriarchalism. The Church could espouse these virtues, doubly so because as a great landed institution she became herself so closely integrated into the whole system. Another factor was the relative cultural retardation of the state which made rulers eager to avail themselves of the services of churchmen for civil tasks. Notably was this true under Charlemagne, and churchmen having been exercised in such pursuits were both ready and willing to perform similar functions under the aegis of the Church.

Into the midst of this situation came the Gregorian reform with its aim to Christianize the world, purify the Church, and revive the monasteries. The Christianizing of the world, however, only in part effected a raising of the general level and in part involved the secularization of the Church. War, for example, was baptized as a crusade. The Church developed into a great administrative organization and the monasteries were no longer retreats for the practice of mortification, but rather a militia for the performance of heroic assignments in the winning and the holding of the West. The outcome was a society ostensibly, at least, Christian.

Thomas Aquinas provided the theoretical justification. His scheme, though built on urban life, was conceived in terms of the small town with an agrarian hinterland, hence still essentially agricultural. Thomas did two things. He made possible the fusion of Christianity and society by blurring the cleavages between the Church and the world. The Christian ethic was toned down and pruned of all radical characteristics. The natural law which Thomas appropriated was equated with the Ten Commandments rather than with the Sermon on the Mount, and on the classical side was much more Aristotelian than Stoic. Hence Thomas was socially conservative.

Secondly, he provided a theoretical justification for the direction of society by the Church. This was based on a new dualism between the natural and the supernatural, with civil society and the state corresponding to the one and the Church to the other. The temporal life and the eternal were similarly contrasted, and as channels of divine knowledge he set over against each other reason and revelation. The Church was always on the upper and the state on the lower side of these contrasts. Her position in society was further enhanced because salvation was channeled through the sacraments, and the sacraments could be administered only by the priesthood of the Church. Consequently sacramentalism necessitated sacerdotalism, and sacerdotalism assumed not only a religious but also a political and social significance in that the clergy became the directors of society.

At the same time Thomas never pressed the dualism so far as to create a gap which would have again split apart the Church and the world. The natural and the supernatural, the temporal and the eternal interlock. Nature leads up to grace, and reason to revelation, and the one is never antithetical to the other. The result is an architectonic system of overlapping pyramids. Civil society is one pyramid based on the serf and peaked by the emperor. The Church is another resting on the laity and culminating in the pope. The heavenly hierarchy starts from the saints and ascends to God the Father. And these smaller pyramids in turn are embraced in another rising from the secular to the ecclesiastical and from the terrestrial to the celestial. Such is the Thomistic picture. It is the Catholic picture, and Catholicism must always be Thomistic or else collapse.

This is Troeltsch's delineation. By way of comment there is little to be said. The picture is essentially sound, but rather too much is made in the course of his study of the secular occupations as religious callings. Karl Holl at this point rightly showed that in the Middle Ages the only occupation which, strictly speaking, could be regarded as a religious vocation was the monastic life. The civil occupations could be described as positions, occupations, or even as giving a status, but there was a dualism running through the medieval synthesis between the monastic sacerdotal, on the one hand, and the lay and civil, on the other, which only the Reformation broke down. In other words, medieval Christian society was marked at certain points rather by dominance on the part of the Church than by a thoroughgoing and equalitarian interpenetration of the Church and the world.

The second section on the Middle Ages deals with sects, and it is at this point that Troeltsch introduces his famous distinction between three sociological Christian types: the Church, the sect and the individualistic or mystical. Troeltsch would not, of course, pretend that these three exhaust all of the possibilities, nor does he contend that overlapping may not occur. For a modern attempt at more adequate categories, consult Joachim Wach, *A Sociology of Religion*. But whatever modifications may be necessary, Troeltsch's distinction is highly suggestive and essentially sound. The Church, in his terminology, is that type of Christian fellowship which seeks to be comprehensive, and therefore contemplates the Christianizing of society as a whole. The primary emphasis is upon the sacraments as the channels of supernatural grace, and not dependent upon the worthiness of the ministrant or the recipient. The Church is able to be comprehensive because the qualifications for membership are not too exacting for ordinary human nature. Infant baptism suffices for entrance into the society, and the moral demands are not rigorous. The sect, on the other hand, aims at the preservation of the primitive Christian ideal in conduct attainable only in small communities. The stress is upon ethical attainment. The ban is rigorously used and any constraint to compel the unworthy to come in is sharply repudiated.

The first clear differentiation of these types, according to Troeltsch, occurs only in the late Middle Ages, and for that reason he deferred the delineation to this point. This generalization may be questioned, although of course the contrast between the Church and the sect was not so marked until the Church had taken on shape in the papal theocracy. But as Troeltsch himself indicates, the two types were in evidence at the outset in Christian history, and had he gone into more detail with regard not only to the Donatists but also to the Novatianists and other sects of the early period, he could have validated his thesis even for the period before Constantine.

Troeltsch derives the medieval sects from the Gregorian reform on the ground that its failures prompted the more ardent spirits to attempt the realization of the ideal on a smaller scale. This is unquestionably sound. But Troeltsch does not grapple adequately with the problem of the resurgence of sectarianism after a slumber of six or seven hundred years. His attention was wholly occupied with the problem of the emergence of the unified Christian civilization, and for that reason he had no eye for the similar and coincident emergence of the principle of separation. Surely there is food for reflection in the fact that the West scarcely knew sectarianism from the time of Augustine to that of Joachim of Floris. The reason may be that the struggle with paganism absorbed too much energy, and many of the aspects of sectarianism found an expression in monasticism. The whole subject might well be accorded a fuller discussion.

As for the ideas which prompted the sects, Troeltsch rightly fastens upon four, namely, these: (1) eschatology, (2) predestination, (3) Christian primitivism and (4) the rejection of sacramentalism. Each of these might have been more fully developed and sharply defined. Eschatology undercuts a great temporal institution like the papacy from the front end and predestination from the rear. In the one case the Church is soon to be superseded; in the other the only true Church ever was or can be the Church chosen by God from before the foundation of the world. The appeal to the primitive Gospel, of course, points up the contrast between the actual and the ideal Church.

Troeltsch might well have paid greater attention to the revival of eschatology, for here we have another riddle; namely, why the eschatology of the early Church should have been sublimated by St. Augustine and should then have slumbered from his time until that of Joachim. Did the revival of sectarianism produce eschatology or the reverse? Again Troeltsch very significantly notes that for the first time in Wyclif predestination took on sociological significance. But the crucial point is not observed by Troeltsch, namely, that predestination is never subversive unless there is some concrete way of telling who are the elect. Wyclif's great radicalism lay not in the doctrine of predestination so much as in a combination of predestination with an ethical test whereby presumably bad Popes were excluded from the elect.

The emphasis on Christian primitivism is thoroughly sound, but Troeltsch is very misleading in tying up this idea with his terminology of absolute and relative natural law. He makes in this connection a most significant admission which is commonly forgotten by his followers when he says, "In the literature of the sects there are no allusions to these things." Quite right! The sects did not talk the language of natural law, even though there might be an occasional appeal to the behavior of Adam. What Troeltsch has done is to set up a pattern of ideas somewhat arbitrarily imposed upon classical antiquity and most arbitrarily imposed upon late medieval sectarianism. If he deemed it expedient to talk of absolute and relative natural law, he might have made it still more plain that he was describing types rather than using the terminology of particular groups.

The importance of the rejection of sacramentalism is noted in connection with Wyclif. It might well be developed, because sacramentalism is the basis of sacerdotalism.

Finally, Troeltsch gave too sharp a picture of the sect over against the Church. He does say, to be sure, that the types may and do overlap, and he devoted a very brief section to the Franciscan movement within the Church. He might well have noted more fully that Franciscanism itself exhibited a pattern of proliferation with some branches remaining within the Church and others becoming definitely sectarian and the whole movement constantly palpitating with tensions.

The reply of course may be that not everything can be said in one book. Yet a great deal more might have been said if there had not been such prolixity of style and repetition in particular sections.

The Reformation Churches

The treatment of Protestantism is divided into three sections, the first dealing with Lutheranism, the second with Calvinism, and the third with sectarianism as exemplified both by the Anabaptist and Puritan movements.

The section on Lutheranism contains some of the sharpest strictures, and here one feels at times that Troeltsch was more the prophet than the historian. He was thinking in terms mainly of the Lutheranism of his own day and seeking to explain its origins and to castigate its defects. He was led in consequence at times to exaggerate certain tendencies in Luther in spite of a formal recognition that Luther and Lutheranism are not to be equated. Troeltsch did note that Lutheranism developed differently in different countries and in all was subject to a degree of modernization which sets present-day Lutheranism off from the founder with his essentially medieval outlook.

The primary difference between Protestantism and Catholicism was defined by Troeltsch as lying in the area of the doctrine of grace. Both Catholicism and Protestantism are religions of grace, but whereas for Catholicism grace is "a mystical miraculous substance" channeled through the sacraments, for Protestantism grace is "a divine temper of faith, conviction, spirit, knowledge, and trust." Such a definition undercuts sacramentalism and, in consequence, also sacerdotalism and the hierarchical system of the Catholic Church. The sociological consequences are, however, not as drastic as might have been supposed because the Catholic extension of the Incarnation in the priesthood was replaced in Protestantism by the extension of the Incarnation in the Bible, and, since the Bible must be preached, a Church as a visible institution necessarily ensues. Whether or no this institution shall be a Church in Troeltsch's special sense or a sect depends on the way in which faith is conceived. If the stress is placed upon faith as an inward and personal quality, then the Christian community may properly consist only of convinced believers and a sect is the result. But if faith can be dormant as in babies, then the membership can be all-inclusive and the Church type is the outcome. The former road was taken by the Anabaptists, the latter by Luther and his followers. Thus he was able to carry over from Catholicism the concept of a Christian society, a *corpus Christianum.*

Then arises the question of the leadership of this Christian society. The doctrine of grace as personal faith open to all believers not only dissolved the unique place of the priest as the mediator of grace but also displaced him from his position as the director of society. The Church itself was relegated to the purely religious sphere and the state assumed leadership. The assumption was that the state would be Christian, but no effective organ was instituted whereby the Church could exercise criticism and restraint.

The state was not left, however, without an ethic, for this was provided through the doctrine of natural law which was equated with the decalogue rather than with the Sermon on the Mount. The coercive role of the state was stressed, and the need for coercion was underscored by Luther's pessimism with regard to mankind. Since in fallen humanity power has become the essence of law, there was a tendency to glorify power for its own sake. The wielder of power was instituted by God, and vested by God with authority. Therefore he should be accorded unconditional respect and obedience. In this glorification of authority there was a certain resemblance to the doctrine of Machiavelli, and Luther instead of recoiling from the exercise of severity actually urged it.

On the part of the citizen Luther recognized the duty of disobedience only if the faith were infringed or in war, in case the subject knew the cause to be unjust. Otherwise there should be obedience, and at no time should there be armed rebellion. On this subject, however, Luther reluctantly yielded a concession at the end of his life, in the case that government should seek to suppress the true religion. He entertained no doubts with regard to the right of the government to suppress the wrong religion and was by no means an advocate of toleration.

By this exaltation of authority and force Luther set up a severe tension for the Christian, who is bound to love by the injunctions of the Sermon on the Mount. The problem was not resolved as in Catholicism by assigning the more exacting standards to the monastery. Luther had instead two forms of dualism. The one was between private and public life. In the private sphere the Christian should be loving and nonresistant and not claiming his own, whereas in the public sphere he should be severe as the instrument of God's anger and justice. The second dualism is within the breast of the individual who, according to his person, turns the other cheek but according to his office, exacts an eye for an eye.

Luther's scheme did not succeed in Christianizing political life. With the years the rulers became increasingly less amenable even to the ethic of the decalogue, and the Lutheran Church in Germany found itself impotent even if disposed to protest. Economic life was even less transformed, because at this point Luther was fighting against the spirit of his own age. He was thoroughly conservative, agrarian, precapitalist in his outlook, and the world passed him by. His influence was felt mainly in private relations in the home where a benevolent and affectionate patriarchalism prevailed, and in the workshop where every man was encouraged to labor in his calling out of gratitude to God rather than to improve his status in life.

The main comment to be made on this whole treatment is that it is overly schematized in terms of Prussian Lutheranism and in terms of everything in Luther which could be regarded as looking in that direction. Luther was a man of unguarded utterance, slow maturing, extreme sensitivity to divergent aspects of the Gospel, and without the least regard for any formal consistency, though guided by steady principles. His glorification of force is quite overdone by Troeltsch, who has forgotten that, although Luther urged decisive action against the peasants, yet when they were defeated he roundly upbraided the princes for wreaking their vengeance upon the vanquished. Luther's utterances as to political authority were conditioned by that which he was at the moment opposing. Over against the Catholics he insisted that the state is independently ordained of God and does not derive authority from the Church nor should it be directed by the Church. This was the sense in which Luther said that no one in a thousand years had so defended the civil power as had he. And when accused by the Catholics of being even more subversive to the civil than to the ecclesiastical authorities, he resoundingly proclaimed his political allegiance. These were the sayings which ever since have been selected to prove that he counseled unconditional submission to government. But Troeltsch himself recognized that in two instances Luther allowed civil disobedience. The other party whom Luther opposed were the Anabaptists with their complete denial of the use of the sword by the Christian. Against them Luther followed the traditional Augustinian thinking on the use of the sword with benevolent intent in the hands, and only in the hands of him who was ordained to wield it by God.

As for the double morality, the dualisms set up by Troeltsch call for some modification. The distinction between public and private is valid, but the line is not between the magistrate and all other callings. Luther used private to refer only to those relations in which a person is involved solely for himself. The moment he becomes responsible for others, whether as a magistrate, a school teacher, or the father of a household, he is acting in a public capacity. The line therefore cannot be drawn between the state as public and the home as private. As for the dualism in the breast of the individual, this is sound enough, but it is not specifically Lutheran since it goes back directly to St. Augustine, who portrayed the inner conflict of the judge in terms which might readily have been borrowed by Luther. Finally, one must bear in mind that the Catholic ethic, as elaborated by Augustine, posited not several ethics but several codes of behavior. In war, for example, the prince makes the declaration of war and habitually wields the sword. The citizen takes it only at his behest, and the priest must never use it because he ministers at the altar, nor again the monk because he is set aside to practice the counsels of perfection. Luther simply eliminated the monk. The other categories remained for him intact. Thus his so-called distinction of two kinds of morality is nothing other than Augustine's codes of behavior. Throughout them all the attitudes of Christian love should prevail.

As to the economic ethic, Troeltsch's picture is sound, and the recent attempt by Benjamin Nelson[1] to prove that Luther aided the development of capitalism appears to me to be basically ill-conceived. Nelson points out correctly that Luther regarded the problem of usury as not settled by the Deuteronomic legislation, which was merely the private law of the Jews, no longer binding upon Christians. Yet although Luther rejected the Biblical author-

[1] Benjamin H. Nelson, *The Idea of Usury* (Princeton, 1949).

ity for the prohibition of usury, his own ethic was that of St. Thomas, who rejected a contract of fixed return and allowed only a contract of mutual risk.

On the domestic ethic Troeltsch is again essentially right but he could have pointed up the discussion had he been able at that time to take advantage of the subsequent studies of Lilly Zarnke, who pointed out that prior to his own marriage, Luther defended marriage on the grounds that the sexual urge is irresistible and not amenable to papal control. But after his own marriage, the emphasis was shifted to the picture of the home as a school for character.[2]

On the problem of religious liberty Troeltsch has obliterated all distinctions as to Luther's phases and all recollection of his hesitations. As a matter of fact he was much later in condoning the death penalty for religious dissent than Zwingli and always more hesitant than Melanchthon.

On the question of natural law Troeltsch is quite right, and the attempt of some to eliminate natural law thinking from Luther's system by calling it something else is far from successful. Luther did hold that there are moral principles instilled into the minds of all men and capable of being attained by even the natural man. For this reason the Romans and the Turks were quite able to provide a thoroughly sound political administration.

In turning from Lutheranism to Calvinism Troeltsch observes that the latter has been more progressive, expansionist, and revolutionary. He sets himself to inquire whether this difference is due simply to circumstances or to initial variations in the outlook on life and religion. Troeltsch feels that the divergencies in the presuppositions are not great because early Calvinism was distinctly an offshoot of Lutheranism. Nevertheless the differences, though small, were very significant. The first was the concept of God. Luther put the emphasis upon the love of God manifest in Christ, and Calvin on the sovereignty of God, the majesty of God, the inscrutable, arbitrary, and absolute will of God. For Luther the problem of man is to know how he may be the recipient of God's grace. But for Calvin the question is how man may fulfill God's good pleasure. Calvin's picture of God, according to Troeltsch, is

[2] Lilly Zarnke, "Der geistliche Sinn der Ehe bei Luther," *Theologische Studien und Kritiken* CVI (1934), 20-39.

altogether unique, even though confirmation for it was found in the Old Testament. Inasmuch as the implementation of the will of God called for rules, these were discovered in the precepts of the Old Covenant.

Troeltsch's picture thus far seems to me basically sound. Whether Calvin arrived at his doctrine of God independently or through a study of the Old Testament is as insoluble as the question whether Luther first reached justification by faith through his own experience or through the study of St. Paul's Epistle to the Romans. But this is plain—that no more powerful, moving, and at times appalling exposition of Calvin's theology can be found than in his commentary on the book of Deuteronomy.

Closely linked with Troeltsch's picture of the sovereignty of God is the doctrine of election. The difference here, on the part of Calvin, from Luther is the impossibility of falling away from grace. Hence in Calvinism there is a greater assurance and a release of energy into the channels of activity. The elect for Calvin, being certain of themselves, could form an elite company dedicated to concrete tasks. Yet even for Calvin the elect were not perfectly assured, and, since he who is elect will certainly exhibit a righteous life, the urge then was great not to earn one's salvation by good works, which was impossible, but to convince oneself of the state of election by a strenuous pursuit of holiness.

This analysis appears to me essentially correct, but it needs sharper formulation. There is only one point which invests the doctrine of predestination with any particular sociological significance, and that is the point of certainty as to who are the elect. The very possibility of assurance at this point was denied by Luther. For that reason he scoffed at the presumption of the sects in forming holy communities of the saints. Calvin, on the contrary, while conceding that there is no infallible test—he repudiated Muentzer's claim that the new birth and the incoming of the Holy Ghost constitute a proof—yet posited three presumptive tests. The first was the true faith, by which he meant not so much Luther's vibrant trust as an orthodox belief, hence the zeal against heresy. The second was an upright life. From this arose the strenuous discipline. And the third was participation in the sacraments. Here was the churchly element. Calvin's tests were all relatively external and attainable, namely, the creed, the deed and the sacrament. Nothing so emotional, subjective and elusive as the inrushing of the Holy Ghost was requisite. Those who could meet the three tests were to regard their election as assured even if they could not be absolutely certain. And they should stop worrying because no one can worship God aright who is everlastingly distressed as to his salvation. To be so concerned displays a lack of confidence and submission to God's selection, even should it be adverse. Some of this language on Calvin's part might have been directed expressly at Luther, who suffered from a perpetual struggle for faith. Plainly Calvin's attitude provided a better basis than Luther's for the life heroic. Subsequent Calvinism, however, did not adhere to these principles, and New England Calvinism, in particular, added as a test for election the emotional signs of grace. The inner turmoil then returned. This was the torment of colonial Puritanism and an important factor in its disintegration.

To return to Troeltsch: another characteristic of Calvinism in his delineation was the disposition to form holy communities in which individuals striving to make their calling and election sure, yet found the possibility of corporate endeavor. The pattern of the community was drawn from the Old Testament. The state should serve the Church after the manner of the kings of Israel, and public life should be controlled by the ministers after the manner of the prophets.

In discussing the holy community Troeltsch verged upon, but did not quite come to grips with what appears to me to have been the most significant difference between Luther and Calvin, and that is the concept of human history as it yet remains to be unrolled. Luther revived the eschatology of the early Church, and without setting dates fully expected the return of the Lord within his own lifetime. Calvin did for Luther's view what Augustine did for the thought of the early Church. The end was indefinitely postponed and thus a vast vista was disclosed of ongoing life on earth. The Church for Augustine was then well-nigh identified with the Kingdom of God as the instrument for the achievement of the divine purpose within the historical process; and likewise for Calvin the Church restored, one might almost say the Church reformed, was virtually equated with the Kingdom of God. The company of the elect had a work to do on earth. Their commission and their success depended not upon their worthiness in the eyes of God, for all men are a mass of corruption, but solely upon God's sovereign will and power to use even the most unsuitable instruments if it be his good pleasure. Thus all the elements in Calvin's system drew together: divine sovereignty, election, the holy community, human depravity and human activity, and all of them focused on a prodigious optimism grounded not on man's goodness but on God's greatness. Here in religious form was the doctrine of progress. It sent men forth into the midst of society ready to resist and slay tyrants, overthrow kingdoms, subdue continents, and erect holy commonwealths.

The next section in Troeltsch's book compares Calvinism with the Anabaptist movement. Similarities are discovered first in the rigid church discipline, in sharp contrast to Lutheranism where the preparation for the Lord's Supper was confession and absolution, but in Calvinism an actual scrutiny of conduct with an exclusion of those whose deportment was faulty. A further common point in Calvinism and Anabaptism was in the area of Christology. For Luther Christ was the mediator, but for Calvin and the sects Christ was the lawgiver, example, and head of the Church. Hence the possibility of the covenant between Christ and the Church. But there were also certain differences between Calvinism and Anabaptism. Calvin had less feeling than had Luther for the Sermon on the Mount, and quite rejected the Anabaptist repudiation of oaths, war, government, and private property. Moreover, Calvin, while believing that the elect could be recognized, nevertheless did not pretend that the wheat could be separated from the tares. The combination of these ideas issued in grades within the Calvinist community. In New England the terminology was that of saints and strangers, and even at Geneva excommunication did not issue immediately in banishment, and thus for a period at least there might be a fringe who were in the town but not of the Church. Moreover, Calvinism did not abandon the world, and while believing that election was wholly in the hands of God and of course predetermined, nevertheless addressed evangelistic appeals to the community at large. Thus Calvinism, though like

Anabaptism in being not of the world, was very much more in the world in its sphere of operations.

This whole picture calls only for slight modification and amplification. A survey and comparison of this sort almost necessarily eliminates all the shadings. And yet one wishes that some statements could be slightly less extreme. It is not true that Christ for Luther was never an example. In fact Luther insisted that every Christian should be a Christ to his neighbor. His objection to the imitation of Christ was simply that it should not be detailed and legalistic. And Calvin on the other hand was not wholly untouched by the discrepancy between the Old Testament severity and the New Testament compassion, for after recounting the frightfulness of the book of Deuteronomy, he not infrequently would interject an expression such as this, "Although this must appear cruel, nevertheless," and so on.

Later on Troeltsch continues his comparison in a very fruitful way as to the concept of the Church. He holds that Calvinism combined the Church and the sect ideas. The Church regards Christianity as coterminus with the boundaries of some civil society. The sect segregates Christians from the world into a select community. Calvinism at Geneva brought together the view that the entire community should be regarded as Christian and the view that the Church should contain only convinced and upright believers. The combination was effected by excluding from the town those who did not conform or attain to the standards of the Church. Banishment and the ban did not immediately coincide as noted above, but a Genevan, if not reconciled to the Church, could not long remain in the town. Thus Geneva, by the expulsion of the unworthy and the reception of thousands of refugee saints, became almost as select a community as an Anabaptist colony. When, however, larger territories were involved the comparison could not be so exact. In countries like France, Holland, England, Scotland, and New England the strangers commonly outnumbered the saints, and then the holy commonwealth, if attainable, could be based only on a minority control of the community through the rulership of a religious aristocracy.

Troeltsch then went on to take up the ethic and social theory of Calvinism. The ethic, he held, was marked by intramundane asceticism. Here for the first time Troeltsch introduced the exact terminology of Max Weber. The expression "intramundane asceticism" was selected to distinguish the Calvinist ethic from the Lutheran, which is not ascetic, and from the Anabaptist, which is not intramundane. The Calvinist was, more than either of the others, in the world without being of the world. Troeltsch summarized by saying that the Calvinist had a keen interest in politics but not for the sake of the state, was active in industry but not for wealth, was concerned for social organization but not in the interest of happiness and engaged in unceasing labor but not for wealth.

This whole delineation contains profound insights, but one would like to have it broken down and rendered more precise. With regard to alcoholic beverages, for example, Lutheranism and Calvinism stood together in favor of moderation, and only Anabaptism called for greater rigorism. Lutheranism emphasized, at least in Luther's early writings, the gratification of sex, whereas Anabaptism and Calvinism minimized sex and emphasized partnership in the work of the Lord. On the score of personal adornment and stark simplicity in worship, Calvinism stood with Anabaptism on the side of austerity. With regard to the state, Lutheranism and Anabaptism were much more pessimistic than Calvinism, though making different deductions. The practical consequence for Lutheranism was participation in political life with a heavy heart, whereas the Anabaptists withdrew altogether. The Calvinists, however, had no reservations because they looked upon the state as directly commissioned by God as an instrument for the erection of his kingdom. In this instance one may wonder whether the term asceticism is applicable in any sense.

With regard to the callings. Troeltsch drew the great dividing line between Luther and Calvin rather than between Luther and the Middle Ages. Luther, in his view, still regarded the callings as occupations arranged by Providence in which each was obligated to remain, without seeking to improve his status, whereas Calvin saw in the callings room for the exercise of faith through labor.

I question the validity of this distinction and feel that the difference, insofar as there is a difference, arises rather from Calvin's whole picture of man's future upon earth in the midst of a holy community.

Finally, Troeltsch felt that Calvin substituted for the *corpus Christianum* of the Middle Ages an international Christian society organized according to nations, each one of which should be a holy commonwealth in collaboration with the rest. This undoubtedly is the direction toward which Calvinism tended, and this pattern to a degree was actually achieved. One ought not to forget, however, that there was something of an international Lutheranism in Germany, the Scandinavian countries and the United States. The phenomenon is more marked in Calvinism because it spread into those countries such as France, Holland and England which were advanced or advancing in the direction of national organization and colonial expansion. In other words, circumstance is in part responsible for the difference—though once again one must never forget the Calvinist dream of the holy community which knew no earthly confines.

Troeltsch saw a difference between Luther and Calvin on the score of the right of armed resistance to tyranny in that Luther conceded it but reluctantly as implicit in the German constitution, whereas Calvin had fewer reservations and grounded it in natural law. This I think is true, but it must not be forgotten that Calvin also had his reservations and deplored the conspiracy of Amboise. The pressure of events is probably the important factor here, because, when the heat was on, Luther did modify his previous theory, and Lutheranism moved in the Schmalkald War to a qualified endorsement of the right of revolution. But the need for it after the peace of Augsburg ceased because Lutheranism received legal recognition, whereas Calvinism moved out into lands where it was continuously resisted by political authority, and under these circumstances speedily abandoned reservations with regard to the legitimacy of resistance to government.

Throughout the whole discussion Troeltsch spoke often of absolute and relative natural law. In place of this terminology he would have done better to say simply that natural law was a concept of exceeding variability as to its content. The advocates of persecution and the advocates of liberty alike appealed to it in support of their respective positions. One might with propriety speak of a conservative natural law and a radical natural law, but the terminology of absolute and relative harks back to the old distinction of the ideal natural law of the golden age without property, slavery, and war, and the accommodated natural law of man's fallen condition. The writers of the Reformation did not often couch their concepts in these terms. They might pit Aristotle against the Gospel or the Decalogue against the Sermon on the Mount, and to use this terminology would more nearly accord with the sources.

With regard to the political ethic of Calvinism, Troeltsch claimed that it had a facility for accommodating itself to a democratic structure. It was not strictly democratic but rather aristocratic, but there were certain democratic ingredients. The first was an appeal to public opinion and the second was the doctrine of limited sovereignty which justified even tyrannicide if the sovereign suppressed the true religion.

These suggestions are in the main correct, but one might observe that Lutheranism also made an appeal to public opinion and would never have been so widely disseminated had this not been the case. Likewise in Zurich all the decisions relative to ecclesiastical matters were taken in sessions of the Town Council. In other words, the first point, though valid, is not peculiar to Geneva. The second point depended much on circumstance. Calvinism, as already observed, moved slowly and under pressure through a revolutionary temper, whereas Lutheranism, after achieving toleration, went rather in the other direction.

In the economic sphere Troeltsch adopted wholesale Weber's thesis as to the connection between Calvinism and the spirit of capitalism. Calvin, because of the situation of Geneva with its small town industry and commercial life, endorsed alike industry and monied economy. Intramundane asceticism stimulated work and prevented expenditure, thereby ministering to the accumulation of capital. The removal of the ban on usury made possible the rational ordering of economic life directed toward the increase of gain, and this in turn could not be enjoyed but could only be distributed through philanthropy or put back into the business. Hence Calvin, though with some misgivings and some qualifications, gave distinctly a support to the spirit of capitalism.

In this whole picture there is this element of truth that the energy of Calvinism was not without its economic effects. But the contention that Calvinism particularly contributed by lifting the ban on usury is in my judgment quite unsound. Calvin did indeed reject the authority of Aristotle, but nevertheless like Luther he retained the economic ethic of Thomas Aquinas and also allowed usury only in case the enterprise had prospered. Not so much the Protestants as the Catholic casuists of the Renaissance broke down the scholastic restrictions on usury and the spirit of gain.

On the ethic of war Troeltsch could discover no difference between Lutheranism and Calvinism, though he did note that in modern times Calvinism had become congenial to pacifism. I would suggest that the cleft between Calvinism and Lutheranism is to be found at the point of regarding war as a strategy for the achievement of ideal ends. This Luther could never concede because ideal ends cannot be attained in the political order. But Calvin with his view of the Kingdom of God on earth regarded war from the point of view of an instrument, and if ideal ends seemed to be capable of achievement through war, then war became not so much a reluctant necessity as a crusade. But if these same ends were not attainable by war and might be accomplished by nonviolence, then came the swing to pacifism, and this pacifism was grounded much less in any objection to the taking of life than upon nonresistance as a strategy.

On the sex ethic Troeltsch discovered very little difference except that in Calvinism the personality of woman was given a higher independence and the purpose of marriage was conceived in a more rational way in that the concept of marriage as a restraint of sin was replaced by the concept of the family as the means of building up a Christian society. I should be disposed to phrase this a little differently and, as previously indicated, would feel that the element of newness in Calvinism, as also in Anabaptism, is the stress upon marriage as a partnership involving a community of conviction and a sharing in labor.

Troeltsch's study of later Calvinism takes up the situation in England where the Churches of Calvinist descent came to endorse the principle of diversity in religion, and abandon the concept of a uniform Christian society. In England the Calvinists espoused religious liberty and even the separation of Church and state. The question is whether this development proceeded logically out of original Calvinism or was an accommodation to defeat. Troeltsch favored the latter hypothesis. Calvinism can never accept the world. Either it must dominate or else withdraw, and if it fails to dominate, then withdrawal is the necessary result. This does not mean, however, the adoption of a sectarian pattern on principle but only an accommodation to circumstance, and if subsequently the opportunity returns of coming into power, then Calvinism will revert to the system of theocracy.

Early Congregationalism, according to Troeltsch, was no exception, because the only Calvinist ingredient in Congregationalism was the concept of the holy community. The remaining ideas were Baptist in origin.

By way of critique this may be said: original Calvinism was modified even in idea by the impact of events, because in England several Churches, all Calvinist in theology, confronted each other, and the alternative then was either toleration or else that Calvinism should devour itself. Under these circumstances toleration came to be defended by Calvinists. At the same time one must not overlook, as Troeltsch does, that all along the line an Erasmian strain ran through Protestantism and even through Calvinism. And that this strain tended to modify the original asperity and to humanize the picture both of God and of man.

Developing Congregationalism was described by Troeltsch as midway between the Calvinist church type and the sect type. At this point Troeltsch would have profited had he been able to avail himself of the studies of Perry Miller, who has clearly demonstrated that early Congregationalism was never a unity. At the very outset separatist and non-separatist constituents were present. Consequently Troeltsch's picture of New England Congregationalism moving in a separatist direction and British independency seeking to operate within the established Church offers all too sharp a contrast. The distinction was less between British and American than between separatist and non-separatist constituents in both.

Cromwell was regarded by Troeltsch as a Calvinist theocrat for whom Independency was the religion of the state. The essential

newness in Cromwell appears to me to be missed by this description. Independency was not a single Church but was conceived in
terms broad enough to include Congregationalism, Presbyterianism, and the Baptists. In other words, Cromwell substituted for a
state Church a national religion, and to this degree the medieval
pattern of a single state and a single Church was gone.

Still more significant historically was the collapse (to which
Troeltsch turns) of Cromwell's attempt and the transition subsequently to a system of thoroughgoing toleration in which the state
gives no favor to one group more than to another. This was the
principle espoused by Locke and later exemplified in the United
States. Here the separation of Church and state was motivated
more by the actual multiplicity of sects than by any hostility of the
two institutions to each other. The state in the United States is still
regarded as in some sense Christian in character. Thus the separation of Church and state on this side of the water has not been
marked by that antagonism which is so characteristic of Latin
lands, where the Church has had to be forcibly disendowed and
disestablished. This observation is acute.

Sectarianism and Mystical Movements

The final section of the book dealing with sectarianism and
mystical movements was probably at the time of its appearance the
most significant portion, because for a representative of the established Church in Germany to give equal space and equally
respectful treatment to the sects was an event. And yet today this
section is the least worthy of reading for its own sake, because in
the interim so many excellent studies have appeared, some of them
directly traceable to Troeltsch's influence. At this point he has
come to occupy a position something like that of Christopher
Columbus whose achievement in crossing the ocean in a Spanish
galleon appears to us increasingly stupendous as we develop easier
modes of travel. But while we give ever greater honor to Columbus,
we are less and less disposed to make the voyage in a similar bark.

So we may judge that Troeltsch's treatment of the Anabaptists is sketchy and his treatment of Methodism is woefully
brief. One does have the feeling somewhat that in this section of

his work Troeltsch was becoming more interested in fitting the proliferating sects into his schematization than in tracing their social teaching and influence. There are indeed many very illuminating suggestions, but the work is not carried through with uniform acumen.

Take for example the section on Thomas Muentzer. Troeltsch makes the suggestion that Muentzer combined the mysticism of Tauler, the eschatology of Joachim, and the revolution of the Hussites. This is a very intriguing analysis, but the course of Muentzer's inner development is vastly better traced in a more recent study by Annemarie Lohmann.[3]

As for the Methodists, Wellman J. Warner provides a much better guide to the economic ethic,[4] and the total impact of Methodism on the life of England is admirably handled by Halévy in his *History of the English People in 1815,* for he points out that Methodism integrated the life of England, reclaimed the working classes for Christianity and the Church, and imparted to the labor movement itself a Christian terminology and a Christian ideology. Nothing of the sort occurred on the Continent, for Pietism failed to recover the masses and the working class movement embraced Marxist materialism.

Finally the treatment of Christianity in the United States is very scant. There are illuminating hints. If Troeltsch be right, and I think he is, that in this country we have an almost unique situation with a separation of Church and state without hostility, and if he be right that the greatest activism is to be found in Calvinism and the United States was the peculiar sphere of Calvinist operation, then this country ought to be one of the best to study in order to discover the impact of Christianity upon civilization.

But this is something for American historians to undertake, as indeed they have been and are doing.[5]

[3] Zur geistigen "Entwicklung Thomas Muentzers," *Beiträge zur Kulturgeschichte des Mittelalters und der Renaissance,* XLVII (1931) .

[4] Wellman J. Warner, *The Wesleyan Movement in the Industrial Revolution* (London, New York, 1930) .

[5] I have devoted less space to his treatment of sectarianism because to do so would be either to give a bibliography of better works or else to develop my own views. I might suggest, for example, what would have been done in a contrast of Mennonites, Brethren, and Quakers. But this would be to make a start on another book, and that is scarcely called for.

To repeat, this is a great pioneer work. If it is at many points inadequate, the reason is frequently that it has itself inspired many other superseding studies. For its own sake it is still worthy of careful study for the methodology and the many pregnant suggestions.

11. Alexander Campbell and the Social Order

Alexander Campbell in his social outlook was a highly representative American of the first half of the nineteenth century. He combined all of the dominant attitudes of the time, many of them disparate in origin and incongruous at least in their implications. Somehow he managed to hold them all together and to arrive at a conclusion which added up about to this: that society is riddled by evils, that these evils are capable of redress, and that America offers a better opportunity than anywhere else in the world for their elimination. In this land, by the effort of man and the grace of God, the millennium will shortly be introduced.

Into this amalgam went some surprising ingredients. Alexander Campbell was a Bible Christian, a Protestant of the left, a sectarian who believed in the separation of Church and State because the Church might be sullied through association with an agency of this present evil world. Nevertheless, at the same time he endorsed without qualm the views of Jefferson stemming from the Enlightenment, who desired the separation of Church and State lest the State be subject to clericalism, who demanded universal suffrage, universal education, and proclaimed the fundamental and universal rights of man. Campbell was tinged by the Romantic Movement which looked upon nature as relucent with God, and regarded the American wilderness as that free environment in which the soul of man would not be stifled. Yet he recorded with pride America's material progress and enormous increase in population. He shared with the puritans the belief in the possibility of a Holy Commonwealth and merged this ideal, as did many of them in the eighteenth century, with the thousand-year

First published in *The Sage of Bethany*, ed. Percy E. Gresham (St. Louis, 1960).

reign of prosperity and peace which should precede the coming of the Messiah. Thus left-wing Protestantism, the rationalism of the Enlightenment, Romanticism, Puritan Theocracy, and Millenarinism formed a fluctuating and yet fairly stable union.

Let us begin by examining his view of nature and of America. Campbell shared with the Romantics of his generation the view of nature as the garment of God. He has a rhapsodic passage on sunrise at sea, couched in a diction too florid for the taste of our generation.[1] Somewhat more restrained, though no less vibrant, is the report of his biographer on his feelings as he first contemplated the American forest.

In the exaltation of his youthful feelings he seemed to have reached a land of enchantment. The moon, already high in heaven and nearly at the full, seemed to mingle its silvery beams with the sun's golden radiance reflected from the western sky. The mighty trees, in all their wild luxuriance, stood around him, forming aloft, as it were, a new heaven of verdure; while, beneath, he trod upon the soil of a new world—the land of liberty and of Washington, whose liberal institutions had long been the object of his admiration. All nature around him seemed to sympathize with his emotions. The balmy air, fresh from the wild mountain slopes, the new varieties of birds, which from almost every tree seemed, to his fancy, to chant their evening song in praise of the freedom of their native woods, the approaching shades of evening, veiling the distant landscape in a gentle haze—all seemed to speak of liberty, security and peace.... Keenly susceptible as he was to impressions of grandeur, and tending still, in the habitual workings of his mind, to religious thought, as he ranged through the deep, untrodden glades, or paused beneath the canopy of verdure which the wild vine had woven as the woof upon the spreading warp of branching oaks, his heart overflowed with gratitude and reverence.[2]

Alexander Campbell took care, however, to seal off his Romanticism in such fashion that it compromised in no sense his biblical faith. There is no such thing, said he, as natural religion. God illumines nature, but nature does not reveal God. Without revelation we cannot so much as arrive at his existence. For that reason there cannot be a rational Deist, for whatever he believes

[1] Richardson, *op. cit.,* II, 419-420.
[2] *Ibid.,* I, 207.

in the way of religion is derived precisely from that revelation which he rejects.

But when it came to the cult of America, Campbell was not so successful in compartmentalizing. His view was a blend of cultural primitivism, the idea of progress, the ideal of the Holy Commonwealth, a sense of national mission, and the expectation of Christ's kingdom. The cultural primitivism centered not on the *bon sauvage,* the American Indian, but on the sturdy frontiersman. We see him

moccasined with his deer-skin boots, wrapped in his hunting-shirt, with a tomahawk suspended from his girdle on his right side, and a scalping-knife, sheathed in a deer-skin scabbard, dangling on his left, with rifle on his shoulder, his faithful dog by his side, [as he] sallies forth from his cabin or his fort, at early dawn, and, with cautious step and listening ear, surveys his environs. If neither man nor savage beast greets his watchful eye, he grounds his rifle, seizes his axe, and begins to girdle the forest-tree, or, with mattock in hand, engages in grubbing the virgin earth in quest of his daily bread. Gathering courage as he proceeds, day after day the forests bow beneath his sturdy strokes, and an opening is made through which the sun penetrates the newly-opened soil and quickens into life the precious seeds which, with so much parsimony, he had hopefully deposited in the bosom of his mother earth. Thus began, twice forty years ago, the settlements around us.[3]

At this juncture one might have expected Campbell to have interjected perhaps a lament over the passing of the forest primeval. There were Americans during this period who bemoaned "the primordial hills shorn of their locks." Campbell was not of their number. He goes on to exult in the march of civilization.

On every side around us, far as the eye can reach, a thousand hills and valleys, waving in rich harvests or covered with green pastures, overspread with bleating flocks of sheep or lowing herds of cattle, interspersed with beautiful villas and romantic hamlets, shaded with venerable oaks, the remains of ancient forests, or enclosed with evergreens of other climes, that vie with each other in lending enchantment to the scenes that environ the homesteads of the rugged pioneers of the great and mighty West, present themselves to our enraptured vision. . . .

[3] Alexander Campbell, *Popular Lectures and Addresses* (Cincinnati, 1863) , p. 175.

And what shall we say of the sons and daughters of those brave and magnanimous pioneers? We are unable to do them justice. The beautiful towns and cities spread all over the new western world, "with glistening spires and pinnacles adorned," pyramidal trophies of industrial art, monuments of generous liberality, piety and good sense, in solemn and majestic silence, speak their praise.[4]

On another occasion he lauded the amazing resources of the land, the astounding growth in population at a rate which might bring the total to 7,000,000 within the lifetime of some there present. He spoke of the great increase in commerce without and within, for "the Father of Waters with his unnumbered tributaries" bore to New Orleans the gleanings of shores twelve thousand miles in extent. "Already we travel on canals more than four thousand miles, and on railroads over five thousand, and in this land we have four thousand four hundred and eighty eight post offices!"[5]

In both of these addresses he breaks off at this point to extol America's spiritual greatness. The greatness of America, declared Campbell, lay in her system of universal education, including women as well as men, in her defense of human rights, and here he inserted praise for Jefferson whose name will descend "to the latest generation in that halo of glory which encircled the sun of our destiny on the first morn of its rising."[6] How different from the attitude to Jefferson of the New England Congregationalists! Our land, said Campbell, is peculiarly blessed because peopled by Anglo-Saxons to whom God has given the scepter of Judah and by Protestants, for Catholicism had made France into a nation of infidels. The very heart of popedom is gangrenous. America enjoys also the separation of Church and State. All of these astounding advantages have given to her a singular opportunity and a unique mission. Let her perceive the hour of her destiny; *kairon gnoothi.* (For all his scorn of sophistication Campbell did not disdain to quote Greek) . This is the *kairos* of America.[7]

Naturally, American utopianism with its secular strain could

[4] *Ibid.,* pp. 175-176.
[5] *Ibid.,* pp. 495-496.
[6] *Ibid.,* p. 181.
[7] "Address on the Destiny of Our Country" (1852) , *ibid.*

easily be combined with Christian millenarianism. The millennium, said Campbell,

... will be a state of greatly enlarged and continuous prosperity, in which the Lord will be exalted and his divine spirit enjoyed in an unprecedented measure. All the conditions of society will be vastly improved; wars shall cease, and peace and good will among men will generally abound. ... Genuine Christianity will be diffused through all nations; crimes and punishments will cease; governments will recognize human rights, and will rest on just and benevolent principles ... [There will be] one extended and protracted series of revivals ... [and even] the seasons will become more mild; climates more salubrious, health more vigorous, labor less, lands more fertile, and the animal creation more prolific.[8]

At the same time Campbell was a vigorous critic of his culture and his land. One would expect this in a descendant of Protestant sectaries, congenital Elijahs immolating the priests of Baal. Harold Lunger has called attention to the fluctuations in Campbell's rhapsodies over America. He was disillusioned by Georgia's violation of the rights of the Cherokee Indians, Virginia's dilatoriness in taking any action to alleviate the lot of the slave. The Jacksonian Spoils System betokened political degeneration, and one of the "antedeluvian signs of the times was that 'the earth was filled with violence.' " Yet he remained always an activist who believed that something could be done about it.

One agency to that end is the State, to which he accorded a somewhat grudging acquiescence. He was strongly persuaded of the separation of Church and State and the absolute inadmissability of any tampering with religion on the part of the State. Equally was he clear that the kirk is not to give laws to Caesar. He verged, at times, almost on the old Anabaptist view that the State is ordained of God because of sin and should be run by sinners. "Would to God that [Christians] would set their affection on the politics of heaven, and leave the politics of earth to those who cannot soar above the Allegheny Mountains." Nevertheless, on important issues the Christian might vote, and Campbell himself was willing to be a delegate to the Virginia Constitutional Convention of 1829-30, because the making of a fundamental political

[8] *Millennial Harbinger*, 1841, p. 9.

framework was of greater significance than the choice between candidates equally undesirable. And he was willing to accord to government certain of the functions in the economic sphere which we associate with the welfare state.[9] In general, his attitude *vis à vis* the State grew less intransigent with the years.

He never ceased to regard the Church as the primary sphere for Christian activity, and that was why he so sharply disapproved of societies. One might have expected him to be cordial because they originated in part to obviate that very denominationalism which he deplored. Men of all religious persuasions or of none were invited to unite on a single point of agreement and endeavor. There was a society to emancipate Negroes, a society to educate Negroes, a society to repatriate Negroes. In such a project to send the Negroes back to Africa cooperation could be enlisted from Baptists, Methodists, Presbyterians, Catholics, and infidels. But that was just the trouble, in Campbell's eyes. Alliances were being made with the sons of Ashdod, and in any case membership in a society of whatever sort was a diversion of interest and effort from the Church. In later life he relaxed at the point of missionary societies and slightly as to temperance.[10] But he was never of the view that the Church herself should espouse social reforms after the manner of societies; rather her task was to make Christian citizens.

As a Christian citizen Campbell was active in sponsoring many social reforms. The two chief reforms were antislavery and war. His views on slavery have been so well delineated by Lunger that I may content myself with a summary and a comparison with the position of some New Englanders in the same period.

Campbell was thoroughly convinced that the slave trade is evil and blazed out against those who would raid the African coast and separate families. But he did not feel that the holding of slaves is of itself wrong, if their treatment be humane. The primary ground for this position was biblical. Neither the Old Testament nor the New Testament forbids slaveholding. On this point Campbell was unquestionably right. He held further that slavery in the United States was not worse than in the days of the Apostle Paul.

[9] *See* Lunger, *op. cit.*, pp. 191-192.
[10] *Ibid.*, pp. 44-48.

That assumption is almost certainly wrong, because the word used by Paul for *slave* is often so mild in meaning that in English it is better rendered simply by the word *servant*. On the basis of these assumptions Campbell could not be persuaded to stigmatize slave-holding as necessarily a sin.

Of course it might be a sin, and he heartily concurred in the action of his father who had moved out of the state of Kentucky because of interference with his activities in instructing Negroes. To hold them in servitude and to keep them illiterate was indeed a sin. Moreover, Alexander Campbell held that although slave-holding might not be a sin, yet slavery was inexpedient and should as speedily as possible be abolished. The arguments which he used referred mainly to the deleterious effects upon the white population rather than to the injustice to the Negroes. Servile governesses were not the best guides to the youth of a free people. Slave insurrections kept the master in continual fear of his property and life. More important even than the emancipation of the slave was the emancipation of the master. Economically the system of slavery was unproductive and would be the very ruin of Virginia.

Some strictures have been leveled against Campbell at this point because he burned with concern for the self-interest of the white rather than blazed with indignation against the oppression of the black. The criticism is not altogether unjustified, but one must not forget that in his own mind this was an instance in which Christian and non-Christian motives converged, and he may have felt that his plea would be more heeded if based on grounds appealing to the entire populace and not merely to churchmen.

Several courses of action commended themselves as feasible. The first was private emancipation and this course Campbell took himself until he came to have no slaves. The second was a gradual emancipation to be undertaken by the government. Campbell did not favor emancipation without indemnification because the slave is property. He would devote federal funds to the reimbursement of owners and then to the colonization of the emancipated slaves in Africa. This was the great scheme of colonization which for several decades was the method most approved by many of the South and also of the North. Another way was the system of gradual emancipation. In 1849 Campbell gave support to a plan proposed by Henry Clay whereby all slaves born after 1855 or 1860 should be free on attaining the age of twenty-five.[11] This was the system by which slavery had been terminated in Connecticut, so that by 1850 there was not a slave remaining.

Thus far Campbell's position was entirely in accord with that of the Northern moderates—the Yale circle and such men as Nathaniel W. Taylor, Leonard Bacon, and Moses Stuart. These men also held that slaveholding is not, as such, a sin. Stuart, who was a great biblical scholar, stoutly maintained like Campbell that the New Testament has no more by way of prohibition than the Old Testament. Taylor considered *Uncle Tom's Cabin* a gross exaggeration, and Leonard Bacon, when asked whether he would receive to his pulpit a slaveholding Presbyterian minister from the South, said that he would not admit him simply because he was a Presbyterian nor reject him simply because he was a slaveholder, but would inquire why. Attention was called by these Northerners to the dilemma of the Southern Christian who had inherited slaves, who treated them humanely, who would like to set them free but feared to do so lest in a hostile society they should find nowhere to lay their heads. George Park Fisher of the Divinity School declared that to tell the South to liberate all the slaves at once was like telling an eagle in midair with a lamb in its talons to let go before coming down. These Northerners were all in favor of gradualism. They, too, endorsed and strenuously fostered the colonization plan, but the trouble here was that after fifteen years the number of Negroes transported to Africa did not equal the natural increase in the United States. The Abolitionists, therefore, began to stigmatize the plan as a diversion. They rejected it also for precisely the reason which commended it to the moderates; namely, that southern slaveholders would cooperate. Anything in which they would join, said the abolitionists, must be wrong because slaveholding is *sin*. Campbell countered by saying that abolitionism is sin because of its intolerant spirit and unbiblical basis.

Colonization was, as a matter of fact, so unfeasible that by 1840 it had been dropped in the North. Campbell continued to advocate it as late as 1850. But in the meantime a much more

---

[11] Campbell's position on slavery is well set forth by Lunger.

serious question had arisen as to whether the Fugitive Slave Law should be obeyed. The North was seriously divided at this point. There were some like Daniel Webster and Moses Stuart who counseled obedience. So also did Alexander Campbell, and of course the South in general. The reasons adduced were different. The argument in the North was not merely that obedience would preserve the Union but also that obedience was a path to the ultimate emancipation of the slaves as a whole. It was pointed out that there were only two ways in which the slaves in the South could be freed. One was by persuasion of the owners; the other was by force. But that would mean war. There was, to be sure, a third course open, namely, the disruption of the Union and secession. This would save the North from pollution, but would not emancipate the slaves in the South. The best method then would be to preserve the Union and induce the South to take voluntary action. To that end property rights would have to be respected and fugitive slaves returned. Any other course would end in secession or war or both.

Campbell appears not to have defended compliance as requisite for mass emancipation but rather on the ground that disobedience would disrupt the churches and the nation. He had a frightful dread of division in the churches. The Methodists, the Presbyterians, and the Baptists were splitting over the issue. He would take no position which would cause Disciples of Christ also to divide. His church unity program, in other words, made him less sensitive to the claims of justice. The other concern was for peace. He was aghast at those who were resolved that the matter

shall only be discussed by the light of burning palaces, cities, and temples, amidst the roar of cannon, the clangor of trumpets, the shrieks of dying myriads. . . . the horrid din and crash of a broken confederacy . . . and the agonizing throes of the last and best republics on earth![12]

So also in the North, Leonard Bacon only a few weeks prior to the attack on Fort Sumter felt that secession was to be preferred.

Since we know only too well the outcome we may pass over to Campbell's views on war. He was not an extremist and did not

[12] *Millennial Harbinger*, 1835, p. 587.

reject even capital punishment, because it is inflicted upon the guilty. The difficulty with war is that it includes in its penalties the innocent. Much of his critique is of the sort which one finds today among Catholic conscientious objectors, who so long as they are Catholic cannot deny the legitimacy of the just war, but deny that any modern war can satisfy the conditions. Campbell was more radical in that for him no war ever did or ever could meet the demand that only the guilty should be made to suffer.

The considerations which he adduced were a blend of a strict New Testament literalism resting on the Sermon on the Mount and the rationalism of the Enlightenment, which deemed it more prudent to obtain peace by purchase than to have recourse to war. Witness the policy of the great Jefferson in the Louisiana Purchase. War is contrary, said Campbell, to the spirit of Jesus. War is unbefitting men endowed with reason and sense. War is destructive of property, devastating of life, and debauching to morals. Lunger has well summarized Campbell's main arguments in his *Address on War* where it is urged that "war is *folly,* because 'it can never be a satisfactory end of the controversy,' and 'peace is always the result of negotiations.' " Campbell argued further the wickedness of war "on the rational and pragmatic grounds that 'those who are engaged in killing their brethren, for the most part, have no personal cause of provocation whatever;' 'they seldom ... comprehend the right or the wrong of the war' and act therefore 'without the approbation of conscience;' 'the innocent are punished with the guilty;' the soldier is constrained 'to do for the state that, which, were he to do in his own case, the state would condemn him to death;' and wars 'are the pioneers of all other evils to society, both moral and physical.' "

One can disparage, if one will, the pacifism of Alexander Campbell on the grounds that it was only the mood of the moment. One cannot deny, of course, that he lived in the period when first opposition to war took hold of the American mind, except, of course, the traditional peace churches—the Quakers, the Mennonites, and the Brethren. Notably the Congregationalists and the Presbyterians had been far removed from pacifism and had looked upon the French and Indian War and the Revolutionary War as crusades. There were, to be sure, Tories in New England but they were primarily Episcopalians who objected to resistance to the Lord's anointed. The first revulsion against war came after the conflict of 1812 which had been highly unpopular on the Atlantic seaboard. The formation of the American Peace Society, by which Campbell was so much influenced (even if it was a society), occurred in 1815. The Mexican War received general disapprobation in New England and Campbell heartily concurred. He was not as remote as New England but still not near enough to the Rio Grande to be going against the current of popular opinion by his opposition. The great test was the Civil War. He was an old man then and, in the words of a friend, in almost imperceptible decay. His writing grew diffuse and rambling. But the question of war so affected him that he rallied into lucidity and in 1861 made this statement in the *Millennial Harbinger:*

> Of all the monstrosities on which our sun has ever shone, that of professedly *Christian* nations, glutting their wrath and vengeance on one another, with all the instruments of murder and slaughter, caps the climax of human folly and gratuitous wickedness. Alas! Alas! man's inhumanity to man has made, and is still intent on making, countless millions mourn![13]

[13] *Ibid.,* 1861, pp. 345-348.

12. The Churches and Alcohol

One of the major social problems of our time is that of alcoholism. The attitudes of the churches on this subject can be distinguished as to periods. The great wave of rigorism in this country was at the peak during World War I, issuing in national prohibition. The failure of that experiment has led to a wave of laxism not only in our culture as a whole but to a large degree also in the churches. Another line of demarcation is confessional. The common assumption is that Protestantism is marked by rigor as to drink but latitude as to sex in the matter of birth control, whereas Catholicism exactly reverses the stands. This prompts the suggestion that Protestant asceticism is directed toward drink, Catholic asceticism toward sex. A movie entitled *Going My Way* illustrates the point. In the story, a young priest by a vow of celibacy wounds a heart. An old priest has concealed in a bookcase, behind the works of General Grant, a whisky flask. A Protestant clergyman would have married the girl, but in many denominations he would never have been able to grow old in the ministry if he were caught with the flask. The Protestant clergyman is expected to be abstinent, the Catholic to be celibate. Of course, each is free to emulate the virtues expected of the other, but the pressures are differently weighted. The Catholic priest is subject to obligatory celibacy. The Protestant clergy is well-nigh subject to obligatory matrimony. Such differences in practice make one wonder whether Protestant rigorism may not be directed to drink and Catholic rigorism to sex.

If this be true, the explanation might be that Catholicism is prevalent among southern peoples more prone to sexual excess, and Protestantism in northern climes more disposed to intemper-

This article is a combination and reworking of two previous articles. The first, with the above title, appeared in the *Quarterly Journal of Studies on Alcohol* VI, 1 (June, 1945). The second was first published as "Total Abstinence and Biblical Principles," in *Christianity Today* (July 7, 1958).

ance in drink. The mores required of the clergy represent, in each case, a recoil against abuses. This explanation, although plausible, is at every step too simple. To begin with, Catholicism and Protestantism are not to be neatly equated with south and north, for Catholicism has a great hold in Ireland and Poland, and Protestantism was once strong in France. Neither can we be too confident that excess in sex is southern and excess in drink is northern. Statistics for the year 1927 reveal that in the total consumption of alcoholic beverages France was first, Spain second, Italy third, and Germany in the twenty-first place.[1]

On the other hand, the generalization may be defensible for the days in which the Catholic and Protestant ethics were formulated. In the time of St. Augustine, who did so much to fashion the Catholic view, the Germanic invaders were reputed to be more chaste than the Romans. The Vandals were lauded by the vanquished for having closed the brothels of Carthage,[2] whereas in the period when the Protestant ethic was taking shape at the hands of Martin Luther the Germans were notorious for drunkenness. These considerations perhaps support an explanation ultimately in terms of climate. But this again is too simple. Religious ideas mould conduct even in defiance of climate.

A more serious objection to the generalization is that the lines do not fall neatly between Catholic and Protestant on the matter of drink. The Lutherans and the Anglicans have stood in the Catholic tradition. For the most part early Protestantism and even Puritanism were not rigoristic. The movement culminating in total abstinence and prohibition had its rise in the eighteenth century, due on the one hand to the increased sensitivity induced by the evangelical revivals and on the other hand to the increased evil of drunkenness due to the introduction of distilled liquors. Nor has the Catholic Church been devoid of movements for total abstinence. The only valid generalization is that on ethical questions an absolutist stand is to be expected only from small groups

[1] Statistics from the article "Alkoholfrage" in *Die Religion in Geschichte und Gegenwart*, 2d ed.

[2] Salvian, *On the Government of God*, IV. 5 and VII. 20-23, tr. Eva M. Sandford (New York, 1930).

with a highly select constituency, whereas churches embracing entire populations will tend toward leniency, if not laxity.

All Christian groups in determining their stand have had an eye to Biblical precepts and practices and some have a great reverence for tradition. Both the Bible and tradition down to the eighteenth century supported moderation rather than total abstinence. This practice may be defended on Christian assumptions because of the particular circumstances of our own time, but not on the basis of the example and teaching of the Scripture and the Church during the greater part of her history. The absolute abstainers have sought, however, to wrest the Scripture to their purpose and to impose upon it a meaning conformable to their practice, but only by doing violence to the plain meaning of the words. Their attempt represents the final stage in Biblical literalism. The first was to say that whatever the Bible does not prohibit may be allowed; the second was that whatever the Bible does not enjoin must be rejected; the third that whatever the Bible has at any point enjoined or allowed should be reinstated. The final stage in biblicism was not openly recognized. It consisted in imposing upon the Bible a meaning which would justify current practices actually adopted on non-biblical grounds. For example, George Fox refused to lift a hat as a mark of deference to persons in authority. His real motive was social equalitarianism, but when challenged for a biblical warrant he replied, "Shadrach, Meshach and Abednego were cast into the midst of the burning fiery furnace with their coats and their hose and *their hats* on."

More insidious has been the use of this method by the temperance reformers of the nineteenth and twentieth centuries to wrest the meaning of Scripture in order to find in it an explicit warrant for their practice. Since several words, used in the Hebrew and in the Greek of the Old and New Testaments, describe drinks of juice, the assumption has been that some referred to fermented and some to unfermented beverages and that wherever a drink was commended or not condemned, it must have been nonalcoholic.[3]

---

[3] Ernest Gordon, *Christ, the Apostles and Wine* (Philadelphia, 1944).

Biblical Attitudes

The validity of this contention can be tested only through an examination of the meaning of words, but words can be understood only in the context of ideas and attitudes. The determinative belief alike of Judaism and Christianity for this question is the affirmation of the goodness of creation. God made the world and saw that it is good. It can be abused and is to be used only under discipline. Over against this view are two others. Ascetic religions affirm that creation is bad and is not to be used. Orgiastic religions are lacking in discipline. Judaism has no affinity with either. Ascetic religions frequently proscribe contacts with women, war and wine, because sexual relations, killing and intoxication are defiling. Of this attitude there is scarcely a trace in the Old Testament. The psalmist praises the Lord for "He causeth the grass to grow for the cattle and herb for the service of man ... and wine that maketh glad the heart of man" (Ps. 104:13-15).

Judaism, on the other hand, is not an orgiastic nature religion, discovering particular evidence of the divine in the processes of fertilization, vegetation and fermentation and seeking communion with God through the excitements of sex and drink. This type of religion was found in Canaan in the Baal cult, and in the Hellenistic world in the rites of Dionysus. Against all such orgies the prophets of Israel were flint, even to the point of slaughtering the priests of Baal. Drunkenness in Judaism, whether connected or unconnected with religion, met with the sternest rebuke. Noah, Lot and Nabal were subjected to reprobation for their lapses. Incidentally, one of the problems for Biblical commentators has been to explain how Noah could be sober for 601 years and then get drunk. The classical denunciations of drunkenness in the Old Testament are to be found in the Book of Proverbs: "Wine is a mocker and strong drink a brawler.... Look not upon the wine when it is red, when it sparkleth in the cup, when it goeth down smoothly: at the last it biteth like a serpent and stingeth like an adder" (Prov. 20:1; 23:31).

The only cure for drunkenness contemplated in the Old Testament is moderation. We do hear, however, of two groups of total abstainers, the Nazirites and the Rechabites. The Nazirites, in the interests of holiness, vowed to hold themselves aloof for a limited period from razors, corpses and wine (Num. 6:1-6). Here there is a suggestion of ascetic religion. In the case of the Rechabites abstinence was a survival of nomadic mores. The Israelites before their invasion of Canaan had been desert tribes for whom liquor was difficult to manufacture. On entering Canaan they adopted the agricultural pursuits and the drinking habits of the Canaanites. The Rechabites held out sternly for the good old ways, refusing to build houses, sow the soil, plant vineyards or drink wine (Jer. 35:1-11). This point is worthy of note because not infrequently in Christian history reformatory movements have been couched in terms of cultural primitivism, a return to some simpler mode of existence. Commonly in our day, however, the cry is from the city to the country, not from the country to the desert.

To sum up: Judaism steers a middle ground between an ascetic religion renouncing wine as evil *per se,* and a nature religion using wine to produce religious ecstasy. Drunkenness is reproved; moderation is commended. Total abstinence is represented only by rigoristic minorities.

Christianity inherited this ethic and very largely reproduced its pattern. Jesus was no Nazirite or Rechabite like John the Baptist, for "the Son of Man came eating and drinking," and could be slandered as "a winebibber and a glutton" (Mat. 11:18-19). At the same time Jesus upbraided the drunken stewards (Mat. 24:49) and introduced an ethical rigorism more exacting than that of Judaism in that an offending eye is to be plucked out and an offending hand to be cut off (Mat. 5: 27-29). The Apostle Paul is more explicit because he was confronted with actual drunkenness within the Christian congregations at a very dangerous point, the celebration of the Lord's Supper. Here was the peril that Christianity might degenerate into an orgiastic nature cult (I Cor. 11:21). The Apostle sternly rebuked inebriety. "Let us walk becomingly as in the day, not in revelling and drunkenness" (Rom. 13:13). Among the offenses which exclude from the Kingdom of God is drunkenness (I Cor. 6:10). The antidote in the New Testament is not total abstinence, for Timothy may take a little wine for his stomach's sake (I Tim. 5:23), but first the avoidance of evil company. With the drunkard the Christian should not eat (I Cor. 5:11). The real cure is that "ye be not drunken with wine ... but filled with the Spirit" (Eph. 5:18). As a rule for conduct Paul formulates a principle destined to play a great role in the temperance movement, the principle of consideration for the weaker brother. "Let no man put a stumbling block in his brother's way. ... All things indeed are clean ... but it is good not to eat flesh, nor to drink wine, nor to do anything whereby thy brother stumbleth" (Rom. 14:13-23).

The above passages in the Old Testament and the New alike inculcate a disciplined use of fermented drinks. But the extreme temperance reformers seek to obviate this conclusion by drawing a distinction between two words in the Old Testament in Hebrew —*yayin* and *tirosh*—and two in the New Testament—*oinos* and *gleukos*. The contention is that in each language the one word refers to unfermented and the other to fermented juice and that only the unfermented is approved.

A careful study of the context in which these words occur does not bear out the distinction. In Hebrew *tirosh* is the word alleged to represent unfermented grape juice. The various usages of the word indicate that it does mean the juice of the grape whether in the grape or in the vat. It is the raw product out of which wine is made as bread is made out of flour. *Tirosh* is commonly translated "new wine." But this is not to say that it was not intoxicating. We have one passage in which very clearly it was so regarded. Hosea says, "Whoredom and *yayin* and *tirosh* take away the understanding" (4:11). Here *tirosh* is distinguished from *yayin* but both are compared to fornication.

With regard to *yayin* there is no question that it was intoxicating. Noah drank of the *yayin* and was drunken (Gen. 9:20-21). The daughters of Lot made their father drunk with *yayin* (Gen. 19:32-35). Eli said to Hannah, "How long wilt thou be drunken? put away the *yayin* from thee" (I Sam. 1:14).

Such drunkenness was roundly condemned alike in Proverbs and in the prophets (Prov. 20:1; 23:29-32; Isa. 28:1-7; Joel 1:5; Hab. 2:5).

But if the temperance interpreters were correct, *yayin* should be universally condemned; but such is not the case. The lover in the Song of Solomon sings to her beloved, "Thy love is better than *yayin*" (1:2).

The clearest passage is in the 104th Psalm: "He causeth the grass to grow for the cattle, and herb for the service of man; that he may bring forth food out of the earth, and *yayin* that maketh glad the heart of man, and oil to make his face to shine, and bread that strengtheneth man's heart" (vs. 14).

And then there is the great passage in the prophet Isaiah: "Ho, every one that thirsteth, come ye to the waters, and he that hath no money; come ye, buy and eat; yea, come, buy *yayin* and milk without money and without price" (55:1).

As far as the words are concerned, the attempt to distinguish between a fermented wine which is condemned and an unfermented which is approved simply will not hold. The temperance interpreters are driven to say quite arbitrarily that whatever is approved must be unfermented.

The attempt to find a distinction between two kinds of beverage in the New Testament, the one intoxicating and the other unintoxicating, likewise breaks down. The Greek equivalent of the Hebrew *tirosh* is *gleukos*. The word is used once in the New Testament and the context certainly indicates that it was intoxicating. The occasion was the preaching with tongues at Pentecost. Some of the bystanders were amazed. Others mocked saying, "They are filled with *gleukos*" (Acts 2:13). What point was there in the sneer if it meant that these men were talking gibberish because they had had grape juice for breakfast?

The common word for wine in the New Testament is *oinos*. This is the Hebrew *yayin*. As in the Old Testament only the abuse and not the use is condemned. Drunkenness is of course reproved.

In addition to the passages already cited one may note that in the pastoral epistles bishops are not to be quarrelsome over wine (I Tim. 3:3); that elderly women should not be enslaved to *too much* wine (Titus 2:3), and I Peter condemns *winebibbings* (4:3).

The temperance interpreters have maintained that the wine into which water was turned at the wedding feast at Cana must have been unintoxicating. But can one suppose that the guests at an oriental wedding, having already freely imbibed, would have considered the last wine to be the best if it were unfermented?

Finally the wine used at the Lord's Supper must have been fermented unless Jesus was going flatly counter to current Jewish usage. The word *wine,* by the way, is not used in the accounts of the Lord's Supper. Its presence is inferred from the references to the cup.

The case is so abundantly clear that so lengthy a refutation might well appear superfluous. One notes that the contributors to Kittel's *Theologisches Wörterbuch* do not so much as consider whether *oinos* might have been unfermented, nor whether *nepho* could have meant "totally abstinent" rather than simply "not drunk." The only reason I have discussed the matter at such length is that in this country biblical literalists still persist in their effort to make of the Bible a book enjoining total abstinence. It is argued that since intoxicating wine is a drink of death and Christ is the Lord of life, he simply cannot have turned water into intoxicating wine. There is really no use in discussing the meaning of words in that case. The matter is settled by the presuppositions.

Early Christianity

The practice of the Old and New Testaments continued in the churches until the time of the industrial revolution. In the period immediately following the New Testament, when the Church tended toward greater ethical rigorism as preparation for martyrdom, total abstinence was not enjoined. The normal attitude is represented by Clement of Alexandria in a book called *The Instructor,* in which he inveighs against all excesses and indelicacies in eating and drinking and especially upbraids drunkenness, while recognizing that a moderate use of wine rejoices the heart. Incidentally in the course of his discussion he displays a rather broad acquaintance with at least the names of the choicest varieties. At the same time voluntary abstinence is commendable, especially in the young.[4]

Total abstinence was made obligatory in the early Church only by ascetic heretics who in an age of persecution readily fell

---

[4] I. W. Raymond, *The Teaching of the Early Church on the Use of Wine and Strong Drink* (New York, 1927).

into the error of regarding the material world as evil. Various Gnostics abstained from contact with women, war and wine for the sake of holiness, and in the celebration of the Lord's Supper substituted water for wine. Hence they were nicknamed Aquarians. The same practice prevailed for a time in the orthodox churches of northern Africa where the motive appears to have been not asceticism but the fear that in persecution the Christian would betray himself through the smell of wine on his breath at an unusually early hour of the morning. Bishop Cyprian replied, "Are you ashamed of the blood of Christ?"[5] The sacramental use of wine soon displaced that of water.[6] The danger that actual intoxication might receive a religious sanction was obviated by sublimation into a spiritual intoxication, a *sobria ebrietas* which runs all through the works of the Greek and Latin fathers to reappear in the great medieval mystic, Bernard of Clairvaux.[7]

The Catholic Ethic

The reconciliation of Christianity with the state made the new religion popular and led to accessions with unseemly haste and all too little preparation. The way was made easier by relaxing the standards. St. Augustine tells us that frequently, when the heathen hesitated to embrace the faith for fear of having to renounce the tippling of pagan festivals, the Church relaxed and countenanced drinking in commemoration of the martyrs. Augustine was doing his best to stamp out the practice in his diocese of northern Africa.[8] St. Basil was similarly outraged by the revelry accompanying the celebration of Easter.[9] But neither enjoined a

[5] *Ep.* LXII, 15.

[6] A. Harnack, "Brod und Wasser," *Texte und Untersuchungen,* VII (1892). Harnack endeavored to prove that the practice extended beyond northern Africa and could be discovered in the works of Justin Martyr. In this position he was opposed, and I think cogently, by Adolf Jülicher, "Zur Geschichte der Abendmahlsfeier in der ältesten Kirche," *Theologische Abhandlungen für Carl von Weizäcker* (Freiburg, 1892).

[7] H. Lewy, "Sobria Ebrietas," *Beihefte zur Zeitschrift für die neuentestamentliche Wissenschaft,* IX (1929).

[8] *Ep.* XXII and XXIX.

[9] *Hom.* XIV and *Sermo* XVI. Summarized in Raymond, *op. cit.,* p. 105.

total abstinence. St. Basil, even in his monastic rule, recommended only self-discipline and variation in practice according to individual need. St. Augustine, writing against a new variety of religious ascetics, the Manichaeans, defended wine as a gift of God.[10]

The rise of monasticism introduced no essential change. The movement was a protest against the corruption of secular and even of ecclesiastical society. To escape contamination the monks fled to the desert. So great was their despair of any Christian society upon earth that they renounced propagation and lived in segregated communities of men and women. In consequence, the quelling of sexual desire became, for a period, a positive obsession, and the means employed was mortification of the flesh by fasting and abstinence. Yet the Rule of St. Benedict did not prohibit wine and the earlier rigor was soon so far relaxed that the Benedictines and the Chartreuses became famous for their vintages.

The Middle Ages offered nothing new in principle, only a constant recurrence of the ancient abuses and the traditional correctives. The holy days of the Church were celebrated with conviviality. There were church-ales, Whitsun-ales. What we now call a bridal party was then a bride-ale. The Church inveighed against all such abuses. Occasional drunkenness was branded as a venial sin and habitual drunkenness as a mortal sin. The drunkard was pilloried from the pulpit. All of the burlesques of the English stage and novel have their prototypes in the medieval satires of the pulpit. The drunkard was ridiculed who, seeing two candles and extinguishing one as superfluous, was amazed to find the other disappear as well. More serious was the situation of the inebriate who came home to find four children instead of two. He accused his wife of irregularity and called upon her to demonstrate her innocence by holding a plowshare which he heated red hot in the fireplace. She consented if he would hand it to her, which he did.[11] The preacher assured his auditors that the Virgin would turn away

[10] *On the Morals of the Manichaeans*, XVI, 44, and *Against Faustus*, XX, 13.

[11] G .R. Owst, *Literature and Pulpit in Medieval England* (Cambridge, 1933) , pp. 425-441.

[12] G. G. Coulton, *Five Centuries of Religion* (Cambridge, 1923) , I, 163.

her face from the prayer of a monk whose breath was redolent of wine.[12] The ideal of temperance was at least so well established that satires on clerical intemperance were as funny then as they have been ever since. No more blasphemous piece of buffoonery could be conceived than a parody called *The Mass of the Drunkards.* The lines of the mass, which read *per Dominum nostrum qui vivit et regnat per saecula saeculorum* (through our Lord who lives and reigns through the ages and ages), were turned into *per dominum nostrum reum Bachum, qui bibit et poculat per omnia pocula poculorum* (through our lord Bacchus who drinks and guzzles through the cups of the cups).[13] As an example of the same type of literature in modern times we have the skit of Alphonse Daudet concerning Père Gaucher, who imperils his immortal soul to invent a choicer cordial for the profit of the monastery; or the hilarity of Dickens in the *Pickwick Papers* over the exploits of the rednosed Pastor Stiggins at the session of the Brick Lane Branch of the United Grand Junction Ebenezer Temperance Association.

But to return to the earlier centuries. A new possibility was introduced when the Roman Empire gave its patronage to the Church. Christian ideals could then be embodied in secular legislation to be enforced by the state. In other words, the door was open for prohibition. No ruler attempted it in the Christian Roman Empire, nor in the west during the Middle Ages, but regulation of the sale and consumption of liquor by rulers, whether ecclesiatical or secular, was very common during this period. Sumptuary legislation was frequent enough long before the period of the Protestant Reformation.[14]

During the Middle Ages instances of total abstinence are hard to find. The end of that period saw the resurgence of ascetic sects such as the Cathari, resembling the ancient Gnostics. They may have been total abstainers. Bernard of Clairvaux says of them

---

[13] T. Wright, *Reliquiae Antiquae* (London, 1845), II.

[14] K. R. Greenfield, *Sumptuary Legislation in Nürnberg* (Baltimore, 1918). Much information on this point is contained in the admirable study of Edward G. Baird, "The Alcohol Problem and the Law," *Quarterly Journal of Studies on Alcohol,* IV, 535-556 and V, 126-161.

that their faces were pale with fasting. One may perhaps infer that their noses were not red with tippling.[15] But that they were complete abstainers is not clear since they allowed the use of wine in the sacrament.[16]

Early Protestantism

The Protestant Reformation brought at first no great change in the picture. Martin Luther, when he abolished monasticism and inaugurated that attitude which was to make matrimony almost a prerequisite for a Protestant clergyman, did not compensate by rigorism as to drink. On the contrary, he was somewhat convivial. Once, when at table with his colleagues, he pointed to a stein girt with three rings. The top one, he said, stood for the Ten Commandments, the middle ring for the Apostles' Creed, and the bottom for the Lord's Prayer. Then Luther drained the stein at a draught and refilling it handed it to his friend Agricola who, to Luther's intense amusement, could not get beyond the Ten Commandments. But Luther was no drunkard. Melanchthon testified that he was abstemious and, under the stress of work, would often fast for days. Luther had no use for drunkenness and scathingly denounced his fellow Germans and even his own prince for lapses.[17] Luther's matured attitude is well expressed in his commentary on the miracle at Cana. Jesus turned water into wine. Let us not be scandalized, commented Luther, if some one should take a little more than was necessary for thirst and grow merry, but alas! in our day we drink until we are soused. We are swine, not men.[18] He suggested facetiously that the only way to cure the

---

[15] H. C. Lea, *History of the Inquisition in the Middle Ages,* 3 vols. (New York, 1922), I, 101.

[16] H. J. Warner, *The Albigensian Heresy* (London, 1922), p. 81. But our sources are meager and their practice may not have been uniform. They had also one standard for believers and another for the perfect.

[17] *See* the relevant sections in the biographies of Luther by Preserved Smith (New York, 1911) and A. C. McGiffert (New York, 1907). Especially consult Adolf Allwohn, *Luther und der Alkohol* (1929), and for early Protestantism Fritz Blanke, "Reformation und Alkoholismus," *Der Fürsorger,* VI (1949).

[18] *Weimarer Ausgabe,* XVII, 2. 63-64. Cf. H. Schmidt, "Die Erzählung von der Hochzeit zu Kana," *Die Alkoholfrage in der Religion,* IV, pt. 1 (1931).

Germans of drunkenness would be to command them by edict of the princes to get drunk. Then, such is the contrariness of man, they would willingly be sober.[19] Yet total abstinence appeared to him preposterous. In a plea against violence in abolishing the mass and destroying images he argued, "Wine and women bring many a man to ruin and make a fool of him. Shall we therefore despatch all women and spill out all wine?"[20]

Not to Luther nor to Lutheranism are we to look for the origin of the modern Protestant campaign against all drink. Nor is the source to be found in the Anglican Church. On this point the Lutheran and the Anglican Churches are at one with the Roman Catholic—all of them churches which include the masses.

Another type of Protestantism arose, in the sixteenth century, which insisted that the Church should be a city of the saints no matter how small, and should exclude the unworthy from her membership. The code of conduct demanded of the saints was exacting. This has been the pattern of English and American sectarianism. Its prototype in the Germany of the Reformation was Anabaptism. The movement was not ascetic in the sense of the ancient Gnostics. The Anabaptists did not eschew marriage, and required only moderation in food and drink, but they were ethical rigorists who criticized the Lutheran Reformation for failure to produce a manifest change in moral demeanor. One of the marks of the true Christian is sobriety. The rule of the Hutterian Brethren (1545) forbade any member of the society to be a public innkeeper or to sell wine and beer.[21] The Lutheran Formula of Concord enumerated among the errors of the Anabaptists that a Christian might not keep an inn. A Lutheran minister in 1531 testified that the best way for an Anabaptist suspect to clear himself was to indulge in frequent drinking bouts.[22] One of the Hutterite preachers was detected because of his refusal to drink in an inn. The Hutterites and the Swiss Brethren appear to have been the most rigoristic among the Anabaptists. Of the latter Bullinger testified that they would drink only sweet cider. The Mennonites

[19] *Tischreden* III, No. 3468.
[20] *Weimarer Ausgabe*, X, 3. 33.
[21] J. Horsch, *The Hutterian Brethren* (Goshen, Indiana, 1931) , p. 139.
[22] J. Horsch, *Menno Simons* (Scotdale, Pennsylvania, 1916) , p. 114.

were less severe. Menno inveighed against the consumption of alcohol without demanding total abstinence and in a later period many Mennonites were brewers. The only writer in the sixteenth century requiring total abstinence was an independent detached from all of the churches, Sebastian Franck.[23]

But the Anabaptists, though ruthlessly suppressed, were not altogether without their influence. Their memory afforded an impetus to German Pietism, which in turn affected English Methodism. The sectarian Protestantism of Germany reappeared in the English sectarianism of the seventeenth century among the Quakers. In view of such connections we need feel no surprise to discover the Methodists and the Quakers as the pioneers in the modern temperance crusade.

They were to enlist the support of the churches of Calvinist derivation, and Calvinism itself owes much to its competition with Anabaptism. In order to meet the Anabaptist criticism Calvin adopted a strict discipline. His whole demeanor was more austere than that of the convivial Luther. To be sure, Calvin was no teetotaler. He allowed wine in moderation and did not decline the present of a cask from the town council. At the same time he revived and went beyond the sumptuary legislation of the late Middle Ages.[24] Taverns were suppressed in favor of hostels where food and drink were served only to those who looked as though they would be able to say grace after as well as before partaking, and who agreed to depart from the premises at 9 P.M. Even though the hostels lasted but 3 months,[25] the Genevans were proud of their austerity. A satire composed by Calvin's colleague Theodore Beza pictured a Catholic spy coming to Geneva to discover to his amazement how pale were the faces of the heretics. Beza was not slow to point the contrast with the leader of persecution against the Protestants in France, whose nose was the hue of a cardinal's hat.[26] Calvinism contributed to the ultimate temperance campaign a

[23] Cf. Blanke, *op. cit.*, and the article "Alcohol" in the *Mennonite Encyclopedia*.

[24] On the discipline applied to drunkenness in Geneva before Calvin, see H. Naef, *Les Origines de la Réforme à Genève* (Geneva, 1936) , p. 235.

[25] G. Harkness, *John Calvin* (New York, 1931) , p. 28. I have not been able to consult Peter Brunner, *Die Alkoholfrage bei Calvin* (1950) .

[26] *Le Passavant* (Paris, 1875) . Reprinted by Isidore Liseux.

deep moral earnestness, and a readiness, not characteristic of Anabaptism, to make use of the state to institute and enforce a code of
conduct. But initial Calvinism was not committed to total abstinence. The modern movement of Prohibition is really a combination of the Anabaptist code with the Calvinist program.

But the modern movement did not come until the late eighteenth century. Calvinism was a long time in adopting the Anabaptist code. The Calvinism of Scotland under Knox was no different from that of Geneva under Calvin. Knox had his wine cellar.
The Calvinism of English Puritanism exhibited the same general
pattern. The Roundheads, indeed, stigmatized the Cavaliers as
rowdy and dissolute, but the worst of their offenses appear to have
been Sabbath breaking and "God-damn-me oaths" together with
pillaging.[27] When King James promulgated a "Book of Lawful
Sports" to be played on Sunday afternoons in order to wean the
people from "filthy tippling and drunkenness" the Puritans were
so outraged by this proposed profanation of the Lord's day that
the "Book of Sports" was burned.

New England Puritanism exhibits no marked change. A
housewarming had reference to the use of ardent spirits. Even the
ordinations of ministers were often unseemly occasions. The shep-
herd of souls was sore tried to do justice to the hospitality of his
flock and get home with the aid only of his crook. Ministers, such
as the Mathers, inveighed against drunkenness. Colonial assemblies
regulated the hours of taverns, the quality of beer and the sale to
domestics and the Indians, among whom rum wrought havoc. The
name Manhattan, by the way, is said to be a corruption of a
sentence in the language of the Delawares meaning, "Here we got
drunk," referring to their first experience of the hospitality of
Hendrik Hudson.[28] Despite all regulation, excessive drinking continued even among churchmen in New England until the reform
movement of the early nineteenth century.

[27] *See* the passages collected in my article "Congregationalism: from the
Just War to the Crusade in the Puritan Revolution," *Andover Newton Theol.
School Bull.*, XXXV, 3 (April, 1943; Series II in this collection).
[28] E. H. Cherrington, *The Evolution of Prohibition in the United States
of America* (Westerville, Ohio, 1920).

The Temperance Crusade

The initiative in the temperance crusade came from the Methodists and the Quakers, with the Calvinist churches swinging into line later. The Catholics, Lutherans and Episcopalians were reluctant to demand one practice only of their constituents, let alone of society at large. The first temperance reformers were not ascetics fleeing contamination, nor saints aspiring to perfection. Their motivation might rather be called sociological. The evil of drink had grown worse in the eighteenth century due to the displacement of fermented by distilled liquors. A report to His Majesty's Justices of the Peace in 1735-36 lamented the surprising increase of gin-drinking in London in which whole families were involved, parents, children and servants.[29] No one was better acquainted with the prevalent excesses than John Wesley. In the campaign for correction, the alliance of religion with medicine is noteworthy. The inaugurator of the American reform was Benjamin Rush, the Quaker doctor of Philadelphia.

If the program of the reformers became ever more drastic, the reason lay not in any ascetic presuppositions but in the lessons of experience. First came total abstinence from hard liquors, coupled with moderation as to the soft. But when it was found that drunkards on the way to reform could lapse as readily on soft as on hard, the ban was placed on both, and those who might be able to drink in moderation were urged to refrain entirely out of consideration for the weaker brother. The same moral was deduced from the failure of the Duke of Wellington's attempt to oust hard liquor in Britain through the encouragement of beer. Inebriety was only increased by the Free Beer policy of 1830-1869. The failures of regulation likewise drove the temperance movement to the advocacy of prohibition. The course of the movement was very similar in England, Germany and the United States, except that prohibition was achieved only here.[30]

[29] M. D. George, *English Social Life in the Eighteenth Century* (London, 1923) , pp. 34-35.
[30] On the movement elsewhere, *see:* H. Carter, *The English Temperance Movement* (London, 1933) , I; M. Helenius, *Die Alkoholfrage* (Jena, 1903) ; also the articles "Alkoholfrage" in *Die Religion in Geschichte und Gegenwart* and in the *Lexikon für Theologie und Kirche.* The series *Die Alkoholfrage in der Religion,* 4 vols. (1926-1931) is only very partially available in this country.

In England the Methodists took the lead. John Wesley, who so well knew the debauchery of the English countryside, lashed out against the sellers of spirituous liquors as poisoners of the people. The Rules of the Society called Methodists, in 1743, required members "to avoid buying or selling spirituous liquors, or drinking them, unless in cases of extreme necessity."[31]

In the United States several Quakers were the most notable exponents of reform. The reputed father of the temperance movement in this country was the Philadelphia doctor Benjamin Rush. Having observed all too well the evils of excessive drinking in the Revolutionary Army he came out with a tract entitled *An Inquiry into the Effects of Ardent Spirits* (1785). His objection was only to the use of distilled liquors. As a substitute he recommended first water, and if that did not suffice, then cider or light wine. Much medical observation was introduced. He closed with a ringing plea to all the churches to join in the crusade. In the following six decades his tract circulated 200,000 copies.[32] Another notable Quaker pioneer was Neal Dow, one of the fathers of American prohibition. He was a citizen of Maine. His first enunciation of the principle of prohibition was in 1839. He lived to see it embodied in the law of his state in 1851. Thereafter the cry of the temperance reformers was, "Remember the Maine Liquor Law."[33]

The Society of Friends as a whole, however, was loath to impose an absolute on the consciences of its members. In 1751 the Yearly Meeting testified against *excessive* drinking. In 1835 the Epistle suggested abstention from *distilled spirits*. Not until 1906 did the testimony for total abstinence reach the level called "General Advice."[34]

Among the churches of the Calvinist tradition which rallied to the support of the Methodists and the Friends come first the

[31] H. Carter, *op. cit.* (n. 30 above), I, 33.

[32] C. H. Moehlman, *When All Drank and Thereafter* (New York, 1930).

[33] H. S. Clubb, *The Maine Liquor Law* (New York, 1956). The Society of Friends as a whole, however, was loath to impose an absolute on the consciences of its members. In 1751 the Yearly Meeting testified against *excessive* drinking. In 1835 the Epistle suggested abstention from *distilled spirits*. Not until 1906 did the testimony for total abstinence reach the level called "General Advice."

[34] Bernard Canter, *Consider Whether,* Friends Temperance Union (London, 1953).

Congregationalists, who were the leaders of the movement in New England from 1810 until the formation of the Temperance Society in 1826. The year 1810 was marked by the indignation of Lyman Beecher when, at his ordination, the sideboard was loaded with decanters containing every liquor in vogue. The talk was jocose and convivial. This, said he, "woke me up for the war."[35] He was ardently seconded by Leonard Bacon who, in New Haven in 1829, preached his sermon on "Total Abstinence from Ardent Spirits." By ardent spirits he meant distilled liquors. Beer and wine were not discussed.

But when it was found that inebriates were incapable of maintaining sobriety on soft liquors these too were placed under the ban. The pledge was made more inclusive: "So here we pledge perpetual hate to all that can intoxicate." One society had two levels of membership; the names of some were marked with the letters "O.P." for "old pledge"; others with a "T." for total. Hence they came to be known as "T-Totalers."[36]

With regard to other churches of the Calvinist tradition we may note that the Presbyterians in 1827-30 took a strong stand for total abstinence, and in 1854 endorsed prohibition. The pronouncements of the Baptists were the most rigoristic. The New Jersey Association in 1835 declared, "It is morally wrong in all, and especially in a professor of religion, to manufacture, vend or use such liquors [alcoholic, whether distilled or fermented] as a common article of luxury or living."[37]

The churches with the more inclusive membership, the Catholic, Lutheran and Episcopalian, have been less disposed to general requirements binding upon all members, although of course perfectly ready to bless total abstinence movements within their folds. The approval given by Pope Leo XIII to the Catholic abstinents was similar to a papal sanction of a vow of celibacy or poverty, which is commendable in those who take it, but not required of all. The zeal and effectiveness of thousands of Catholics who did espouse the cause are by no means to be minimized. One

[35] H. Blair, *The Temperance Movement* (Boston, 1888), pp. 425-426.
[36] This paragraph is taken from my book *Yale and the Ministry* (New York, 1957), p. 139, where documentation is given.
[37] Blair, *op. cit.*, pp. 442-447.

thinks of the Confraternity of the Sacred Thirst, and the vigorous support of Cardinal Gibbons and Bishop Ireland who declared that, "to Irishmen particularly, because of their comparative native powerlessness to resist alcohol . . . I will never cease pointing out with an undeviating finger, the harbor of peace and security—total abstinence." One may question his appraisal of the Irish, for prior to the great famine Father Mathew well-nigh dried up the island.[38]

The Lutherans have generally confined themselves to the advocacy of temperance, although various synods have taken strong stands against the liquor traffic.[39]

The Episcopalian Church has had a Temperance Society in which moderates and total abstainers alike participated. Episcopalians accepted Prohibition because it was the law of the land, but the majority of the clergy desired modification or repeal of the Volstead Act.[40] They stoutly and very properly resisted the efforts of the teetotalers to impose their code upon the Bible by interpreting the "wine that maketh glad the heart of man" as unfermented, and the wine into which the water was turned at Cana as grape juice.[41]

The Protestant sects with the strong ethical rigorism led the campaign for prohibition by government of the manufacture and sale of intoxicating liquors. The Holy Experiment came and went, and like most lost causes, now is memorialized by a wreath of sneers. The knell was sounded in *The Rubaiyat of Ohow Dryyam,* which concludes with the verse:

> When thyself at last shall come to trip
> Down that dim dock where Charon loads his ship,
> I'll meet thee on the other wharf if thou
> Wilt promise to have something on thy hip.[42]

Prohibition is gone, but the problem of inebriety confronts us still in no less acute form.

[38] *Ibid.*, pp. 474 ff. Also, D. L. Colvin, *Prohibition in the United States* (New York, 1926) , pp. 268-269 f.

[39] *Ibid.*, p. 450.

[40] *Prohibition as We See It* (The Church Temperance Society, New York, 1928) .

[41] E. A. Wasson, *Religion and Drink* (New York, 1914) .

[42] J. L. Duff (San Francisco, 1922) .

The attitudes of the churches throughout the centuries provide us with no absolute rule. The Bible provides us with no absolute rule.

Need For Total Abstinence

Nevertheless a sound case can be made for total abstinence on the basis of biblical principles. These principles have to be applied and reapplied to new sets of circumstances, and what may have been legitimately permissible in one era ceases to be in another. Before considering these principles, we do well to recall the difference between the situation in biblical times and our own.

Drunkenness of course existed in biblical times and was condemned, but it was not so rampant as in our day because we have made such technological advance. First, the discovery of distillation has rendered possible an enormous increase in the alcoholic content of beverages. Secondly, an industry has arisen which depends for its existence on an expanding consumption of alcohol. Thirdly, the temptation to excess has been increased by all of the new strains involved in modern living, and, finally, the menace of inebriation is greater in a society where any blunting of extreme alertness may result in serious accidents.

Whereas in antiquity drunkenness was certainly to be condemned as a destroyer of judgment and a breeder of crime, today in the United States alcoholism is one of our major social problems. In 1949 Dr. Jellenik compiled statistics which added up to nearly four million alcoholics in this country; to be exact, the number was 3,852,000. Of these 3,276,000 were male and 576,000 were female. The alcoholic is defined as one for whom the craving for alcohol has become a disease and who consumes so much as to be recurrently incapacitated for work.[43]

Selden Bacon, writing in 1951, considered the above estimates conservative. He reported also on the financial losses to industry in the year 1946. The most moderate estimate was a billion dollars.

---

[43] E. M. Jellenik, *Quarterly Journal of Alcoholic Studies,* XVIII (June, 1952) , 215-218.

Other "seriously considered estimates ran to more than ten times that figure."[44]

Surgeons report their heaviest time to be on weekends, because of the higher number of automobile accidents in which alcohol is a very frequent causative factor. Ministers must give an inordinate amount of time to the endeavor to keep married couples together in cases where alcohol makes it almost imperative for them to live apart.

Recent investigations have taught us that alcohol is not a stimulant, but a sedative which relaxes the controls of intelligence and will. The consumption of alcohol may develop into the disease known as alcoholism. Some persons by reason of personality factors, perhaps physical factors, are predisposed to this disease. No one can tell in advance whether he is of this type. He can find out only by getting well on the road toward alcoholism, and then to stop is a frightful struggle.

This is the situation as described by sober investigators. To this situation biblical principles must be brought to bear. The first principle is this: "Know ye not that your bodies are members of Christ?... know ye not that your body is a temple of the Holy Spirit...?" (I Cor. 6:15 and 19). Certainly of themselves these tests do not require total abstinence. The question is, what does dishonor the body? Many will hold that a moderate use of alcoholic beverages is no dishonor, but others will reply that although a moderate use under carefully controlled conditions is no dishonor, nevertheless the moderate can lead to the immoderate, and the consequences of immoderate use in our highly mechanized society are so drastic that one is wise to preclude the possibility of excess by refraining from the moderate which may lead to it.

The second great biblical principle is consideration for the weaker brother. The classic passage is in Romans 14:

Let us not therefore judge one another any more. One man hath faith to eat all things, but he that is weak eateth herbs. Let not him that eateth set at naught him that eateth not; and let not him that eateth not judge him that eateth.... Let us not therefore judge one another any

[44] *The Civitan Magazine* (March, 1951), pp. 1-8.

more; but judge ye this rather, than no man put a stumblingblock in his brother's way.... I know, and am persuaded in the Lord Jesus that nothing is unclean of itself; save that to him who accounteth anything to be unclean, to him it is unclean. For if because of meat thy brother is grieved, thou walkest no longer in love.... Overthrow not for meat's sake the work of God.... It is good not to eat flesh, *nor to drink wine,* nor to do anything whereby thy brother stumbleth.

Apparently there were in the early Christian community those who abstained not simply from meat and wine polluted by having been offered to idols, but from all meat and from all wine. They were vegetarians and aquarians. The apostle regarded them as weak. Nevertheless they were to receive consideration, and the strong should adopt the practice of the weak rather than give offense.

If we translate these precepts into the terms of our situation, we may say that there are some who are capable of drinking in moderation, but others either for physical or psychological reasons are in danger of the Lost Weekend. For the sake of such people, those who can drink without excess should abstain in order to create a social environment in which abstinence is not an act of courage but accepted behavior.

The apostle Paul did not draw this specific inference. He was not legislating. He was enunciating principles. These two principles, that our bodies are the temples of the Holy Spirit and that the strong should accommodate themselves to the weak, are the biblical grounds on which I base my practice and teaching of total abstinence.

13. The Churches Shift on War

Very significant shifts have taken place within recent years in the attitudes of Christian groups to the morality of participation in war. The Catholics have been moving toward the Quakers, the Quakers toward the monks, and the Calvinists toward the Lutherans. Such a statement calls for a preliminary exposition of the traditional stands of these bodies, and this in turn requires an initial account of the major Christian answers to the problem of taking life in war.

Broadly speaking, the history of Christianity exhibits three attitudes toward war: the first is one of nonparticipation, pacifism; the second of reluctant participation, the just and mournful war; the third of hearty participation, the crusade. All three draw their inspiration alike from the New Testament, the Old Testament and from classical antiquity; but in the main pacifism makes its primary appeal to the New Testament, the crusade to the Old Testament, and the just war to the classical ethic, especially of Stoicism. All three attitudes are possible for Christians because the Gospels do not settle the question and the proof texts commonly adduced in favor of each position are not sufficiently explicit to exclude the others. Pacifists rely on the Sermon on the Mount, but the difficulty here is that the precepts on nonresistance are set in the framework of private ethics. Only the injunction to love enemies has to do with public relations, and in this instance the problem remains open whether love and constraint at the point of killing are compatible. The crusader appeals to the expulsion by Jesus of the money changers from the temple, but no weapon is mentioned save in the Fourth Gospel only, the whip of cords, which, if it be authentic, is scarcely a bayonet. The just war relies on the texts in favor of civil government such as "render unto Caesar" (Mark

First published in *Religion in Life*, XII (Summer, 1943). Copyright 1943 by Whitmore & Stone.

12:7) and "be subject under the higher powers" (Romans 13:2),
but the use of these texts for the *justum bellum* rests on the analogy between war and civil government which is more than dubious.
All three of these positions, then, have some basis in the New
Testament, but none has an unassailable and exclusive claim.

The reason is that the New Testament was not concerned to
legislate for all contingencies. What we do find is an enunciation
of general principles and specific applications to the situation of
that time only, not of all time, nor of our time. The New Testament inculcates an attitude of love without stint directed toward
the evil as well as toward the good, a quality of mercy patterned
after the mercy of God. The New Testament paints a picture of
peace transcending anything in Hebrew and classical antiquity.
Peace is not simply the opposite of war, but of all contention. It is
not outward merely, but also inward; not negative only, but positive, dynamic, creative. This peace is the principle of harmony, the
bond of all human associations. But whether love can constrain,
whether peace may use the sword in her own defense, here are the
questions unanswered. In a specific instance Jesus disapproved of
war. He could not endorse the zealot rebellion against Rome, but
his reasons may have been prudential, inasmuch as insurrection
was foredoomed. His attitude in this particular case, therefore,
does not preclude the possibility that he might have condoned
some other war with a different objective and a better chance of
success. The three positions, then, have each a toehold, but not an
exclusive foothold in the New Testament.

They were elaborated in the course of the centuries, first
pacifism, then the just war and then the crusade. The period from
Christ to Constantine was marked by pacifism; the interval from
Constantine to the barbarian invasions witnessed the emergence
of the just war; the Middle Ages added the crusade.

The pacifist period was one in which at first the problem of
war was not acute. The Roman Peace was not seriously menaced,
military service was not generally compulsory, and the civilian was
under no pressure to volunteer. The question arose only in case a
soldier already in the army was converted, and even then the situation was ambiguous because the army did the police work of the
Empire. Hence some Christians made a distinction between a per-

missible service in peace time and an illegitimate service in war time. The presence of Christians in the ranks between wars does not, therefore, of necessity demonstrate an approval of war. On the other hand, their absence from the armies need not have been due to pacifism, since there were other motives for abstention, inasmuch as Christians, being persecuted, held aloof from many areas of life, and even in periods of religious toleration military service was difficult to dissociate from pagan worship.

Yet when all the qualifications are in, the fact remains that no churchman, whose works are extant, condoned Christian participation in warfare until after the age of Constantine. Coupled with an increasing evidence of the presence of Christians in the army is an increasing literature of protest. An outsider, Celsus, the pagan critic of Christianity, toward the end of the second century charged that "if all men were to do the same as you, there would be nothing to prevent the king from being left in utter solitude and desertion, and the forces of the Empire would fall into the hands of the wildest and most lawless barbarians." The Church Father Origen in his reply did not deny the accusation of pacifism, but contested only the assumed consequences.

The grounds for such nonparticipation are generally discovered by historians, who do not approve of it, in motives of a very ephemeral validity: in the belief of the early Christians that the world was destined to a speedy end, and in an attitude of pessimism and rigorism inspired by persecution and far in excess of anything in the New Testament. These, however, are not the motives assigned by the Church Fathers themselves. The avowed grounds of their pacifism are love, legalism and optimism. The spirit of love was taken by them to exclude war. "If we are enjoined to love our enemies, whom have we to hate? If injured, we are forbidden to retaliate. Who, then, can suffer injury at our hands?" "If you enroll as one of God's people, heaven is your country and God your lawgiver, and what are His laws? . . . Thou shalt not kill. . . . Thou shalt love thy neighbor as thyself." "Christians do not learn war any more, for they have become the sons of peace." They cannot regard "homicide as a crime when committed by an individual, as a virtue when carried on publicly." Running through all these passages is the incompatibility of love and war.

Added to this general consideration was an appeal, sometimes to legalism and sometimes to optimism. The first is absolutist and has no regard for consequences; the second is utilitarian. The legalist says: "Christ has laid down the law. In disarming Peter, He disarmed every soldier. We cannot strike, no matter what happens." But the optimist argues that in the long run nonviolence is the superior technique for the maintenance of order, the establishment of justice and the preservation of peace. This was the reply of Origen to Celsus, who had charged that if all men were Christians the empire would fall into the hands of the barbarians. Origen retorted, to begin with, that if all men were Christians, the barbarians would be Christians. He could not conceive of a genuine conversion of the Roman Empire without a parallel effort and success among the barbarians, and even while the Christians were a minority, he looked upon them as the preservative of the empire. Rome had achieved only an external peace by suppressing war. Christianity had introduced an inward and dynamic peace, a spirit of concord taming wild passions and rendering men fit and able to live together. Christian love, Christian labor and Christian prayers were doing more in his judgment than arms to preserve Rome, and the winsome Word of God incarnate in Jesus, he believed, would go on to ever more abundant conquests of the minds of men.

The pacifist position, however, was rapidly moving toward the just and mournful war. Christianity itself became the object of war in the two decades of civil dissension leading up to the sole authority of Constantine. As many as seven contestants at one time struggled for the imperial title, and each, to curry favor with one element or another of the population, promised either to tolerate or to persecute the new faith. Little wonder that the sympathies of Christians gravitated to their protectors and that prayers went up for the success of their arms. The next step was Christian participation in warfare, which marked the period from Constantine to the barbarian invasions. The older inhibitions were not surrendered at once, nor ever completely. If by the end of the fourth century Theodosius had decreed that only Christians could be soldiers, the Church still enjoined penance for bloodshed in war, and the monks arose to perpetuate a complete pacifism among a limited group.

The first churchman to justify Christian participation in war was St. Ambrose. He was a true Roman trained in the imperial employ before he became a bishop. He was steeped in the classics, and his treatise on Christian morals was a free reworking of a treatise by Cicero. St. Ambrose began the appropriation of the classical theme of the just war. But the great formulator of the doctrine was St. Augustine, who laid down the essential lines of the Catholic, Lutheran and Anglican positions. He was confronted with a frightful situation. The barbarians were already in Spain and the refugees were pouring into his native Africa. Boniface, the Commander of the Legions, having lost his wife, desired to become a monk. "For God's sake not now," exclaimed Augustine, and then set himself to explain both why God had suffered the barbarians to break in and why Christians should nevertheless resist their further advance. The ultimate explanation is a somber view of history. The optimism of Origen is gone. Man is a fallen being, who has well-nigh obliterated in himself the image of God in which he was created. The Roman Empire was founded on the fratricide of Romulus and grew by rapine. The conversion of Constantine brought an improvement, but not even conversion, whether of an empire or of an individual, produces perfection. This is possible only in the life to come. The corollary is that peace will never be obtained on earth. Nevertheless outrageous villainy can be restrained. To that end the sword of the magistrate is ordained. In making war, the prince is acting as a magistrate.

Not any war is legitimate for a Christian, but only the just war. It must be waged under the authority of the prince who determines its justice. The common soldier is not in a position to judge, and is not bound to raise the question. The war must be just as to its object, which is to punish injustice and restore peace. It must be just in its intention—that is, without vindictiveness; and just in its conduct—no wanton violence. For the prince and the soldier the Sermon on the Mount is conserved only as an inner disposition. Outward resistance is conjoined with inward love. At the same time nonresistance is reserved for private relations, and the civilian must not defend even his own life. He is permitted to use the sword only under the authority of the prince. The clergy and the monk are entirely exempt from military participation. Here, then, is a graded ethic: for public, private and ecclesiastical relations. One point of very great significance must be noted, namely, that for Augustine, unlike Cicero, a war can be just on one side only. He is the father of the war guilt theory.

The war then is just. It is also mournful, for no Christian can feel happy at the taking of life, whether as executioner or soldier. In an imperfect world men, mindful of their own imperfection, must wield the sword of a justice all too relative in its quality. They will do so only with heaviness of heart.

The theory of the just war was elaborated in the Middle Ages. During the predatory raids of an unsettled society the recovery of property was added as one of the objects of the just war. The number of non-combatants was increased to include not only women, children and the clergy, but also travelers, merchants and farmers. A utilitarian note was introduced when a reasonable chance of success was made one of the conditions of the just war, but the most notable development was the implementation of the idea by a machinery for the determination of justice in the courts of the Church and through the arbitrament of the Pope. The papacy of the thirteenth century came closer to realizing the idea of the League of Nations and the Permanent Court of Justice than has any other institution before or since.

At the same time the Middle Ages saw the rise of the third attitude, that of the crusade. The initial ingredient in the crusading idea was furnished by the infusion of new blood. The barbarians were a warlike folk, and though the missionaries might decline to translate for them the books of Kings in the Old Testament, the marauders were ingenious enough to turn the New Testament into a warrior's manual. The first Christian poem in the German language celebrates the exploit of the doughty knight St. Peter, who wielded his broad sword and clave clean the ear of Malchus. King Clovis, of the Franks, transformed Jesus into a tribal war god. The pacifism of early Christianity was utterly incomprehensible to these lusty folk.

The second step toward a crusade was a great peace movement. In the eleventh century the Church made a valiant effort to curb feudal anarchy by restricting the scope of war. Princes should take a pledge to refrain from molesting an ever-enlarging circle of non-combatants. This was the Peace of God. The next move was to limit the time of hostilities. The taboo applied to holy days in such number that scarcely a quarter of the year remained for warfare. This was the Truce of God. It was none too successful, and then a league was made to enforce the peace. Here was the germ of the crusading idea. Unhappily the peace army got out of hand and another had to be raised for its suppression. The Church despaired of curbs upon war. More feasible would be a diversion of bellicose propensities. If the knights must fight, let them cease devouring one another and turn rather against the enemies of the Church, the enemies of the faith.

The great speech in which Urban II summoned France to the First Crusade was a peace speech. He started off with all those exhortations to leave off mutual destruction which had characterized the sermons of the peace crusade, but he concluded with a call to arms and the assembly cried *Deus Vult*. The crusade differed in several respects from the just and mournful war. It was fought, to begin with at least, under the authority of the Church rather than of the prince. Secondly, the common soldier had to volunteer. He took the cross and thus had more personal responsibility for judging the cause. In the third place, the spirit was far from mournful. All qualms were erased. This was a holy cause in which to kill was to benefit Christ; to die was to gain salvation. Finally clerical and monastic exemption broke down and three new orders, the Templars, the Hospitalers and the Teutonic Knights, combined militarism with monasticism. Differences of opinion among the theologians arose as to whether the object of the crusade was to convert the infidel or simply to punish and restrain him from molesting pilgrims, encroaching on the eastern empire and holding the Holy Sepulcher, which objects could be squared with the formula of the just war. The latter was the prevailing view, but however much the language of the just war was retained, the spirit was different.

A reaction set in. Many criticisms were leveled at the crusades, though few were strictly pacifist. Some objected to shipping the scum of Europe to the Holy Land; others upbraided the finan-

cial abuses. Some considered the enterprise ill-starred and preferred to pasture their cows or court Nicolette. A few, especially
among the Franciscans, contrasted the bloodthirstiness of the
crusades with the meekness of the gospel. In the wake of the
crusades some minor pacifist movements arose. The Albigenses
refused even to kill a chicken, and the Bohemian Brethren repudiated war.

The Protestant Reformation continued the process of dissolution by wrecking the unity of the medieval church. Protestantism itself further divided, and different groups supported the
three attitudes to war. The Lutherans and Anglicans adopted the
just war; the Calvinists the crusade; left-wing groups, such as
Mennonites and Quakers, were pacifist. The older positions were
modified naturally in certain respects.

Luther's position can be described as that of Augustine all
over again minus monasticism and with a strong aversion to crusades. Luther believed in war against the Turks, but not under the
auspices of the Church, and certainly not in the name of Christ.
The Turk should be restrained, not because he was an infidel or a
polygamist, but because he had encroached upon the territory of
European states. A Christian prince would be equally resisted were
he to do the same thing. The war against the Turks was thus a war
of defense to be waged under the authority of the prince.

The common soldier could fight without peril to his salvation, yet not lightheartedly, for war is, after all, a concession to the
depravity of man. If all the world were Christian there would be
no war. Christians have no need of the sword for their own protection since they are as sheep. But inasmuch as the majority of mankind act like tigers, the Christian, out of love for his neighbor,
must assist in providing that protection which the non-Christian is
not willing to forego. The conduct of the war must be free from
barbarism, and the Christian must always preserve love in his
heart. One recognizes the familiar Augustinian lines.

The main difference is that no class of men is set aside to
exemplify the ideal of peace. The clergy, to be sure, do not bear
muskets, yet they do assist in war, for their role is to curse. The
monastery for Luther was completely eliminated, and the nearest

functional substitute was the home. Here there is no mine or thine; here all the tender virtues find their scope. But the cleavage between private and public morality is thereby intensified, and the resultant type is that of a Bismarck, practicing the Sermon on the Mount at home and *Realpolitik* in the office.

The purveyor of the crusading idea in Protestantism was to be primarily Calvinism, though Lutheranism for a time veered in that direction because any revolution on behalf of religion against the constituted authorities tends to become a crusade. The just war theory of fighting under the authority of the prince is scarcely tenable when the revolt is actually directed against the prince. Three devices have been employed by way of harmonization. The first is to say that the revolt is not really against the prince, but only against his evil counselors. This was at first the contention of the English Puritans in their struggle with Charles I. The second is to say that the prince by tyranny has forfeited his position and may be resisted as a private citizen. This is the doctrine of tyrannicide. The third rests on a theory of constitutional government and distributed sovereignty. If the prince violates the constitution he may be resisted by some other organ of government which equally is ordained of God to bear the sword.

The political situation in Germany in Luther's day lent itself readily to this device because the country was in a transitional period. The Holy Roman Empire was enfeebled, though far from extinct, and the centralized national state had not yet arisen as in Spain, France and England. A goodly number of mutually independent princes and free cities acknowledged the tenuous overlordship of the Holy Roman Emperor. The question was whether he might be resisted if he undertook to exterminate Protestantism. Luther was very hesitant on the point until the jurists convinced him that the emperor was a constitutional monarch who might be resisted by the princes since they were even more indubitably ordained of God through hereditary right than he who ruled only by election. Thus arose a doctrine destined to have an enormous vogue that the higher magistrate might be resisted by the lower, identified in Germany with the princes, in France with the nobles, in England with parliament. The theory was convenient in Germany during the Smalcald war, but lost its relevance when the Peace of Augsburg in 1555 accorded toleration to Lutheranism in designated areas.

Calvinism then became the purveyor of the idea. Calvin himself, to be sure, had much the same reservations as had Luther at first. Calvin declared that he would rather see the Reform wiped out than that it should survive through revolution, but hardier spirits, like Beza and Knox, justified not only revolt, but even tyrannicide. The struggle became acute in France where the theory of the lower versus the higher magistrate was applied to the resistance of the Huguenot nobility to the crown. Wars of religion devastated the land for three decades, where religious fanaticism extinguished the gentler virtues. A similar spirit fired British Calvinists. Here Cromwell's men issued a "Soldier's Bible," in which "love of enemies" was subordinated to "Doe not I hate them O Lord that hate thee? ... I hate them with an unfained hatred, as they were mine utter enemies." American Calvinists transplanted the same mood to the wilderness where the red men were the Amalekites whom Jehovah had given to the sword.

The Calvinist crusade differs formally from that of the Middle Ages in that it was not fought under the auspices of the Church, though this made little difference since appeal was made to the will and glory of God. Monastic military orders were, of course, out of the question, but the discipline of the monasteries was maintained by the Ironsides. The volunteer element was the same; Cromwell desired only the godly in his army. Particularly the absence of all qualms of conscience in the holy war is the persistent characteristic of this type.

Pacifism is represented by such groups as the Mennonites and Quakers. The incompatibility of love and war is stressed by them all, but the Mennonites make more of legalism and separatism; the Quakers more of optimism and utilitarianism. The Mennonites recognize the state as ordained of God for the ungodly and to be administered by the ungodly. The Christian should pay taxes, but should not act as a magistrate, let alone as a soldier. The Quakers, however, have been of all pacifist groups the least aloof from political life. They sat in the Pennsylvania legislature until the French and Indian War and have frequently been represented in the

British House of Commons. Like the Calvinists they regard the state as divinely ordained for something more than the mere restraint of evil and have been willing to co-operate in the making and administration of all remedial legislation. They do not object to the use of force when subject to the restraints of orderly government, but deny the validity of the analogy between government and war, where the determination of justice rests with the contestants themselves. Quakers have commonly protested against capital punishment and are very critical of resort to the sword because it is a carnal weapon inconsistent with reliance upon the Spirit, not only as a source of divine guidance, but also as a means of restraining evil. They believe in the power of love to overcome at last all that is contrary to itself. Hence their pacifism can be described as a long-term utilitarianism. They are not so naïve as to suppose that if they turn the other cheek it will never be hit, but they do believe that ultimately love will triumph. Of all pacifist groups they are probably the most inclined to respect Christian warriors. Too many Quakers came out of Cromwell's army to be willing to disclaim the disinterestedness of their former zeal or to dispute the sincerity of friends still in the ranks.

One sees thus how close is pacifism to crusading. The objects are the same; the hopefulness of achieving something on earth is the same. Only the means differ. Perhaps that is why these two attitudes have been most characteristic of American Christianity. The obvious reason, of course, is the transplantation in force of Calvinists to New England and of pacifists to Pennsylvania, whereas the representatives of the just war were comparatively few. In addition the exhilaration of the frontier inspired the dream of Holy Commonwealths to be planted with or without the sword. A certain oscillation is observable in our history according as one method failed and recourse was had to the other.

The main lines of the traditional attitudes were still intact in the North during the Civil War. The crusading spirit was exemplified by those who fought the war to free the slaves. Among them were the Congregationalists, Presbyterians, Baptists, Methodists, Unitarians and Universalists. Pacifism was represented by the Quakers, Mennonites, Brethren, and the like, who wanted to free the slaves as much as the crusaders and abetted the underground railway, but shrank from the sword. The just war theory was maintained by those who fought to preserve the Union. The Catholics, Lutherans and the Episcopalians took the view that the constituted authority ordained by God had been assailed by a rebellion which must be put down, because we are "subject unto the higher powers."

During World War I all save resolute pacifists swung to the crusading position. Since that time the traditional lines have been breaking down; as suggested earlier, the Catholics have been moving toward the Quakers, the Quakers toward the monks, and the Calvinists toward the Lutherans.

Some Catholics have been moving toward the Quakers without abandoning the formula of the just war. The point is rather that modern war is incompatible with the traditions of the just war as laid down by such theologians as Thomas Aquinas. Perhaps this is only another way of saying that Catholicism is incompatible with modern life (which is not to condemn Catholicism). Franziskas Stratmann[1] remarks that "the old teaching of St. Augustine, and the Thomists, supported by Suarez and Bellarmin, may seem strangely out of place in the world of today, fit only for the cloister from which it came—so much the worse for the world!" One by one he examines the conditions of the just war to see whether they are realizable under modern conditions. Sole guilt? If one takes into account the long antecedents of war, where will this be found? Exemption of noncombatants? Poison gas is not discriminating. A reasonable chance of success in vindicating justice? When one considers the millions of the innocent who are engulfed in the punishment of the guilty, can the end be achieved? A similar position was taken in 1933 by John K. Ryan.[2]

The Rev. Cyprian Emmanuel in a pamphlet called *The Ethics of War*, written for the Catholic Association for International Peace (1932), concludes: "It is becoming ever more difficult to find all the conditions [of the just war] verified simultaneously in any given case. And in few, if any, modern wars have they been observed; nor has even an honest attempt to observe them

---

[1] Franziskas Stratmann, *The Church and War* (New York, 1928).
[2] *Modern War and Basic Ethics* (Washington, D. C.).

been made by the nations that initiated hostilities. It is particularly the growing brutality of modern warfare and the comparative ease with which unbiased arbitration can be had in practically all instances that render the justification of war so difficult at the present time."

Obviously all this does not mean that the Catholic Church as an institution nor that many Catholics as individuals are joining the Quakers, but there is certainly a growing appreciation of the grounds for declining to participate if not in all war, then at any rate in all modern war.

Coincidentally the Quakers have been moving toward the monks. That is to say, they are coming to think of themselves as a group with a vocation, with a special task which will not and cannot be undertaken by the community as a whole.[3] The Quaker would prefer that all should be as he. In that respect he differs from the monk, who has been known, like St. Augustine, to urge Boniface, the general, to remain and discharge his tasks in the world. The Quaker would like to see all men adopt his way, but he knows that they will not, and that being so he would prefer to have them fight than that they should connive with evil. So long as England and France had not repudiated the military method they would have been on higher moral ground preventing the Italian appropriation of Ethiopia, than emulating Pilate's washing of hands.[4]

But if the Quaker takes this attitude, he must withdraw from politics, certainly in wartime. If he believes that those who are willing to go to war ought to fight rather than connive with injustice, he has no business to hinder military appropriations by adverse votes or lobbying. Those who are committed to war must not be hampered from doing it effectively. The Quaker must withdraw to whatever moral equivalent he can discover for the monastery. He tries to find it in constructive work for the victims of war and of social inequality.

[3] Compare Trueblood in the *Atlantic Monthly*, December, 1940, and more particularly the article "Vocational Christian Pacifism," *Christianity and Crisis*, November 3, 1941.

[4] Bertram Pickard, "Peacemakers' Dilemma," *Pendle Hill Pamphlet*, No. 16.

While he cannot participate actively in what others are doing, yet he recognizes that they, too, are working toward ends which are also his. Much as the Catholic Church looks to the prince to suppress disorder and to the monk to exemplify the way of peace, the Quaker believes that the use of force even in war can be in some measure disciplined for moral ends and that after a tortuous course some sort of justice can be achieved. The Quakers were able to respect a Lincoln as he respected them. Functionally this is very close to the Catholic solution.

Finally the Calvinists have been moving toward the Lutheran position, which is another way of saying that crusading is gone. We are left only with pacifists and mournful warriors. Despite the fact that aggression is this time so much more brutal than before, we are all so chastened by our own previous failures that no one now is repeating the remark of R. H. Tawney in 1917: "Either a war is a crusade or it is a crime; there is no half-way house." The word which is most common today is not "holy" but "grim."[5] This is a war without music. Those who, like John Bennett,[6] call it just will not call it holy. "Much that is holy is at stake in this war." We ought "to do all that we can to defeat the Nazi power." But neither of these statements means that this is a holy war. The war cannot be called holy because so much unholiness is mixed with it. The war can be called just despite the mingled injustice, because justice is at a lower level than holiness. Whether in the end this war can "be regarded as just in the light of its results may depend in large part upon the refusal of Christians to call it a holy war now," since those who fight a holy war are so imbued with righteous hate that they cannot make a stable peace.

Many like Bennett, very many, indeed, in Britain and in the United States, formerly either crusaders or pacifists, have now become mournful warriors. All this may leave us unsettled and confused, but at least there is this ground for hope that the churches are facing the problem with openness of mind and heaviness of heart.

[5] "American Preaching in Wartime—I," Federal Council, *Information Service,* June 6, 1942.
[6] *The Christian Century,* October 8, 1941.

14. The Appeal to Reason and the American Constitution

The Constitution was a product of the Age of Reason.[1] The term has three major meanings. Reason is a faculty of man; reason is a quality of the universe; reason is a temper in the conduct of human affairs. The first sense is basic for the Constitution, the second for the Bill of Rights, and the third for both.

Reason as a faculty of man lies behind the essential theory of

First published in *The Constitution Reconsidered*, ed. Conyers Read (New York, 1938).

[1] Reason is an elusive term and no comprehensive history of the concept is available. The article "Vernunft" in Rudolf Eisler's *Wörterbuch der philosophischen Begriffe* (Berlin, 1930) does not go far beyond a catena of definitions from the outstanding philosophers. The article "Ragione" in the *Enciclopedia italiana* is useful. The work of Allan J. M. Macdonald, *Authority and Reason in the Early Middle Ages* (London, 1933), shows that reason did not fare so badly as the handmaid of revelation. On the use of the word ratio in the Middle Ages, see G.-Ed. Demers, "Les Divers sens du mot 'Ratio' au moyen âge; autour d'un texte de Maître Ferrier de Catalogue" (1275), *Études d'histoire littéraire et doctrinale du XIIIe siècle* (Publications de L'Institut d'études médiévales d'Ottawa, 1932), 1 Ser. I, 105-139. The various types of rationalism in the eighteenth century are analyzed by Arthur O. Lovejoy, "The Parallel of Deism and Classicism," *Modern Philology*, XXIX (1931-1932), 281-299. On the concept of reason in modern philosophical systems, see Jean de la Harpe, "L'Idée de la raison dans les sciences et la philosophie contemporaine," *Recueil de travaux ... Université de Neuchâtel*, XV (1930).

For the rôle of reason in law, see Otto Gierke, *Natural Law and the Theory of Society, 1500-1800, op. cit.* (Ch. 1, n. 62), pp. 39, 235; and Giorgio del Vecchio, *Il concetto della natura e il principio del Diritto*, 2d. ed. (Bologna, 1922). Paul Vinogradoff ("Reason and Conscience in Sixteenth-Century Jurisprudence," *Law Quarterly Review*, XXIV [1908], 273-384) points out that reason and conscience as normative principles in the application of law in England survived the collapse of the canon law. W. S. Holdsworth (*A History of English Law* [5th ed., 10 vols., London, 1931-1932], II, 602-603) indicates, however, that the discontinuance of the canon law meant the separation of reason from nature. (Compare Hale's discussion of reason in application to law, *ibid.*, V, 482, 500-506). Charles McIlwain (*The High Court of Parliament* [New Haven, 1910], in the chapter on "The Fundamental Law") has many citations in which the law of reason takes the place of the law of nature.

the Constitution, which is government by consent, the federal theory of the consent of the states, the compact theory of the consent of the individuals. Each separate member of the body politic should acquiesce in the association. Now why should the voluntary assent of individuals be regarded as requisite? On the assumption that there is in man an inviolable something, call it reason, conscience, or faith. The early sixteenth century preferred to talk of faith. This is something spiritual which can neither be created nor cut by the sword of the magistrate. The age of the religious wars spoke more of conscience. Here is the seat of man's integrity, and if it be sapped his character will disintegrate. The eighteenth century appealed to reason. This, too, is inviolable by the civil sword, for "only light and evidence can work a change in men's opinions."[2]

The shift in terminology from the religious to the secular concept was aided by the spawning of sects with their rival claims to truth. For that reason Grotius, though a man of personal piety, sought a basis for government independent of religion. He found it in natural law, long associated with divine law, but pre-Christian in its origins.[3] The Stoics believed in the law of nature, the expression of the universal reason pervading the world and man. Grotius declared that this would be valid even if there were no God.[4] And

[2] "Four Letters on Toleration," *The Works of John Locke* (London, 1888), III, 6.

[3] The literature on natural law is very extensive. The best bibliography is in Charles Grove Haines, *The Revival of Natural Law Concepts* (Cambridge, Mass., 1930). The fusion of Stoic natural law with divine law in Hellenistic Judaism and in early Christianity is traced by Ernst Troeltsch, *The Social Teachings of the Christian Churches*, tr. Olive Wyon, 2 vols. (London, 1931). The development of the idea in Europe is covered by Otto Gierke, *Johannes Althusius und die Entwicklung der naturrechtlichen Staatstheorien*, "Untersuchungen zur deutschen Staats- und Rechtsgeschichte," VII (Breslau, 1880), and in his *Natural Law and the Theory of Society*, cited above. The American development is given by Benjamin Fletcher Wright, Jr., *American Interpretations of Natural Law* (Cambridge, Mass., 1931), who points out that until 1776 Americans identified natural law with the British constitution. Compare Charles F. Mullet, "Fundamental Law and the American Revolution, 1770-1776," *Studies in History, Economics and Public Law* (Columbia University (New York, 1933), No. 385.

[4] Hugo Grotius, *De Iure Belli ac Paris* (Paris, 1625), Prolegomena, sig. e. "Et haec quidem quae jam diximus, locum aliquem haberent etiamsi daremus, quod sine summo scelere dari nequit, non esse Deum." Otto Gierke (*Johannes*

Burlamaqui, who enjoyed a vogue in the colonies, asserted that natural law is evident to the mere light of reason and requires no revelation, because constant and independent of the caprice of the divine will.[5] Here, I suspect, we have the explanation of the polite shelving at the federal convention of Franklin's plea for prayer. The framers were not averse to religion, but they resented the attack on the adequacy of the human understanding to operate unassisted in the area of natural law.[6]

The shift to reason in the eighteenth century was aided likewise by the decline of the doctrine of human depravity. The fall of Adam was believed by the followers of St. Augustine to have vitiated not only the moral but also the intellectual capacities of man. The Renaissance began to challenge this conception. One of the humanists declared that morally indeed Adam fell down, but intellectually he fell up, for he ate of the tree of knowledge and his eyes were opened.[7] The eighteenth century came to have great confidence in man's ability to understand and plan his world. Yet this confidence alone would scarcely explain the inviolability of individual reason had not the secularized concept trailed with it the aura of sanctity with which faith had been invested. This belief in something sacred in each person accounts for the voluntary character of all associations. Marriage is a social compact, not a family arrangement.[8] The church is a covenant of believers, not a

---

Althusius, p. 74) points out that Gabriel Biel said practically the same thing. This is significant because Biel belonged to the "Moderni," the late scholastics who sundered faith and reason. Locke owed much to Occam, the founder of the school.

[5] Jean Jacques Burlamaqui, *The Principles of Natural and Politic Law* (London, 1763; first English translation, London, 1748-1752) , p. 185: "If these laws were not a necessary consequence of the nature and constitution of man a very clear revelation would be necessary, but it is agreed that the law of nature is and ought to be known by the mere light of reason."

[6] Max Farrand, *The Records of the Federal Convention,* 3 vols. (New Haven, 1911) , I, 451-452. Luther A. Weigle, "The Pageant of America," *American Idealism* (New Haven, 1928) , X, 124-125, shows that godlessness was not the cause of the omission. The Continental Congress observed daily prayer.

[7] Sebastian Castellio, "De Arte Dubitandi," *Per la Storia degli eretici italiani del secolo XVI in Europa;* testi raccolti da D. Cantimori e E. Feist, Reale Accademia d'Italia, "Studi e Documenti," VII (Rome, 1937) , 367.

[8] John Locke, *Two Treatises on Civil Government,* II, Ch. VII, §78.

community of those baptized in infancy,[9] and the state is likewise a voluntary society composed of those who yield certain alienable rights in order to safeguard the inalienable. Here is the root of government based on individual consent.

Nevertheless the framers entertained no extravagant notions of human reason and here, too, they were representative of their period, for it is the paradox of the century that the Age of Reason debased reason. At the outset exuberant and sobering currents were in conflict. Optimism attached itself to the method of Newton,[10] and men were naïve enough to suppose that even the truths of Christianity were demonstrable.[11] But many factors operated to demean the domain of reason. When man ate of the tree of knowledge and his eyes were opened, what did he behold? The appalling vastness of the universe of Copernicus and Galileo, before which the affrighted human atom recoiled[12] to take refuge in a homier and more manageable world.[13] The mood was reinforced by the revulsion against abstract theological speculation popularized by Erasmus,[14] and more markedly by the attempt of the Scottish school to salvage something from the onslaught of Hume by having recourse to common sense, to which reason was assimilated or subordinated. The Scotch signer of the Constitution, James Wilson,

[9] John Locke, "Four Letters on Toleration," *Works*, III, 7.

[10] The optimistic strain is described by Ernst Cassirer, *Die Philosophie der Aufklärung* (Tübingen, 1932), in the chapter "Natur und Naturerkenntnis," but he shows how the line runs from Newton to Hume. The optimism is emphasized likewise by Carl L. Becker, *The Declaration of Independence* (New York, 1922).

[11] The progressive disintegration of the attempt to demonstrate Christianity is illustrated in the documents collected by John M. Creed and John S. B. Smith, *Religious Thought in the Eighteenth Century Illustrated from Writers of the Period* (Cambridge, Eng., 1934).

[12] Blaise Pascal, *Pensées*, Ch. I. "Je vois ces effroyables espaces de l'univers qui m'enferment . . . comme un atome, et comme une ombre qui ne dure qu'un instant sans retour."

[13] Arthur O. Lovejoy (*The Great Chain of Being* [Cambridge, Mass., 1936], p. 122) discusses man's sense of his "inexpressible unimportance" before the "incalculable vastness" of the new astronomy. In the article "'Pride' in Eighteenth-Century Thought," *Modern Language Notes*, XXXVI (1921), 31-37, he takes up the picture of man as the "Yahoo" and the "featherless human biped."

[14] The influence of Erasmus on the eighteenth century is shown by Werner Kaegi, "Erasmus im 18. Jahrhundert," *op. cit.* (Ch. I, p. 57).

was contemptuous of philosophy. The theories of Locke, Berkeley, and Hume reminded him of My Lord Peter's brown loaf, which was one day mutton, the next beef, and the third plum pudding. Reason, he thought, should never be allowed to conflict with common sense. And what is common sense? It is that degree of reason which makes a man capable of managing his own affairs.[15] Wilson was not the only framer who entertained a moderate view of man's capacities.[16] Hence the constant search of the convention for checks and balances, not only upon the departments of government, but also upon the irrational tendencies of man. The almost religious concept of reason as an inviolable quality of man supported the theory of government by consent. The waning of the Age of Reason dictated restraint upon the contracting parties.

The second meaning of reason as a quality of the universe is basic for the Bill of Rights. For why should the reason, conscience, or faith of the individual man be respected as inviolable? To say that they cannot be created or cut by the sword of the magistrate does not settle the question. Why should society care whether they be either created or cut? The answer is that the reason in man corresponds to and is a part of the reason of the universe. To violate this principle in man is to transgress the universal law of life. This was again the old Stoic doctrine and had been potent enough to inspire intransigeance toward tyranny. One recalls the stalwart resistance of Paetus Thrasea to the despotism of Nero. Nevertheless, Stoicism did not develop a list of the rights of individual men. The explanation, I surmise, lies in the pantheistic diffusion of reason. Two steps were taken in the early sixteenth century toward a sharper demarcation. First the jurists set off man from the world by excluding the animals from the sphere of

[15] *The Works of James Wilson*, ed. James DeWitt Andrews, I (1896), 232-236.
[16] Franklin regarded the deadlock as a "melancholy proof of the imperfection of the human understanding" (Farrand, *op. cit.* [above, n. 6], I, 451). Distrust of reason as a temper in human affairs is most marked in Hamilton, who was in the tradition of Hume (*ibid.*, I, 381). G. Morris said, "We must remember that the people never act from reason alone" (*ibid.*, I, 514), though he did think that a reasonable plan would commend itself to reasonable minds (*ibid.*, I, 529). Madison was alive to the corrupting influence of power (*ibid.*, I, 584).

natural law.[17] The second and more decisive step was taken by a man of religion, when Martin Luther proclaimed the naked isolation of the individual soul before the face of that God who sitteth upon the circle of the earth to pass judgment upon the ways of men. Here is a principle of transcendence sufficient to set the individual man against society and to sustain him in his defiance. The Calvinist doctrine of election still further intensified the immediacy of each man's relation to the Supreme.[18] The classic American expression is found in the Biglow Papers:

> Ef you take a sword an' dror it,
> An' go stick a feller thru,
> Guv'ment aint to answer for it,
> God'll send the bill to you.

The finality of such sheer individualism is basic for the inalienable rights of man. Oddly enough by the time such rights had reached their maturest formulation, the religious overtone was waning, if not forgotten.[19]

[17] Otto Gierke, *Natural Law and the Theory of Society*, p. 233, n. 22.

[18] Ernst Troeltsch, *Kultur der Gegenwart*, Teil 1, Abt, IV, 1, II Hälfte, pp. 577, 585; Hans Maier, *Die geistesgeschichtlichen Grundlagen der Konstitutionellen Theorie* (Tübingen, 1914) , p. 22.

[19] Georg Jellinek precipitated a lively controversy as to the origin of the rights of man in his *Die Erklärung der Menschen und Bürgerrechte* (1st ed., 1895, tr. Max Farrand, *The Declaration of the Rights of Man and of Citizens* [New York, 1901]) . The discussion down to 1919 was summarized by his son in the preface to the third edition. Jellinek contended that the French declaration of 1789 was not derived from Rousseau, but from the American declarations, that the natural law tradition was inadequate to explain the source, that the real impetus came from the struggle for religious liberty, which he traced through the colonies to the Agreement of the People of 1647. Émile Doumergue ("Les Origines historiques de la déclaration des droits de l'homme et du citoyen," *Revue du droit public et de la science politique en France et à l'étranger*, XXI [1904], 673-733) drew the line forward from Calvin to the French declaration. David G. Ritchie (*Natural Rights* [London, 1903]) quite independently supported Jellinek as to the religious influence. J. Walter Jones ("Acquired and Guaranteed Rights," *Cambridge Legal Essays* [Cambridge, Eng., 1926], pp. 223-242) drew the line backward through the American colonies to the Agreement of the People of 1647.

Jellinek was criticized by Adalbert Wahl ("Zur Geschichte der Menschenrechte," *Hist. Zeitschrift*, CIII [1909], 79-85) on the ground that religious liberty was not conceived as a universal human right in the American colonies. Rationalism and individualism effected the change and these stem from Locke. But

But the day was largely won. The framers of the Constitution did not quarrel with the content of the Bill of Rights. Some objected merely that the rights of individuals were the proper province of the states and not of the national government. Others brought forward the deeper criticism that fundamental rights cannot be secured by codification. Eternal law must be unwritten.

---

this still leaves the problem of the origins of Locke. Gustav Hägermann ("Die Erklärungen der Menschen und Bürgerrechte in den ersten amerikanischen Staatsverfassungen," *Hist. Studien*, LXXVIII [1910]) found the impetus for the American declarations in the economic situation and the source in the philosophy of the Enlightenment. Justus Hashagen ("Zur Entstehungsgeschichte der Nordamerikanischen Erklärungen der Menschenrechte," *Zeitschrift für die gesamte Staatswissenschaft*, LXXVIII [1924], 461-495) pointed to the incomplete attainment of religious liberty in the colonies. Men like George Mason and John Adams were more liberal as to civil than as to religious rights. The source of the rights of man is not American but European, and not religious but secular, in spite of Puritan elements in Locke. The root lies in natural law. Yet Hashagen recognized that the rights of man and natural law do not necessarily coincide. Gustav Adolf Salander ("Vom Werden der Menschenrechte; ein Beitrag zur modernen Verfassungsgeschichte unter Zugrundelegung der virginischen Erklärung der Rechte vom 12. Juni 1776," *Leipziger rechtswissenschaftliche Studien*, Leipziger Juristenfakultät, XIX [1926]) pointed out that Virginia, which made the first declaration of rights was dilatory as to religious liberty and the religious clause in the declaration of 1776 would have been more conservative had not Madison revised Mason. Otto Vossler ("Zur Erklärung der Menschenrechte," *Hist. Zeitschrift*, CXLII [1930], 516-545) found the source of the rights of man in English law, which was never sundered from the tradition of natural law. Roger Williams hindered, if anything, by severing the sacred and the secular so that the achievement of freedom in religion meant nothing for civil liberties.

The following discussions of Jellinek are interesting though not relevant to our immediate concern. James Sullivan ("The Antecedents of the Declaration of Independence," *Annual Report of the American Historical Association*, 1902, I, 67-81) went back to the Greeks, but he was discussing rather the origin of natural law than of the specific rights of men as individuals. Fritz Klövekorn ("Die Entstehung der Erklärung der Menschen- und Bürgerrechte," *Hist. Studien*, XC [1911]) supported Jellinek on the derivation of the French from the American. Robert Redslob (*Die Staatstheorien der französischen Nationalversammlung von 1789: ihre Grundlagen in der Staatslehre der Aufklärungszeit und in den englischen und amerikanischen Verfassungsgedanken* [Leipzig, 1912]) maintained that the French declaration owed something to Rousseau because there was more of the sense of community than in the American declarations.

One observes that much of the criticism of Jellinek applies to the immediate American situation in 1776, when the lines of the previous three centuries were already interwoven and the original motives obscured. The

A code, in the nature of the case, is positive law, the product of time and circumstance. James Wilson did not regard the American Constitution as fundamental law; rather, it was municipal, or in medieval terminology, *ius civile.*[20] Roger Sherman referred to the "sublimity of nonsense and alarm" on the subject of a bill of rights which are "much too important to depend on mere paper protection."[21] For him the only guarantee was popular control over Congress. And John Dickinson said, "Trial by jury and the dependance of taxation upon representation, those cardinal stones of liberty, were not obtained by a bill of rights, or any other records, and have not and cannot be preserved by them. They and all other rights must be preserved by soundness of sense and honesty of heart. Compared with these what are a bill of rights, or any characters drawn upon paper or parchment, those frail remembrances?[22] Here we are brought back to the first meaning of reason as a faculty of man. The eternal and universal reason of the world gives

---

critics themselves recognize the need of going back to Locke, but they do not undertake to analyze the struggles of the seventeenth century which he epitomized. Jellinek called attention to the fact that the first "native right" of the Agreement of the People in 1647 was "that matters of religion and the ways of God's worship are not at all entrusted by us to any human power, because therein we cannot remit or exceed a tittle of what our consciences dictate to be the mind of God without wilful sin." The point made by many that Calvinism was concerned not for universal religious freedom as a right of man, but for the recognition of Calvinism as the truth of God, does not invalidate the point that as a matter of fact Calvinism contributed mightily toward the recognition of an inalienable something in man, the more so because Calvinism did not sever religious and political life.

The best commentary on the whole controversy to my mind is that of Carl Schmitt (*Verfassungslehre* [München und Leipzig, 1928], pp. 158-159) : "Dass die Religionsfreiheit das erste aller Grundrechte darstellt, ist also ohne Rücksicht auf die geschichtlichen Details der Entwicklung in einem systematischen Sinne unbedingt richtig. Denn damit ist das fundamentale Verteilungsprinzip aufgestellt: der Einzelne als solcher ist Träger eines absoluten Wertes und bleibt mit diesem Wert in seiner privaten Sphäre; seine private Freiheit ist infolgedessen etwas prinzipiell Unbegrenztes; der Staat ist nur ein Mittel und daher relativ, abgeleitet und in jeder seiner Befugnisse begrenzt und von Privaten kontrollierbar."

[20] *Works*, I, 94.

[21] Paul Leicester Ford, *Essays on the Constitution of the United States* (Brooklyn, 1892) , pp. 218-221.

[22] Paul Leicester Ford, *Pamphlets on the Constitution of the United States* (Brooklyn, 1888) , p. 186.

validity and inviolability to the reason in man, but the reason in man is the only guarantee that the reason in the world will be understood and obeyed in human affairs.

Once more, however, we are recalled to the sober picture of man's reason, so easily a prey to error and to passion. In almost the same breath with the above proclamation of "soundness of sense" Dickinson declared that by the "superior will of the people" he meant a "reasonable not a distracted will." But how preserve a reasonable will? The answer of the age was education. Here is the great faith of the century of reason in the enlightenment of the people. Jefferson was its prophet. "It is an axiom of my mind," said he, "that our liberty can never be safe but in the hands of the people themselves, and that, too, of people with a certain degree of instruction."[23]

We have already touched upon the third meaning of reason as a temper in the conduct of human affairs, the round-table mood of matching mind with mind in the common quest for truth. It is the Socratic application of intelligence to life, Stoic equanimity and Christian forbearance. All these strains combined in Erasmus and again in Benjamin Franklin,[24] who was influenced alike by the Quakers and by the Enlightenment. Jefferson, too, spoke in similar vein. The Constitutional Convention elicited his admiration because "We are yet able to send our wise and good men together to talk over our form of government . . . with the same *sangfroid* as they would a subject of agriculture. The example we have given the world is single, that of changing our form of government under the authority of reason only, without bloodshed."[25] Had he lived later he would have realized that the discussion of agriculture can engender warmth, and had he been on the spot he would have known that the *sang* was not so *froid*. But Franklin, on the floor of the convention when the deadlock came, commended the previous coolness and reminded his colleagues that they had been sent

---

[23] *Writings of Thomas Jefferson*, XIX (Lib. ed., Washington, 1904) , 24. Compare Roy J. Honeywell, *The Educational Work of Thomas Jefferson* (Cambridge, Mass., 1931) .

[24] Gertrud Philippi, "Imperialistische und pazifizistische Strömungen in der Politik der Vereinigten Staaten von Amerika 1776-1815," *Heidelberger Abhandlungen z. mittleren u. neueren Geschichte,* XLV (1914) .

[25] *Writings of Thomas Jefferson,* VII (Lib. ed., Washington, 1904) , 73.

to consult, not to contend. In international relations Franklin rejoiced in the peace with England and hoped that mankind "as
they call themselves reasonable creatures will have reason enough
to settle their differences without cutting throats." Jefferson wondered whether the nations would not someday devise a "more
rational umpire of differences than force," and Samuel Adams
drafted a plan to invite Europe to compose national disputes
"without the necessity of war ... to the destruction of human
happiness and the disgrace of human reason. . . ."[26]

This appeal is not popular today. One attack has come from
those philosophies which rely on experience alone and eschew
metaphysics. Unable, therefore, to arrive at universal principles of
truth and right they regard every controversy as a clash of con-
jectures each of which has as much claim to be correct as the other,
and the only arbitrament is a test of strength. If Locke is the parent
of the bills of rights by his transmission of the mood of religious
intransigeance, on the other hand by his empiricism he fathered
the skepticism of Hume and the utilitarianism of Bentham. The
only premise which gives point to the round-table method is the
assumption of an ultimate and universal truth in some measure
accessible to the mind of man.[27]

Even more fatal in our own day, because invested with a
religious fervor, is the revolt of the Romantic movement against
the individualism of the Enlightenment, with its universal reason
diffused in every individual man. This atomism was swept out by
the cult of the community, the *Volkgeist,* which, when identified
with the state and personified in the ruler, banishes reason and
tramples on the rights of man.[28]

[26] These and other passages are collected by Edwin D. Mead, *Washington,
Jefferson and Franklin on War.* World Peace Foundation, Pamphlet Series III
(May, 1913) , 5.

[27] Morris Cohen protests against many varieties of contemporary irration-
alism in *Reason and Nature* (New York, 1932) , and Harold Laski points out
that Duguit escaped the consequences of his denial of metaphysics only by
inconsistency. "M. Duguit's Conception of the State," in *Modern Theories of
Law* (London, 1933) .

[28] Ernst Troeltsch ("The Ideas of Natural Law and Humanity in World
Politics," *op. cit.,* ch. 1, n. 62) in 1922 found the greatest difference between
Germany and the Anglo-Saxon peoples in the survival of natural-law concepts
among us and the disruption of that tradition by the Romantic movement and

But if I break a lance for Minerva in her contemporary conflict with Mars and Dionysus, I would not be naïve. Reason, too, has her pitfalls. There was a touch of belligerency in the crusade against superstition which caused triumphant reason to extinguish fanaticism on the guillotine.[29] Seldom has a tone of aristocracy been lacking in the cult of reason. Locke based the power of the father over the child on the fact that the child was devoid of reason.[30] How easy to transfer that to the "little brown brother"! And reason is not above blindness and hypocrisy. The natural-law school taught that since war is a work of unreason, any nation which starts a war is necessarily bereft of reason.[31] They failed to foresee that, since no nation ever starts a war, in every conflict each side would regard the other as a senseless brute to be treated like a wolf or a mad dog.[32] Well did Benjamin Franklin heed the stricture of a Quaker on his pride and add to his list of virtues to be emulated the quality of humility.

---

the *Volkgeist* in Germany. A similar observation couched in quite different terms is made by Randolph Greenfield Adams, *The Political Ideas of the American Revolution* (Durham, N.C., 1922), p. 147.

[29] J. Peter and C. Poulet, "L'Église constitutionelle du Nord pendant la terreur," *Revue d'histoire ecclésiastique*, XV, 1 (1929), pp. 677-707.

[30] *Two Treatises on Civil Government*, II, §63.

[31] Emerich de Vattel, *Le Droit des gens ou principes de la loi universelle*, "The Classics of International Law," 3 vols. (Washington, D.C., 1916), Liv. III, §34, Vol. II, pp. 26-27.

[32] Much is made of these pitfalls in the rationalism of Jefferson by Otto Vossler, "Die amerikanischen Revolutionsideale im ihrem Verhältnis zu den europäischen," *Hist. Zeitschrift Beiheft*, XVII (1929), 132 ff.

IV. Christianity in New England

15. The Puritan Theocracy and the Cambridge Platform

Our land might better be called New Canaan than New England, because our fathers braved the deep, not so much to transplant old England as to erect in this wilderness the commonwealth of the new Israel of God. The Cambridge Platform was a modest outline of their plan. It came late in the venture because at the outset they needed no blue-print, since English divines of their persuasion had already delineated the essential contours. Not until the enterprise was threatened with interference from across the seas did they state the main features in order to forestall intervention. Under such circumstances they did not set forth in solemn cadences the vast design of God to be realized by his chosen people. They did not even confess their faith but were content to subscribe to the Westminster Confession. They did not disclose their dissensions lest they invite interference. Nor did they betray and probably did not perceive the imminent disintegration of their theocracy. In terse terms they outlined their structure of church and state. That and no more!

The particulars of their system will not engage the present essay because they have often been discussed and are perhaps less urgent at the moment inasmuch as some have been discarded and some have grown axiomatic. We do not need to reiterate the dethroning of the clerical caste, because if today the minister enjoys any deference, it is more by reason of his message and quality than because of his office. We cannot wax excited as to whether discipline should be administered by congregations or by elders because we seldom administer discipline at all. We cannot endorse the view that the magistrate has jurisdiction over cases of idolatry, blasphe-

First published in *The Cambridge Platform of 1648*, ed. Henry Wilder Foote (Boston, 1949).

my, heresy and schism because with us toleration has triumphed. We do accept the independence of the congregations but we do not now stress their liberty so much as the duty to act in unison against the prevalent secularism. We heartily subscribe to the demarcation of the spheres of church and state in a spirit of cooperation. This has come to be an American axiom. It is today challenged and needs to be re-examined. But I have chosen rather to deal with the problem which was central for our fathers as to whether a Christian commonwealth, with "the Lord God our Governour,"[1] is so much as possible.

That was their belief and they aspired to plant a theocracy. The very attempt, the word in fact, is big with hope. The word means the government of God. It assumes that the Kingdom need not wait until the new Jerusalem descends from heaven but that in this present time a new Canaan can be reared in the wilderness. It is not a Utopia based on unbounded faith in human goodness and capacity, because the instruments of God may be weak and unworthy. It is an act of faith that the Creator of the ends of the earth will not abandon His people. As He formerly manifested Himself in Christ Jesus our Lord, so now His Spirit will operate through a society chosen to execute His plan for the ages. Theocracy is therefore a creed of hope.

The mood was immensely heightened by the circumstances of the New World. Our founding fathers had sought to rear their New Canaan in old England, but finding the people to be a perverse generation rejoiced that in the New World "God hath set before us an open doore of libertie."[2] Their endeavor to take advantage of it was unique in the history of the world, and even in the history of America. They did not in a despairing mood seek to withdraw from the contamination of the world into the cloister or into a segregated community in some unnoticed spot, but under the eyes of all England set out to reap the unprecedented opportu-

---

[1] [John Davenport], *A Discourse about Civil Government in the new Plantation whose Design is Religion* (London, 1673), p. 14. The title page attributes the tract to John Cotton.

[2] [Richard Mather], *Church-Government and Church-Covenant Discussed, in an Answer of the Elders ... Together with an Apologie ... in the yeare 1639 ...* (1643, n. p.), p. 51.

nity afforded by the discovery of a new continent. Their hope rested not on its natural resources; for they well realized that they were not going to a land flowing with milk and honey nor one where "fountaines should streame forth Wine, or Beare," which were more to their taste. No room over there for "a dainty tooth, a beggars purse, and an idle hand!" Their concern was for "his glory as a principall, and all other outward good things but as accessaries."[3] The venture would not be easy but the opportunity was unparalleled to erect on these shores a society in which God should be King among His chosen people.

But who were His chosen people? The answer to that question caused more difficulty than the subduing of the wilderness. All theocracies rest on the assumption that there is a chosen people but differ as to the marks. There are three types—the first is the Jewish, where the chosen people is the nation. However much Israel's relation to God rested ideally on the Covenant, in practice the Jew was a Jew by reason of birth—"We have Abraham to our father"—and by reason of circumcision, a rite administered in infancy, and in part, too, by reason of dwelling in the land. The Puritans, for all their predilection for ancient Israel, would have none of this. They were not chosen because they were Englishmen. They were not chosen because they dwelt in the Bay. There is now no land, said they,

> . . . like unto the possession which the Jews had in Canaan appropriated unto a holy people, the Seed of ABRAHAM: in which they had their days prolonged. But now there is no land of that sanctimony; but now we are all strangers and sojourners. Our dwelling is but a wandering; and our abiding but as a fleeting, and our home is nowhere but in that house not made with hands, whose maker and builder is GOD.[4]

The second great type of theocracy is the Roman Catholic, based on the sacraments as exclusive channels of grace to be administered solely by a class itself constituted through the sacrament of ordination. The priest, in consequence, assumes a unique place

[3] E. Winslow, *Good Newes from New England* (London, 1624) , p. 66.
[4] R. Cushman, *The Lawfulness of Plantations,* preamble, third page. Reprinted in Edward Arber, *The Story of the Pilgrim Fathers* (London, 1897) , p. 497. The passage has been condensed.

in society. Because the life to come far overshadows the present and because the priest alone can insure eternal blessedness, he wields a power exceeding that of kings, who should yield to his command in things spiritual and to his direction in things temporal. The clergy, then, are the chosen people, and through them God's will is realized on earth. The framers of the Cambridge Platform set themselves stoutly against such a view as an abomination of Antichrist. The minister for them enjoyed his office not by virtue of ordination but because of the call of a congregation. He was not a minister at large but only to his own congregation and only for so long as he remained in its service.

The third type of theocracy is characteristic of Protestantism and rests on inner experience. It is the most powerful but the most intangible of all and for that reason tantalizing, tormenting and unstable. There are variations in emphasis and all had appeared prior to the erection of the Puritan commonwealth, whose uniqueness lay only in its peculiar combination of previous elements. The theocracy of inner experience was first espoused by a man whom no group is willing to acknowledge as a progenitor—that firebrand of the Peasants War, Thomas Muentzer. He it was who declared, to the horror of Luther, that the wheat could even now be separated from the tares because the hour of the harvest had already come. The saints could be recognized and formed into a church. The test was the new birth through the incoming of the Spirit. The Bible was not necessary, though it might serve as a confirmation. The saints, once assembled into a church, should set up God's Kingdom, if need be even through the extermination of the ungodly. Here was a manifesto of theocracy and revolution.

This program in its entirety commended itself to none, but certain ingredients were appropriated by many. The Anabaptists also believed that the saints could be recognized on the basis of inner experience in the new birth. The genuineness of the experience must be evidenced by holiness of life. Aberrations should be controlled by the norm of Scripture. The saints could never hope to convert the world and should not aspire to rule the world but should withdraw, if they could, into small segregated communities, in order there to cultivate the way of the Lord.

The reformed churches also took over some of these ideas.

Zwingli believed that the predestined could be approximately identified and the test was faith in God and in the written word of Scripture. Since such faith was preeminently manifest in Zürich, he tended to identify the chosen people with the inhabitants of the Swiss city. Little wonder that he compared baptism to circumcision as the outward sign of membership through birth in a divine society! The danger was imminent that the theocracy of Zürich would degenerate into the Jewish type, but from this it was saved by the introduction of a selective principle. Catholics were excluded from office and a nucleus of the saints controlled alike church and state.

Calvin made the tests more comprehensive and less interior. For him there were three: faith, holiness and participation in the sacraments. He did not pretend that the tares could ever be completely excluded but held nevertheless that his three tests would reveal those who were presumably the chosen. Like Zwingli, he associated the elect with a particular community but on a much more selective basis. Non-conformists were banished and refugee saints were admitted in such numbers that Geneva became as highly selective as a Catholic monastery or an Anabaptist colony. The saints alone administered church and state, but the spheres were nevertheless precisely demarked. The most distinctive characteristic of Calvinism emerged only outside of Geneva where it was not in power but constituted a militant minority seeking to impose its way by the driving force of intense conviction. The optimism of the Calvinistic theocracy was akin to that of the Catholic because it aspired to realize the divine plan not in the restricted area of Canaan, Zürich, or Geneva but for the continent of Europe, the New World, and in fact the whole earth.

The basic pattern of the New England theocracy was Calvinism. These Puritans did not agree with Muentzer in his contempt for the Bible and in his espousal of violence. They did not agree with the Anabaptists that the ideal could be realized only in segregated groups. They did not, like Zwingli, identify, the theocracy with a particular community, but rather, like Calvin, took the world as their sphere. They were agreed with him, likewise, on the relations of church and state, but there was one respect in which they diverged from the Calvinist pattern and took their stand with the Anabaptists, namely in that they discovered the final mark of the saint in an inner experience. To be sure, like Calvin, they required faith and holiness and fellowship with the church but above all else they demanded an inward regeneration. Candidates for church membership must give evidence that "they have been wounded in their hearts for their originall sinne, and actuall transgressions, and can pitch upon some promise of free grace in the Scripture, for the ground of their faith, and that they finde their hearts drawne to beleeve in Christ Jesus, for their justification and salvation."[5] What a ring of personal experience there is in the "solemne and publick promise before the Lord, whereby a company of Christians, called by the power and mercy of God and fellowship with Christ, and by his providence to live together, and by his grace to cleave together in the unitie of faith, and brotherly love, and desirous to partake together in all the holy Ordinances of God, doe in confidence of his gracious acceptance in Christ, binde themselves to the Lord, and to one another, to walke together by the assistance of his Spirit, in all such wayes of holy worship in him and of edification one towards another, as the Gospel of Christ requireth of every Christian Church and the members thereof."[6]

How could a society founded on such requirements hope to endure? Bear in mind that the above declaration was really more than a church covenant. It was essentially a compact alike of church and civil state because the franchise was extended only to church members in the Bay and at New Haven and, if Hartford was more liberal, it mattered little because the community had few if any who were strangers to the covenant. The question then was not simply how could a church endure on such a basis but how could a community so grounded preserve its integrity and continuity.

There are two ways in which systems of this sort have endured. One is through converts only. The Jewish theocratic principle of continuity through birth is completely rejected. Catholic

---

[5] Thomas Lechford, *Plain Dealing* (London, 1642). Reprinted Boston, 1867, ed. J. H. Trumbull, p. 19. *See* Edmund S. Morgan, *Visible Saints* (New York, 1963).

[6] *An Apologie,* p. 3. *See* note. 2.

monasticism and Protestant sectarianism, as in the case of the Shakers, embraced celibacy and depended wholly on a convinced membership replenished through new recruits. The Shakers are extinct, but the Catholic monks emphatically are not and it is very instructive to observe that young Catholic chaplains, after the ordeal of war, are joining in the United States the rigorous order of the silent Trappists. A religious body can survive on the basis of converts only. But the Puritans emphatically did not take this way. They were fruitful and multiplied and replenished the earth.

The second way in which a religious community has succeeded in perpetuating itself is by segregation. The descendants of the Anabaptists, the Hutterian Brethren and the conservative Mennonites have maintained their pattern by protecting their children from automobiles, telephones, movies and funny-papers and they have succeeded in preserving their way of life throughout four centuries.

The Puritans were not willing to go this way. The reason was partly one of circumstance, for the Anabaptists had originated under the death penalty when fraternization with the world was impossible, whereas the Puritans arose in the midst of the democratic ferment which gave them an opportunity to survive without withdrawal and even to make an imprint upon public life. The migration to New England was of course in a way a withdrawal from old England, but in no sense intended as an abandonment of "deare *England*, left indeed by us in our persons, but never yet forsaken in our affections."[7] Neither did the colonists desire to separate from the Church of England. The preface to the Cambridge Platform declared that "wee, who are by nature Englishmen, doe desire to hold forth the same doctrine of religion (especially in fundamentals) which wee see and know to be held by the Church of England according to the truth of the Gospel."[8] Their hope was to stir up old England by their "hazardous and voluntary banishment into this remote wilderness."[9] The emigrants sought

[7] William Hooke, *New Englands Teares for old Englands Feares,* 1640 (London, 1641) , p. 23.

[8] The Preface, reprinted in Williston Walker, *Creeds and Platforms of Congregationalism* (New York, 1893) , p. 194.

[9] John Cotton, *The Way of Congregational Churches Cleared* (London, 1648) , p. 102.

not even to segregate themselves from the Indians; for the purpose in coming had been "chiefly to display the efficacy and power of the Gospel, both in zealous preaching, Professing and wise walking under it before the faces of these poor blind infidels."[10] Neither did they separate themselves from the "unregenerated, that are Aliens to the Common-wealth of Israel, strangers to the Covenant of promise."[11]

Here was the initial weakness of the entire venture, for the communities had never been properly homogeneous and contained at the outset saints and strangers, "profane men, who being but seeming Christians, have made Christ and Christianity stinke in the nostrils of the poore Infidels."[12] Ought not such to have been cast out of Israel? Not so, was the answer, for the power of Congregationalism is manifest "in blessing the Ministry of our Preachers with like fruits of conversion (as in our native Countrey) of sundry elder and younger persons, who came over hither not out of respect to conscience, or spirituall ends, but out of respect to friends, or outward inlargements: but have here found that grace which they sought not for."[13]

The New Canaan then was resolved to maintain itself without celibacy and without segregation by making converts from without and by holding its own children from within. To do the latter proved particularly difficult. It is not easy to make Isaacs out of Abrahams, particularly if the Isaacs have been sacrificed on the altar of their fathers' idealism. And it is not easy for one generation to convey its convictions to the next if the children are thrown much with strangers to the covenant. But extremely difficult is it to transmit from parent to child an inner experience which in the nature of the case must be personal and individual. The Puritans made their problem the more difficult by passing on to their offspring a rugged honesty which made no pretense to an experience which had not been experienced, even though the lack of it meant

[10] R. Cushman, *The Lawfulness of Plantations, op. cit.* (above, n. 4), p. 502.

[11] Thomas Hooker, *The Saints Dignitie and Dutie* (London, 1651), p. 98.

[12] E. Winslow, *Good Newes from New England, op. cit.* (above, n. 3), end of the dedication.

[13] John Cotton, *The Way of Congregational Churches Cleared* (London, 1648), p. 102.

exclusion from the church, and from the government and from eternal life. And those Puritan parents, however much they yearned to have their children beside them at the table of the Lord, continued to be exacting and did not receive any on the basis of blood without the proof of inward regeneration. Even a good life did not suffice, for that might be pure hypocrisy. "There must be an expression of inward goodnesse of the heart, . . . a good sap in the botome"[14] of the tree.

But might not this be demanding a little too much? Anne Hutchinson thought not. She brought forth the distinction between the covenant of grace and the covenant of works and would base the church solely on the former. John Cotton wavered, but he came to see that the distinction is exceedingly difficult to discern. "A poore Christian will be put to much exercise to find a difference between himself" and a hypocrite.[15] The practical conclusion was that if so high a degree of inwardness were demanded the church would dwindle from a holy commonwealth into a holy conventicle. The Cambridge Platform recommended therefore that "severity of examination is to be avoyded . . . and such charity and tenderness is to be used as the weakest Christian if sincere may not be excluded." The tests should be only vigorous enough to satisfy "a rational charity."[16]

In this spirit the saints were defined as first: "Such as have not only attained the knowledge of the principles of Religion, and are free from gross and open scandals, but also do together with the profession of their faith and Repentance, walk in blameless obedience to the word, so as that in charitable discretion they may be accounted Saints by calling (though perhaps some or more of them be unsound, and hypocrites inwardly:) ;" and second; "The children of such, who are also holy."[17]

Yet how could infants meet the tests of even the most "charitable discretion," and should they then in no sense be regarded as members of the church? The Anabaptists said that they should not,

[14] Thomas Hooker, *The Faithful Covenanter* (London, 1644) , p. 16.
[15] John Cotton, *A Treatise of the Covenant of Grace* (London, 1671) , p. 47.
[16] Cambridge Platform XII, 2 and 3; Walker, *op. cit.* (above, n. 8) , p. 222.
[17] *Ibid,* III, 1 and 2; Walker, pp. 205-206.

and one would have expected the Congregationalists, with their theory of the gathered church, to take the same position. But they argued that children are "under the wing of the covenant."[18] Such children must, on attaining years of discretion, make their own profession before admission to communion but from infancy they are under "church watch" and "if not regenerated, yet are in a more hopefull way of attayning regenerating grace."[19] So far so good for the second generation, but how about the third? Suppose the child of a saint were unable to make the profession? Should his child in that case be pushed out from under the wing of the covenant or received on the basis, not of his parents' but of his grandparents' faith? The more lenient answer was of course that of the Half-Way Covenant. So far the Cambridge Platform was not prepared to go. Only the first generation of the offspring of the saints might be included,[20] and yet the Platform suggests a movement in the direction of the hereditary principle when it compares baptism to circumcision,[21] the rite of initiation into a national community. The framers were starting down the road which was to convert the elect of New Canaan into the elite of New England, but they did not intend or foresee the outcome. They entrenched themselves on the middle lane between the Covenant of Grace and the Half-Way Covenant and that lane after two decades faded out.[22]

Was it because they refused to simplify their program and adopt either celibacy or segregation? Was it simply that increasingly the strangers invaded the land and came to outnumber the saints? But have we any right to ask such questions which betray too great a concern for numbers and the survival of outward communities? We do better to discern that what was envisaged for New England has in many respects become a pattern for the United States. Essentially that Puritan theocracy was the attempt of a

---

[18] John Cotton, *Treatise of the Covenant of Grace* (London, 1671) , p. 205.
[19] Cambridge Platform XII, 7; Walker, p. 224.
[20] *Ibid*, III, 2; Walker, p. 206. Cf. *Church-Government and Church-Covenant* (London, 1643) , p. 22. Scripture "seemes to limit this faederall sanctity or holynesse to the Children whose next Parents one or both were Believers. . . . And if we should goe one degree beyond the next Parents, we see not but we may goe two and if two, why not 3, 4, 20, 100, or 1000? For where will you stop?"
[21] Cambridge Platform IV, 5; Walker, p. 209.
[22] The claim to constitute a middle way is very common in the history of

determined minority to set the tone for a community by the use of a maximum of persuasion and a minimum of constraint. The Mayflower Compact is itself very instructive at this point. Even on that first voyage the strangers began to murmur against the saints. And the saints did not throw them overboard but assembled the entire company, drafted a constitution and insured consent by the sheer force of moral conviction. So it was very largely in that New Canaan. The intolerance has been grossly exaggerated, for in the century and a half of colonial history the exercise of severe measures was rare and banishment was a more lenient penalty then than ever before or since, because in virgin territory there was somewhere else to go.

That Puritan venture, rooted and grounded in faith, has left a residue of faith which survives as "reverent unbelief" even at Harvard and Yale. The reverence is not for unbelief but for faith. In this land of ours those who cannot believe are ready to yield direction in some measure to those who can, and that is why convinced minorities are able to exert an influence out of all proportion to their numbers. By reason of such nuclei the whole of the United States has come to think of itself as in some sense a chosen people with a mission and a responsibility to the world. The danger of hypocrisy is patent. The need for sincerity is urgent. All of the world looks to us as a land now actually flowing with milk and honey that we may not only feed the hungry but restore faith to the desolate.

The resolve of John Cotton was not vain when he said: "And therefore it is for us to doe all the good we can, and to leave nothing to those that shall come after us, but to walk in the righteous steps of their fore-Fathers. And therefore let us not leave, nor give rest to our eyes, until in Family, Church and Commonwealth we have set a patterne of holinesse to those that shall succeed us."[23]

Such was the mood of the framers of the Cambridge Platform. The external lineaments of their holy commonwealth have

---

the Church. Cotton made it for Congregationalism as lying between Brownism and Presbyterianism, *The Keyes of the Kingdom* (London, 1644), A 4.

[23] John Cotton, *An Exposition upon the thirteenth Chapter of the Revelation* (London, 1655), p. 77.

perished, yet a spiritual heritage survives, and if over the outward
structure we must write the word "failure," then one should add
that the failures of history are often more significant in the eyes of
God than the successes.

16. The Covenant in the Wilderness

The figures in the margin are from prints of the Yale Campus around 1790. At the bottom is a football game with President Timothy Dwight watching on the right.

On the twenty-fifth day of April, it being the Sabbath, in the year 1638, a band of immigrant Puritans gathered for the worship of God under a great oak on the shore of Quinnipiac Bay. The spot was near the present corner of College and George Streets in New Haven, Connecticut, and is commemorated by a plaque. There were two ministers in the company. The first, John Davenport, preached in the morning on the text, "Then Jesus was led up of the Spirit into the wilderness." The second, Peter Prudden, spoke in the afternoon on, "The voice of one crying in the wilderness." Evidently they were agreed as to where they were!

The scene is no less significant for Congregationalism and for the American way of life than the landings at Plymouth Rock and Boston Bay, particularly because the Puritan pattern survived unbroken longer in Connecticut. Pictorial representation of the event was delayed for over a century, and first appeared in the quaint cut from a broadside issued on the eve of the American Revolution (p. 230). Observe that the sexes are segregated like Adams and Eves on either side of the Tree of the Knowledge of Good and Evil. The practice of separate seating in churches was thus projected backwards into the wilderness.

The purpose of those founding fathers was in after years greatly misunderstood, and the broadside which vaunted them as the founders of civil and religious liberty was talking the language of another day. They were Englishmen who came here to realize a plan which in the homeland had been frustrated. They had sought to congregationalize the Church of England. Their objection had not been to a national church, nor were they violently opposed to bishops, provided the bishops respected the will of congregations. These reformers were even more concerned that the church should not be conceived as including everybody born within the parish, but should be the gathered company of those quickened by the spirit of God. Such persons should constitute the church and should give the tone to the state and the community. Thwarted in the effort to inject this pattern into the structure of the Church of

This paper was first published by the Printing-Office of the Yale University Press for presentation by the New Haven Association of Churches and Ministers to those attending the General Council of the Congregational Christian Churches, June 23-30, 1954.

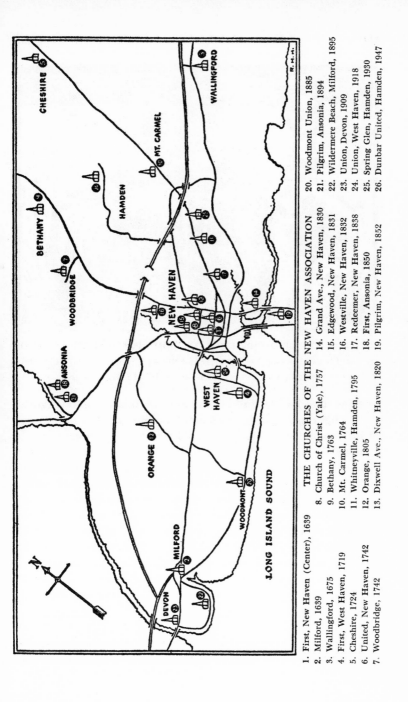

THE CHURCHES OF THE NEW HAVEN ASSOCIATION

1. First, New Haven (Center), 1639
2. Milford, 1639
3. Wallingford, 1675
4. First, West Haven, 1719
5. Cheshire, 1724
6. United, New Haven, 1742
7. Woodbridge, 1742
8. Church of Christ (Yale), 1757
9. Bethany, 1763
10. Mt. Carmel, 1764
11. Whitneyville, Hamden, 1795
12. Orange, 1805
13. Dixwell Ave., New Haven, 1820
14. Grand Ave., New Haven, 1830
15. Edgewood, New Haven, 1831
16. Westville, New Haven, 1832
17. Redeemer, New Haven, 1838
18. First, Ansonia, 1850
19. Pilgrim, New Haven, 1852
20. Woodmont Union, 1885
21. Pilgrim, Ansonia, 1894
22. Wildermere Beach, Milford, 1895
23. Union, Devon, 1909
24. Union, West Haven, 1918
25. Spring Glen, Hamden, 1930
26. Dunbar United, Hamden, 1947

CUT FROM THE BROADSIDE ENTITLED "SOME POETICAL THOUGHTS ON
THE DIFFICULTIES OUR FOREFATHERS ENDURED IN PLANTING RELIGIOUS
AND CIVIL LIBERTY IN THIS WESTERN WORLD" (1770).

England, they had fled first to Holland and then to the New World.

They came cherishing a magnificent dream. Here unimpeded
by bishops and archbishops they could erect a holy commonwealth,
a divine society under "God as governor" and living in accord with
His ordinances as delivered in His Holy Word. The great purpose
of God once partially achieved in ancient Israel should at last
reach consummation through a people chosen with no reference
to blood or soil but solely because their hearts had been warmed
and their lives refashioned by the grace of God in Christ.

The two outstanding leaders of the little company to land
at Quinnipiac were a minister and a layman, John Davenport and
Theophilus Eaton. They had been school friends together in
England. Davenport, the minister, had finished his university
education. Eaton, son of a minister, had prospered in business.
They arrived first in Boston and were cordially received. But
somewhat disquieted by the disputes there raging and intrigued
by reports of a goodly land to the south, they set out on their own,

taking with them another company lately come from England under the minister Peter Prudden. They had no charter from the Crown but settled in territory already vaguely assigned to their Boston friends.

Land in the Quinnipiac area was secured from the Indians by purchase. To Momauguin they gave "Twelve Coates ... Twelve Alcumy spoones, Twelve Hatchets, twelve hoes, two dozen of knives ... and four Cases of ffrench knives and sizers," and to Montowese smaller amounts. Momauguin had only forty-seven braves and Montowese only ten, so greatly had the Indians recently been depleted by the plague. The names of these two sachems are today attached to places near New Haven. The relations of the colonists with these Indians were peaceful for forty years. The case was different with the more powerful tribes to the north, with the result that a sentry had always to sit in the belfry of the church, and the rear seats were reserved for men at arms.

The church was not immediately formed; only after prayer and heart searching was so solemn a step to be undertaken. In

MAP OF NEW HAVEN GREEN, 1748

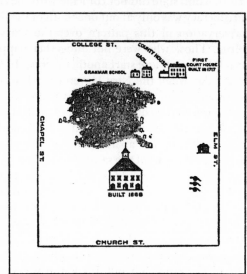

Robert Newman's barn (where Silliman College now stands at the foot of Hillhouse Avenue, marked by a plaque) the company gathered, and on the twenty-second day of August, 1639, the First Church came into being. Twelve men of heartfelt religion and upright deportment were chosen as the nucleus. They should then admit others at discretion. Joining the church was by owning a covenant following a rigid doctrinal examination. The candidate was called upon to enter into holy covenant with God, to forswear all former pollutions and "to give up your selfe to the Lord Jesus, making him your onely priest and atonement, . . . your onely guide, and King, and Lawgiver, and to walke before him in all professed subjections unto all his holy Ordinance, according to the rule of the Gospell, and to walke together with his Church and the members thereof in brotherly love, and mutuall edification and succor according to God."

The institution of civil government had slightly preceded that of the church. The system was theocratic. Only church members could be citizens, and only those of fervent faith and godly deportment could qualify. Church and state were one, and Governor Eaton lived, appropriately, on Elm between Church and State streets. But church and state did not coincide with the community. The ruling aristocracy was only about one-tenth of the inhabitants.

The preservation of this pattern over the years presented grave difficulties. Those who were not altogether happy over the arrangement might depart and start another colony. In fact, on the afternoon of the day when the New Haven church was organized in Robert Newman's barn, another company gathered under Peter Prudden and organized the church which settled at Milford with a more liberal policy as to the suffrage. Again in 1643 another church was planted at Guilford. Yet apart from withdrawals, a serious problem arose when the sons of the saints found themselves ranked among the strangers. The son of a minister, for example, was deeply grieved because he could not vote for the officers in the militia, the reason being that he could not meet the religious tests for church membership. The pillars of the New Haven commonwealth were resolved to keep the standards high and were more disposed to cast out the unworthy than to admit the unqualified. Even the wife of Governor Theophilus Eaton was censured and excommunicated. Her offense was twofold. She denied the validity of infant baptism, and she slapped her husband's mother. When taxed with having disobeyed the Fifth Commandment enjoining honor to father and mother, she replied with a "contemptuous carriage" that her husband's mother was not her mother.

There were various ways coming into vogue among the New England communities for minimizing the gap between the saints and the strangers. One was the Half-Way Covenant. The Whole-Way Covenant allowed baptism only to the children of the elect, who alone were qualified to give religious instruction. The Half-Way Covenant extended the privilege to the grandchildren. The elect were degenerating into the elite. Within the church higher and lower levels of membership were recognized. The lower grade constituted ecclesiastical societies to deal with matters temporal. The church proper dealt with matters spiritual.

Against all such attenuations Davenport was as flint. No relaxation of standards would he tolerate, and no extension of privileges in the commonwealth. He looked askance at Milford and even more at Hartford, where the non-elect, though excluded from office, might share in town affairs. Then came a crisis in the colony. The Puritan regime in England fell. Charles II ascended the throne. What now would become of the New Haven colony, which had never had a charter in the first place? The prospects were the more gloomy because New Haven did not shrink from imperiling her fortunes by harboring the regicides. Colonels Whalley and Goffe (for whom two streets in New Haven are named) were among those who had signed the death warrant for Charles I. When his son ascended the throne, they fled to Boston. Tidings came that they were excluded from amnesty, whereupon they escaped to New Haven and received asylum with John Davenport. When royal emissaries came to hunt for them, they hid in a cave on the summit of West Rock. Davenport disingenuously explained to the authorities that there had been no lack of will or industry "in apprehending the two colonels, but God's overruling providence had prevented." The agents of King Charles had good reason to suspect who had been the instrument of "God's overruling providence," and New Haven could look for no special favor.

Governor Winthrop of Connecticut went to England to

obtain, if possible, charters alike for the colony of Connecticut at Hartford and for the colony at New Haven. He came back with a charter only for Connecticut. There was consternation. Should New Haven unite with so lax a regime as that of Hartford? Better it were to flee to the Dutch, and plans were made for migration to the territories of Peter Stuyvesant. But then New Amsterdam was taken by the English and converted into New York. There was nothing for it. New Haven was incorporated with Connecticut. A group of dissenters thereupon left and founded Newark, New Jersey, while John Davenport himself removed to Boston.

The external structure of the theocracy was giving way, but there were other and better methods whereby the elect of the Lord could give the tone to the community than by restricting the suffrage. One was by strengthening the churches. An attempt in this direction was made in the Saybrook Platform of 1708, which introduced a mildly Presbyterian structure, in that consociations of churches and associations of ministers supervised discipline and ordinations. That candidates might the better qualify for ordination steps were taken to provide superior training. John Davenport had long envisaged and labored for a college at New Haven "to fit youth (by learning) for the service of god in Church and Com̃onwealth." Governor Hopkins had been persuaded to leave his estate "for the breeding up of hopeful youths in a way of learning." But some feared Harvard would be weakened, and the outcome was the founding of a preparatory school which functions to this day as the Hopkins Grammar School, now located on Forest Road.

The college contemplated by Davenport was realized only after his time, and was named for the grandson of that Anne Eaton who had been excommunicated. Her first husband had been David Yale. Her grandson Elihu, reared in England, was an Anglican, who was dubious whether he should contribute to a dissenting academy but was persuaded on the ground that proper books might occasion a return to the Church. For so slight and half reluctant a donation he acquired an immortality which history, had she been just, would have conferred upon John Davenport.

The plea by which Elihu Yale's scruples were overcome was not fatuous. Still further books were solicited from England. Now the only men in England who could give books were men of sub-

YALE COLLEGE, CONNECTICUT HALL, BUILT IN 1752

stance, and the only church to which men of substance belonged
was the Anglican. The new acquisitions contained defenses of the
national church. They were read by the rector and tutors of Yale
College, who at the commencement in 1722 announced their defection to the Episcopal Church. New Haven was more aghast than
if the French had taken Boston. The church in West Haven
(founded in 1719) was almost shattered by the event because one
of those tutors, Samuel Johnson, was at the same time its pastor.
Later he became the president of King's College, which developed
into Columbia University. One of the results at Yale was a closer
watch over Episcopal students, who were required to attend
services at Center Church. When parents objected, President Clap
thwarted them at length by establishing a separate college church
(1757), where the services included an hour's lecture on systematic
theology, which the Episcopal students could be required to attend
as an academic exercise.

There was a method still more fundamental of recovering
the control of the church over the life of the community, and that

was a revival. Instead of letting down the bars to the level of the people, why not raise the people to the level of the bars? The attempt was made in the Great Awakening. Its inaugurator was Jonathan Edwards. He sought to win men by making them sensible of their condition. He simply preached theology. He set before his hearers the supreme glory and excellency of God. He declared the depravity of man, who rejects his high destiny of union with God (Edwards had had a taste of the depravity of man at Yale, where he reported "Monstrous impieties, And Acts of Immorality Lately Committed in the Colledge, Particularly stealing of Hens, Geese, turkies, piggs, Meat, Wood &c, — Unseasonable Nightwalking, Breaking People's windows, playing at Cards, Cursing, Swearing, and damning") yet such petty derelictions did not constitute the major charge against mankind, but rather that in man there is a fire of rebellion blazing with spite and malice against God. Nevertheless the mercy of God extends even to the malicious, and the angry God who holds sinners over hell keeps his hand beneath them precisely that they may not fall into the abyss which they deserve, but may enjoy another chance of salvation.

In response to such pleas the Great Awakening began, moving down the Connecticut River from Northampton and even unto Yale. But there were some disconcerting manifestations, shrieking, swooning, despondencies and even a case of suicide. Some, alienated by the extravagances, decried the revival, and that very movement which might have united church, state and community served actually to split the churches. The revivalists were called the New Lights and the critics the Old Lights. New Haven Congregationalism was divided. United Church on the Green stems from the New Lights and Center Church from the Old. The Milford Church likewise was split, and two churches were formed, which only recently have been reunited.

At Wallingford the controversy occasioned a defiance of the Saybrook Platform. James Dana, a Harvard graduate, an Old Light, savoring of Bostonian defections from orthodoxy, was deemed by the Connecticut stalwarts to be too dim a light to ordain. The Association refused. The church at Wallingford thereupon withdrew and ordained him themselves. He was subsequently a pastor of Center Church in New Haven. Men came to forget his reputed heresies because he visited his people in the plague and was deeply moving in his prayers. When he prayed at the opening of the Legislature, a certain general said he had never heard so impressive a prayer. Someone irreverently wondered how many the general had heard!

By the end of the eighteenth century the Old Lights and the New Lights got together again, perhaps because both had grown feeble. A new revival was in order, and it came in the Second Great Awakening. Among its leaders was Nathaniel W. Taylor, pastor of Center Church and later professor of theology in the newly established Yale Divinity School. He was the architect of what was called the New Haven theology. Without denying predestination he stressed the ability of man to accept God's proffered grace. Leonard Bacon described his sermons as "those solid and massive discourses full of linked and twisted logic, giving out sharp flashes of electric power."

The history of New Haven and Connecticut Congregationalism in the nineteenth century can scarcely be more than sketched. Although the contours of the Holy Commonwealth were gone, and church and state were completely separated in 1818, yet the church continued to give the tone to the community in that ardent souls —they would earlier have been called the elect—inspired and manned many of the great movements of reform, anti-dueling, antislavery, temperance and the like, and were active likewise in the missionary endeavor both at home and abroad. Leonard Bacon, pastor of Center Church in the period leading up to the Civil War, was a great ecclesiastical statesman who preserved the peace of the churches and by his sanity on the slavery issue profoundly affected the mind of Abraham Lincoln. In the late nineteenth century the pastors of United and Center Churches, respectively Theodore Thornton Munger and Newman Smyth, were extremely influential in leading the theological thinking of their day when the doctrine of evolution appeared to imperil the faith.

Just a word about several of the other early churches in this vicinity. The church at Cheshire was separated from that at Wallingford in 1723. It has one of the loveliest church edifices in the state, recently very beautifully restored. The church in East Haven was established in 1710. Its present building, called the Old

Stone Church, was opened for worship in 1774, and is among the oldest in Connecticut. The churches in Woodbridge and Orange in their setting on the old greens are among the most unspoiled in New England.

Thus the churches of the New Haven area link us intimately with the beginnings of American Congregationalism. As we reflect upon the spirit of our sires, we recall the verses of Leonard Bacon's hymn:

> O God, beneath Thy guiding hand
> Our exiled fathers crossed the sea;
> And when they trod the wintry strand,
> With prayer and psalm they worshiped Thee.
>
> . . . .
>
> And here Thy Name, O God of love,
> Their children's children shall adore,
> Till these eternal hills remove,
> And spring adorns the earth no more.

NEW HAVEN HARBOR IN 1786

17. Thomas Hooker and the Puritan Contribution to Democracy

The contribution of Thomas Hooker to democracy and free government is a controverted theme. On the one hand are those who hail him as the first American Democrat, as the precursor of Thomas Jefferson. They regard Hooker as the author of the Fundamental Articles, themselves significant as the first written constitution and the forerunner of the American Constitution. On the other hand are those who say that Hooker in his political thinking differed but slightly from the men of Massachusetts, John Cotton and John Winthrop, and that the Connecticut Colony was only to a degree more democratic than Boston and New Haven.[1]

Our first concern is of course with the facts, for we may rest assured that Thomas Hooker, who would have been embarrassed to be praised of men on any count, would have been doubly disturbed to be praised for the wrong reason. That I might approach the subject with an unclouded mind, I resolved first to read Hooker himself and only afterwards the literature of this debate. I found in him a majesty of discourse, a rhythmic prose, albeit couched in a plain style, for, said he, "In the wilderness if planters find cloth

This paper was delivered as a lecture in the First Church in Hartford, Connecticut, on May 6, 1958. The lectureship was founded by an endowment in memory of Katherine V. Watson, a direct descendant of Hooker. This address was first published in the *Bulletin of the Congregational Library*, X, 1 (October, 1958).

[1] Unqualified claims as to Hooker's contribution to American democracy were made by C. S. Thompson, *Thomas Hooker—Predecessor of Thomas Jefferson in Democracy* (Cheshire, n.d.), and Walter S. Logan, *Thomas Hooker, the First American Democrat* (1904). Similar views were expressed by historians of standing, notably by James Truslow Adams and Parrington. Perry Miller took issue with them all in his essay "Thomas Hooker and the Democracy of Connecticut," which appeared first in the *New England Quarterly* (1931), and was reprinted in *Errand into the Wilderness* (Cambridge, Mass., 1956). Extravagant

to go warm, they leave cuts and lace to those that study to go fine."
I found much piquancy of metaphor as when he compared God to
an itinerant New England salesman. Said he, "God is packing up
his gospel because no one will buy his wares and meet his price."[2]
I found evangelical sermons on such topics as "The Poor Doubting
Christian Drawn to Christ," "The Saints Dignitie and Dutie."
There were all the usual themes of the Puritan sermon: the
covenant of works, the covenant of grace, preparation for salvation
and so on. But in all this I found not one word about political
theory.

Next I looked at his *Survey of the Summe of Church Discipline*. It scarcely differs in essentials from the plan of John Cotton.
In this work Hooker asserts that the civil magistrate should not
tolerate all forms of religion. Evidently Hooker did not believe in
religious liberty. "The civil powers," said he, "have a nourishing
and preserving faculty," which meant that the General Court
could convene consociations of the churches. There was, then, to
this degree a union of church and state. Scarcely here does one
discover any enunciation of democratic principles.

The documentary evidence on which rest the claims for
Hooker's priority as a democrat is actually exceedingly scant. The
whole body of material is comprised within four pages consisting
of one letter and the heads of a sermon the body of which has been
lost. Never have claims so great been supported by evidence so
quantitatively slender, though this of itself does not prove them to
be false.

---

statements as to the early constitution of Connecticut were corrected by Charles
McClean Andrews in "The Beginnings of Connecticut," *Tercentenary Commission,* No. 32 (1934). The same material appears in his *Colonial Period of
American History,* Vol. II. The correspondence of Hooker and Winthrop and
the heads of Hooker's sermon can be found in *Connecticut Historical Society
Collections* 1 (1860), pp. 1-21. The Fundamental Articles of Connecticut are
available in a publication of the *Tercentenary Commission* in 1934. There is a
life of Hooker by George Leon Walker (New York, 1891). Three of Hooker's
sermons are available in facsimile entitled "Redemption," ed. E. H. Emerson,
Scholars' Facsimiles (1958). There is an excellent study of Winthrop by Edmund S. Morgan, *The Puritan Dilemma, the Story of John Winthrop* (Boston,
1958).

[2] *The Danger of Desertion* (London, 1641), p. 14.

The first document is a letter written by Hooker from Hartford to Governor Winthrop at Boston and is related to the question of why Hooker and his congregation ever left Massachusetts. The reason which was adduced at the time was that the pasturage was too straitened to accommodate the cattle. The General Court then granted more land within the confines of the colony, but nevertheless Hooker and his congregation departed. This suggests that there must have been some other reason. Certain persons even then suspected that perhaps the pasturage was too straitened to accommodate Thomas Hooker and John Cotton in the same field and personal friction may indeed have been a factor in the departure. But modern historians, on the basis of the letter about to be examined, have conjectured that the reason was disaffection on the part of Hooker and his group over arbitrary government in Massachusetts. The fundamental reason was the desire to establish a more liberal regime.

This surmise rests on the correspondence exchanged two years after the departure. The occasion was the desire of Winthrop to hasten the federation of the colonies. Connecticut held back. Winthrop suggested to Hooker that the procrastination was due to the error of referring the question to a constituency unduly large in extent, "For," said he, "the best part is always the least and of that best part the wiser is always the lesser." Hooker in his reply agreed in principle that the people should act through representatives but he would make a distinction between matters of greater and lesser concern and would refer the former to a larger council and the latter to a smaller. One observes here a conflict between two ingredients in our present American pattern. We have now a federation of the states and a universal franchise, but at that time in Connecticut the extension of the franchise would defeat the confederation. Hooker was wise enough to perceive that federations without consent cannot be successful. At the same time he agreed in principle with Winthrop and supported him against the anarchic tendencies introduced by Anne Hutchinson in Massachusetts.

In his letter Hooker raised a further point, namely, that although judgment must be rendered by judges, yet judges must decide in accord with law. The reference here may have been to a debate between Winthrop and Vane, who complained that the Massachusetts alien law left the decision as to the expulsion of aliens "to the approbation of majestrates" without specifying reasons. Winthrop countered that since the magistrates were members of the church their judgments were God's judgments. Hooker agreed with Vane that such a principle would lead to tyranny and he would not care to live under a government so arbitrary.

There are two points in this correspondence of great moment. The first is popular participation in government and the second is government under law. The differences between Winthrop and Hooker on these points are neither to be minimized nor exaggerated. Hooker on important matters would take more people into account and he preferred law to magisterial discretion. The difference was less acute because Winthrop did not endorse completely arbitrary government. "I am willing," said he "to listen to advice. My aim is the common good." He acknowledged himself to be bound by "the rules of the gospel." An age-old dispute is involved here. If there be too few laws, the magistrate may become a despot. If there be too many, he may be hamstrung in the administration of justice. Winthrop argued in particular that magistrates must be allowed discretionary powers particularly when the legislative body is not in session. When, for example, fishermen on the Thames asked to be allowed to construct a weir and submitted their plea at a time when the General Court was not meeting, Winthrop gave the authorization on the ground that otherwise a season of fishing would be lost. The magistrate asked for blanket authorization subject to the rules of the gospel. The minister felt that these rules did not sufficiently hedge the magistrate about.

We now turn to the next body of evidence. Two years after the founding of the colony Thomas Hooker delivered a sermon before the General Court which was at the time the ruling body since there was as yet no governor. The date of the sermon was May 31st, 1638. The sermon survives only in a shorthand record of the main points.

The first is this: "that the choice of public magistrates belongs unto the people, by God's own allowance." In other words magistrates should be elected. There is certainly nothing novel here. Election had been practiced in Greece and Rome. Election was employed in the Holy Roman Empire. Election was used in the Swiss Cantons. Election was employed in England for the choice of magistrates and members of Parliament. Election was the device in vogue in the American colonies. Of course the British king was not subject to election but no one as yet in England or the colonies thought of challenging the hereditary principle with regard to the British monarchy.

The second principle of Hooker was that election must not be exercised by the people "in accord with their humors but according to the will and law of God." This would have to be an exhortation rather than a prescription, but it is very important because it shows that Hooker was actually as fearful of the perversity of man in the electorate as in the magistracy. Both in his view must be subject to law, namely to the law of God.

The third point was that those who "have the power to appoint officers and magistrates have power also to set bounds and limitations." This is an assertion of the principle of constitutionalism. Its roots lie in classical antiquity and in the Middle Ages and the demand for constitutional government was in Hooker's day the common concern of the Puritans and the common lawyers in old England. The despotic Tudor monarchy had done its work in achieving a consolidated England and when the Stuarts continued to behave like the Tudors, the cry was general that government must take hands off. Democracy at that moment meant freedom from government, *laissez faire* in politics as well as in trade, the subjection of government to bounds and limitations.

Finally Hooker said that "The foundation of authority is laid in the free consent of the people." This assertion likewise was not original, for the religious struggles of the previous century had led to the contract theory of government in which a covenant is made between God and the King and the people. The use of the word covenant rather than the word contract discloses the specific influence of religious ideas and in particular of the Congregationalist view of the church, built on covenant and consent. There was a theological grounding for this position. Hooker held that man must give free consent even to God.[3] The elect are indeed chosen

---

[3] *Ibid,* p. 16.

by God prior to their consent but consent they must and that freely. The church consists of those who enter into covenant and the state is not simply a coercive agency established by God to restrain evil, but an association of those who consent to form a body politic.

One could wish that Hooker had been more explicit as to the reason for consent. The only ground which he assigned was one of expediency, since government is easier to conduct by consent than by compulsion. Those who consent will show more love for rulers and will yield a readier obedience. Not a word was said about inalienable rights which cannot be abrogated without consent. There was no suggestion of the slogan "No taxation without representation." Hooker again was far from saying that consent constitutes a consensus and that a consensus is an indication of truth, in other words that the majority is necessarily right. Such a conclusion no Puritan could have conceded unless the majority were a majority of the elect only. The consensus of the masses is no guarantee of truth.

This matter of consent raises another question of great moment, namely, whose consent? No one of the colonies was organized on the basis of a universal franchise. They could scarcely have been so constituted because the cornerstone not only of their theology but also of their political theory was predestination. To begin with, the church was to consist only of those presumably elect. How the elect were to be discovered was of course a difficult matter. Calvin had posited three presumptive tests: 1) adherence to the creed, 2) upright deportment and 3) participation in the sacraments. New England Calvinism substituted for the third a heartfelt religious experience without which admission to the sacraments was denied. In consequence many God-fearing folk were excluded from the Lord's table because they could pretend to no emotional experience. Thomas Hooker is reported to have believed that the tests in Massachusetts were too rigid and that a reasonable charity might be more lenient. He quite agreed that those rejected by the Lord should not come to the table of the Lord, but one need not be too rigorous in deciding who they might be. Hooker thus displayed a leaning toward the lowering of the bars for church membership.

This structure of the church affected also the structure of the state because church membership was requisite for citizenship. Such was the system at Plymouth, at Boston and at New Haven. Those who were excluded from the church were excluded from the state. This system provoked restiveness not so much on the part of the original strangers of the first migrations, who never had enjoyed the franchise in England because of the property qualification, as on the part of the sons of the saints who could not pretend to the experience of their fathers. One way to meet the situation was to lower the requirements for church membership, a device with which Hooker appears to have been in sympathy. A second method was to convert the entire community that all might be qualified, but how could this plan ever succeed, if God had predestined some not to be converted? The third way was to give up the religious qualification for the franchise. In the adoption of this solution the Connecticut colony took the lead.

But the degree to which this was done has been misunderstood and exaggerated. The body of the people in Connecticut were divided into three groups. The first were mere inhabitants who had no share in government. Into this class fell automatically women, children, servants and apprentices. The next category was that of "admitted inhabitants" who had to be admitted to the franchise by a town meeting. The requirements were "an honest conversation," and an oath that one was not a Jew, a Quaker, or an Atheist. These admitted inhabitants could then vote for deputies, but not for higher officers nor could they themselves hold office. The third class was that of the free men who were chosen by the court or a magistrate. The free men must be landowners, Trinitarians, and of godly deportment. They only could vote for the higher officials and they only could serve as magistrates.

When, then, Thomas Hooker talked about the consent of the people we are not to suppose that he meant just everybody. The Connecticut colony was ahead of Massachusetts and New Haven in abolishing religious tests, but it was still a long way from the modern secularized state. On the other hand we are not to minimize the difference. It was sufficiently great that when the New Haven colony was incorporated into the colony of Connecticut

John Davenport was outraged and, rather than live under so liberal a regime, moved to Boston. Yet when all qualifications are made, the judgment of Charles McClean Andrews was right when he said "To the Puritan what we call democracy was looked upon as an aberration of the human mind, disapproved of God and his faithful elect. Only those who were Christians, of honest and peaceful conversation, substantial, respectable, and reliable fathers in Israel were worthy to build up a community the design of which was religion."

Finally Hooker is credited with the authorship of the Fundamental Articles of Connecticut. That he was not the author is rendered almost certain by the style. That he was consulted is highly probable. That he approved is almost certain. These orders have been described as a landmark in constitutional government because here for the first time a state was organized on the basis of a written constitution. This claim calls for some modification. What shall one say of the Plymouth colony, based upon the Mayflower Compact, or for that matter what shall one say of the charters granted to the American colonies? Written instruments of government were not altogether new. One recalls Magna Charta or the constitution of the Holy Roman Empire. The newness in our land consisted rather in this, that the colonies were new and could be set up without regard for immemorial precedents. The commonwealths of the New World were like farms in the middle west laid out with T-squares rather than developed from cow paths. The nearest parallel is perhaps to be found in the feudal states which the crusaders set up in the Holy Land unhampered by the vestiges of older structures entrenched in the life of France.

Yet the question of novelty is not our chief concern. There is more point in asking whether a written constitution is essential to a democracy and how it operates. It can scarcely be absolutely essential because by common consent England is a democracy and England does not have a written constitution. A document in writing is a testimony to the resolve to check human caprice and arbitrariness by norms of fundamental law. Our first constitution originated in the period when checks were felt most to be necessary for the curbing of government. But in the course of our history they have operated even more to check the arbitrariness of the electorate. We have a Supreme Court which throws out unconstitutional legislation and thereby thwarts the will of representative assemblies speaking on behalf of the people. The process of legislation is slowed down until the constitution has been amended. A written document is thus evidence of the Puritan distrust of man and the resolve to impose limitations and bounds both upon governors and governed.

As for Hooker, we may conclude that he was a Puritan in accord with his generation in recognizing a certain union of church and state, in recognizing the responsibility of the magistrate for fostering the true religion and suppressing the false. Hooker held that government rests on the consent of the people, but the people for him were those presumably elect, even though he would not be too rigid as to the test for election. There should be creedal tests for the exercise of the franchise and restrictions in terms of fundamental law upon the ruler and the ruled. Thus far Hooker.

But we cannot leave the matter here. Though Hooker is not unduly to be abstracted from his generation, neither is his generation to be written off as having contributed nothing to democracy. Democracy is more than a form of government. It is primarily a way of life which we believe to be best served by a form of government. There are many ingredients in the democratic ideal which go beyond constitutions.

The first is the conviction that government must be an instrument of justice respecting the dignity and the rights of citizens. Hooker's period was the era when great stress was placed on the liberties of the subject, on the birthright of Englishmen, on the inviolability of conscience. The parliamentarians insisted that the king should respect the home of the citizen and the citadel of the saint. If the monarch transgressed, he might be resisted passively and even actively. The absolute intransigence of the Puritan wrecked any pretentions to absolutism on the part of the state.

A second principle was a by-product of Puritanism, namely religious liberty. The contribution here was not direct because the Puritans at first demanded liberty not for any and all opinions but only for the truth and they had no compunction as to the suppression of error. But when there came to be many varieties of Puritanism, each claiming to be exclusively true, the choice lay between mutual extermination or toleration and toleration passed into tolerance, respect for the conviction of another, despite disagreement.

The third ingredient was insistence on morality in the conduct of the state. In our day, even among theologians, there are some who greet this insistence with scorn and tell us the State Department cannot be administered by homilies. We are further told that nations actually follow their self-interest and we should do the same. Agreements are to be kept only so long as we find them advantageous, and the principle of swearing to one's hurt and changing not cannot be regarded as a political maxim. The Puritans would have been aghast at any such political ethic. To be sure they were not always just in their dealings and notably not in the case of the Indians. It is indeed disconcerting to learn that Mr. Pyncheon of Hartford, the author of "The Meritorious Price of Our Redemption," carried the scalps of the murdered Sachems from Hartford to Boston.[4] But in their dealings with white men, with other English colonies and with the Dutch the Puritans of this colony and of the other New England colonies observed the principle that integrity, good faith and magnanimity are sound and essential in statecraft.

Most significant perchance was the Puritan belief in the possibility of a holy commonwealth on earth. The Puritans were certainly not naïve in their appraisal of human nature, otherwise they would never have felt the necessity to set bounds and limitations upon rulers and ruled, but they did believe that the new Israel of God could be erected in this wilderness. They might wring their hands over the dimming of the candles but they never lost faith that they could be kept alight. Here is the root of American optimism, the faith that man can achieve some semblance of God's kingdom upon earth.

This faith entails the view that a commonwealth is like a church in that it is built upon an ideal. To belong to the commonwealth one must subscribe to the ideal. We still take that view in the United States. Immigrants when they are naturalized are given a sermonette by the judge on what it means to be an American.

---

[4] George Leon Walker, *op. cit.* (above, n. 1) , p. 100.

He outlines our ideals of freedom, equality, honor, justice and humanity. Those who do not agree are expected to remain as mere inhabitants. All of this sounds very much like the early constitution of Connecticut.

In the case of those born in this country, however, we do not follow this precedure. They can be enfranchised by the simple expedient of reading a line from Webster's Dictionary, raising a right hand and nodding assent after someone has mumbled an incantation ending "so help me Gawd." Our democracy really combines the Puritan principle of a select electorate with the Jeffersonian ideal of a universal franchise based on the assumption of rationality immanent in all mankind. Such a compromise combination is the best that we can achieve in our secularized society.

Yet we should all agree as to the desirability of placing government, if not in the hands of the elect, certainly in the hands of the elite, but there is no way of placing government in their hands if they do not exist. The most essential operation therefore in a democracy is the moulding of such men and here, rather than in specific political opinion, lies the greatest contribution of Thomas Hooker. He recognized of course that no preacher can manufacture the elect. Nevertheless there is preparation for salvation. The soul, he said, is arable soil encumbered by thistles and weeds and cluttered with trash. Let these be cleared away and the ground ploughed and it is capable of a yield. Hooker thought of himself as a ploughman of arable souls.

How deep he sunk his ploughshare is evidenced from the following two examples from his sermons.

Take the one in which he asked as to the propriety of self-examination to discover "whether you be natural men or spiritual." He approved highly of the exercise and suggested that one test is to examine what is relished.

Now observe therefore what rellish thou findest in the things here below; canst thou rellish base courses and ill company? is any course or advice taken that may adduce thee unto wickednesse? canst thou sweare with the blasphemer, and swagger with the drunkard? canst thou rellish and approve of these courses? but when the Gospell comes and when a man checkes thee for drinking and swearing, and tells thee that these things stand not with the kingdome of God, the kingdome of Christ consists in righteousnesse and joy, and peace in the holy Ghost, and thou must deny thyselfe before thou canst receive the Lord Iesus; if a man shall tell thee that thou must be pure as Christ himselfe is pure, and that the Lord Christ Iesus did not come into the world to make men loose and carelesse, but holy and righteous, to live soberly in this present world, and deny all ungodly and worldly lusts, to renounce and abhorre these, when thou hearest that thou must become a foole that thou mayst bee made wise, and that the Lord came to refresh those onely that were laden with the burthen of their sinnes, when thou hearest these things, how canst thou take them? most men will give this answer, wee thinke not so, wee beleeve is not, nay wee cannot be perswaded of it; is it thus with thee? why then the case is ended, the tryall is done, whoever doth not, nay cannot receive the things of God; the Gospell of God, and the things revealed therein; why the Text saith, and the Lord saith, that man is a natural man.[5]

The following example is a meditation on the text in I Peter 1-12 "Which things (saith the Apostle) the Angels desire to prie into." Hooker commented:

Those blessed spirits that are the subjects of joy and happiness, are so ravished with those glorious mysteries, that they are contented to come to our Congregations, not a step or two, (as we doe, who as soon almost as we are out of our doors are in the Church) but a great journey, even from heaven, and with a great deal of liking and complacencie they behold the services of Gods people, and are glad to see a poor soul converted, and report it again in heaven, rejoycing there together, that a sinner is turned unto God. My brethren, thinke of it; shall we now that have most reason to attend these things (they being that upon which our everlasting salvation depends) to be utterly carelesse of them? Alas, the Angels have the least part in the redemption of a sinner: We are the redeemed, and the saved, and we are they that must be glorified; and shall we have no ears to hear, no hearts to attend to, no desire to imbrace the Word of Salvation? Oh what a shame is it, that we, that have so much interest in mercie, should have so great a neglect of mercie! What then remaineth but this, that we all provoke one another to the performance of this dutie here required of us? that we stop our ears to all carnall counsell, to all delusions of Satan, that we hearken to the Lord onely as our Master, resolving to attend to no advice, to follow no directions, to obey no commands, but what he shall give us?

Oh, but some will say, what is this which you teach us? May not a man hear his carnall friends, may we not follow the advice that they give us? ... [Is not the apprentice to listen to the master, the wife to the

[5] *The Unbelievers Preparing for Christ* (London, 1638), pp. 110-113, reproduced in *Scholars' Facsimiles.*

husband, the child to the parent?] You that stand upon the humoring of your friends and acquaintance, consider it well; Will the perswasions, and counsels, and desires, and commands of a Father, or friend, or husband, or master, stand you in stead at the day of judgement? Will this be a satisfactorie answer at that day, my husband intreated me, my friends counselled me, my master commanded me? No, my brethren, as you are brethren in iniquitie, and causes of sin one to another, so you shall all perish together.[6]

In a striking passage Hooker told his hearers that the narrow way is compared to a needle's eye. "If therefore thou beest a small slender thread, that is, a self-resigned man, thou maist finde entrance, and unite thy Selfe to the Eternal Being; but, if thou beest a huge unwieldly Cable, that is, encombred with thy Selfe ... either look to untwist thy Selfe by Self-denyall, or else despaire of Entrance."[7]

In such passages one finds Hooker the ploughman of arable souls, fashioning the stuff out of which democracies are made.

[6] *Wisdomes Attendants* (London, 1651) , p. 148.
[7] *Heautonaparoumenos or a Treatise on Self-Denyall* (London, 1646) , p. 61.

18. Yale and German Theology in the Middle of the Nineteenth Century

Contact with Germany in the American colonies of the eighteenth century was confined largely to Pennsylvania, since the Quakers there offered an asylum to Mennonites, Schwenkfelders, Brethren and Herrenhuters. New England was in touch rather with old England. A New Englander, writing in 1869, declared that the previous quarter of a century had registered an astounding change. Prior to 1840 German was less known in Boston than Greek. Even the most select schools for youths and maidens neglected it. But now, said he, German is taught all the way from Boston to Omaha. Some educators are saying that it is worth more than Greek or Latin and some, indeed, that it exceeds both of them put together. The Ph.D. degree is no longer the mark of the German exile. The change, said this author, was occasioned in part by a great wave of German immigration. Milwaukee was more German than American, and St. Louis savored of the Rhineland. The passage of these immigrants to the Middle West might have aroused the East to an interest in the literature and scholarly treasures of Germany.[1]

As a matter of fact, New England had already been aroused to a degree even earlier. The first center naturally was Boston, because Boston was close to Harvard, the first American university, and was also a thriving port open to influences from across the sea. In the teens of the nineteenth century George Hedge spent four

First published in the *Zeitschrift für Kirchengeschichte*, Series 4, Vol. 65, No. 3 (1956). To Prof. Hermann Doerries, who always places himself so unreservedly at the service of foreign visitors, this little sketch of American-German relations among theologians of a century past is presented as a token of heartfelt esteem.

[1] Charles H. Brigham, "On the study of German in America," *Christian Examiner*, VIII (1869), 1-20.

years studying in Germany before completing his course at Harvard. It was he who furnished the translation of Luther's *Ein feste Burg* now current among our churches.[2] Yale's earliest contact with Germany began rather by way of books than of boats. Josiah Willard Gibbs, Professor of Sacred Languages in the Yale Divinity School, found that his philological studies could not be pursued apart from the German literature. He mastered the tongue and in 1827 published in London *A Hebrew and English Lexicon of the Old Testament . . . From the German Works of Gesenius.* A pupil of Gibbs and later his successor, George E. Day, traveled to Germany and in 1844, writing to his professor from Tübingen, gave an account of an interview with Ewald, lately dismissed from Göttingen by a reactionary prince:

> [Ewald] is a robust man with a large head, over which his long hair evenly parted in the middle, falls in rather a careless manner. . . . His age, as he told me of his own accord, is forty, and no one, to look at him, would ever dream that he had been such a hard student as his works indicate. He showed me the sheets of the fifth edition of the Hebrew grammar which is just ready for the binder . . . You would have laughed, I know, to have heard our conversation. Sometimes it was in German, sometimes in English, which Professor Ewald speaks in a broken manner, and sometimes in a jumble of both.
>
> It is evident that he deeply feels his banishment from Göttingen . . . At the commencement of the conversation he was inclined to take strong ground against the divisions into denominations abounding in the United States . . . But when I explained to him . . . the perfect freedom of our churches and the manner in which the freedom regulated and restrained its own evils, it was evident that his sympathies were on our side . . . He frankly told me at the outset that with Tholuck and Hengstenberg . . . he had no sympathy. "With Tholuck," said he, putting his thumb on the end of his little finger, "I do not agree so much as this." As he went on to explain his views, I could easily believe him. "My present effort," said he, "is to gain a perfect comprehension of that in which the religious life of the Hebrews consisted, and the conclusion to which I have come is that we must all be prophets and apostles."

Day went on to say that Ewald defended contemporary inspiration as of the same quality as that of the Biblical writers and

[2] Sydney E. Ahlstrom, *The Harvard Divinity School,* ed. G. H. Williams (Boston, 1954), p. 136.

in both instances as not infallible. Day asked what philosophy was uppermost. "None," was the answer. Hegelianism is on the decline. "You Americans," said Ewald, "think that because we are ever changing . . . we make no real progress. Rest assured, it is a mistake. Work has been done which can never be overthrown. Christianity has been placed on higher ground, and in twenty years it will be completed and scientific theology forever after go hand in hand with the Scriptures."

"Do you not agree with me," commented Day, "that these are dreams in Germany as in America?"

Ewald had been disturbed by reading about "an American clergyman named Edwards, who was deposed from the ministry lately by an ecclesiastical council for preaching against some immoralities among his people. The story was so improbable that I inquired into it more particularly and found that he had got hold of the troubles and dismissal of President Edwards!!" [a hundred years earlier].[3]

In the very same year in which this letter was written a German Swiss immigrant to the United States commenced his career in the field of theological education in this country. Philip Schaff, more than any other, was to be a purveyor of German theological scholarship. He had studied at Tübingen under Ferdinand Christian Baur, at Halle under Tholuck and at Berlin under Neander.

In 1857 Schaff published in Edinburgh a book entitled *Germany, Its Universities, Theology and Religion*. The work was reviewed by a Yale man, Noah Porter, Professor of Philosophy and later to be President of the College. The review discloses the enthusiasm for Germany among American students even before the appearance of Schaff's book. The impulse to study there, said Porter, had gained strength for the past ten years in geometrical ratio and was becoming almost a furor. Let it continue, said he. One reason for going is to learn the language, which does not mean that English should be embellished with phrases as cumbersome as Teutonic dressing gowns. But the German language must be learned in order that the Germans may be studied at first hand. They are less dangerous in that way. The second-hand Germaniz-

[3] Manuscript, Sterling Library Yale University.

ing taken from Emerson and Carlyle is more pernicious than a direct contact with a man like Neander. But is not their philosophy a congregation of pestilent vapors? To be sure, their heads are sometimes in the clouds, but that is because they attempt to scale such elevated peaks. Of course, the Tübingen School has generated a portentous smog from a very small fire. Yet we cannot leave German speculation alone. It has fascinated too many minds. Apart from ideas, one can learn from the German habits of solid, exhaustive study. They despise laziness and revere labor. With them enthusiasm for study is a passion. And do not refuse to profit from their sermons because of the candles on the altars.[4]

One of the students swelling the flow to Germany in the decade which Porter reviewed was George Park Fisher, later to be the distinguished Professor of Church History in the Yale Divinity School. We have his diary for the years 1852–53 while he was a student under the theological faculty at Halle. Why he went to Halle, he does not tell, but one may surmise that his reasons were not too different from those of another American student twenty years later, Francis G. Peabody. He was repelled alike by the arid rationalism of Heidelberg and the rabid orthodoxy of Leipzig and turned rather to the median position of Halle. The great figure there was Friedrich August Gottreu Tholuck. Peabody, when he knocked at the door of this professor, was still smarting from chagrin because of his encounter with the rector of the university, who asked about his father. The young American meant to answer *Er lebt nicht mehr;* instead he replied *Er lebt noch nicht.* Another rebuff was in store when he asked the maid for *Professor* Tholuck, and she gave him to understand that he should have said *Ober-consistorialrat.* What was his relief when a gentle little man greeted him cordially in perfect English! Tholuck, said Peabody, was not the most outstanding preacher in Germany nor the most distinguished scholar. "He was preeminent as a saint."[5]

This was the man into whose circle Fisher was to be received, but let him unfold the story for himself through the pages of his

[4] *The New Englander,* I (Nov., 1857) , p. 83.
[5] Francis G. Peabody, *Reminiscenses of Present Day Saints* (Boston, 1927) , pp. 79-84.

diary for the years 1852 and 1853. In the month of June he landed
at Bremen and disembarked on a Sunday to the disquiet of his
conscience. His eye was at once caught by the flower pots in the
windows of the meanest cottages. For some time he ate bread and
milk from a soup plate because he did not know the word for bowl.
Calling on the American consul, he was amazed to find him marry-
ing couples who had lived together for years and had as many as
eight children but had never been able to afford the luxury of the
law. Before migrating to America, they were required to fulfill the
formalities. The Dom at Bremen had four pastors—one Ration-
alist, one Evangelical, and one in between, etc. "They are on good
terms with each other and preach by turns."

Arriving on the nineteenth of June at Halle, he visited the
famous orphanage founded by Francke. He dropped into a book-
store. "Saw there a part of Neander's library which is in process of
being sent to the University of Rochester ... Took lodgings with a
Frau and a Fräulein. The latter spoke English well. The Germans
expect to find Americans either black or copper. When a Professor
from Mercersberg, Pennsylvania, preached in Berlin, a tailor ...
exclaimed, ... "Another cheat! He is not an American! He is
white!"

Professor Roediger is teaching that the speech of Elihu in the
book of Job is not genuine because "it anticipates the speech of
Jehovah and breaks the unity of the book. But how does he know
Job was made according to his laws of unity, any more than the
plays of Shakespeare?"

The following entries culled from the diary are given in the
original order:

June 21, Went to ... church ... Listened but did not understand
the sermon. The congregation was not large—the majority were females
... The persons present appeared devout and the preacher earnest—
though the Lutheran service appears to me to be but a poor imitation of
the Romish ...

I went to tea at Professor Tholuck's ... He was affable and his lady
very social and kind ... Spoke of Coleridge and of his beneficent influence
in stirring up young minds ... With Mrs. Tholuck I talked of Mrs. Stowe's
book [*Uncle Tom's Cabin*]—of slavery in America, etc. She speaks the
English well.

June 26, Hupfeld, who is lecturing on Jewish history, holds that the history in Joshua, etc. was written at a late period—its basis being true, but its details poetical and often irreconcilable with each other . . .

June 27, A sunny day. As I am writing, a woman is at work with a hoe in the garden . . . It is said that a man and woman may often be seen together in the field, the woman digging the holes, while the man drops in the potatoes . . . Yesterday I had my head shaved and am crowned with a wig—an inconvenience greater than I ever intend again to submit to, merely for the sake of beauty . . . My shoemaker and tailor send their bills to "the High-born Mr. Fisher" Germanmanners!

June 28, Last evening talked with the Fräulein of German customs . . . I have been to the Dom Church to hear Professor Erdmann . . .—the singing by the congregation very impressive—the preacher is the Prof. ord. of Philosophy . . . His enunciation was very distinct, so that I could hear all the German, but was able to translate not many sentences. From others, however, I derived a synopsis of the sermon. His introduction was a vindication of the necessity of Philosophy . . . on the part of theological students . . . In his sermon he combatted the notion that we *must* sin, as an introduction to a higher development—saying that we were not commanded to enter the *Red Sea* in order to gain the promised land, but we are already *in* the Red Sea, and the word to us is *Heraus!* (out) . . .

Tholuck's manner in the pulpit is enthusiastic (in the good sense of the word) *and* at the same time dignified . . . I am told there is a party of students "who swear by Tholuck . . ." I have heard Rödiger on the passage in Job "I know that my Redeemer liveth, etc." His idea of it is—"I know that my *Vindicator* liveth!"

This evening I have been walking with Fräulein in the garden. It is a splendid evening. It is quite light here, these evenings, until 9½ o'clock.

July 2, Today . . . I walked from 11 to 1 o'clock with Tholuck. After some pleasant commonplaces he began on the subject of which I had spoken to him—the state of theological parties in Germany—there are 4 principle parties: 1st, the Symbolic Orthodox who hold that the symbols still express the exact truth and allow no progress, except in forms of statement. Hengstenberg is now of this school, also Guericke. (2) The Liberal Orthodox, who hold to a progress in theology, that the symbols do not express the exact truth; they go back to the Bible for instruction: Neander, Müller, Tholuck, Moll, Herzog are of this class. (3) The Rationalists who hold that all religion is but the development of reason —that the Apostles and Christ thought themselves inspired, but mistook their own thoughts for inspiration. (4) The Pantheistic or Progressive Rationalists . . . To the 3d belongs the University of Giessen . . .

Tholuck's own idea of reason in relation to faith is—that the reason of the unregenerate is an unsafe and blind guide and that the heart must be regenerated that one may be led to a full knowledge of the truth . . .

[Walked with] a bright, intelligent youth . . . who asked me . . . if the Americans are not heathens—or how many heathens there are in Massachusetts . . .

July 4, [Discussed]—Is Samuel I fragmentary? Dined with the Fräulein and some friends from the country—good time—began a letter to sister.

July 8, Yesterday went to Leipzic . . . Called on Dr. Fluegel . . . Showed me his dictionary, which is in the course of preparation.

[With another student] walked with Professor Hupfeld. Walked several miles and stopped at a garden where the Prof. treated us to beer and cigars. We asked him about his view of the inspiration of the Old Testament. He said that he objected to the term *inspiration* as mechanical. The whole nation were elevated by Providence and led to the possession of great religious ideas . . . They are not infallible and are sometimes inconsistent . . .

July 14, Tholuck spoke of his unwillingness to remain during the evening at Giebenstein, saying 'A learned man who has a book to write before he dies cannot lose minutes.' . . . *'Leben Sie recht wohl, mein lieber Herr Fisher.'*

July 15, Last evening drank tea at Professor Leo's. Pleasant garden. Prof's remark—'We will speak *Lateinische* . . .'

July 25, Last evening . . . Mrs. Tholuck had *Uncle Tom's Cabin* in her hand . . . She read it until after dark, and although the Prof. scolded that she was so long engaged upon it, for fear it would hurt her eyes, she heard him and then read on . . .

July 29, Mueller, the other day in his lectures on Ethics condemned the American Temperance laws as likely to lead to a reaction . . .

August 4, Monday I called upon Ulrici . . . He says that Hegelianism is fast going down in Germany . . . Also that the interest in philosophical studies is declining . . . Thought it not improbable that Philosophy might emigrate to America.

August 18, 1852. Today I returned from Dresden . . . Was saddened to learn of the death of Fräulein. She was somewhat unwell when I left, but able to come out of her room and bid me adieu; but, alas, how little did I think it was the *last* adieu in this world . . . God only knows when I shall be called . . . I also received . . . the cheering intelligence that my mother and sister are well. May God keep them and love them! And may he keep me, not only in life, but in purity of heart and holiness of walk and conversation. May I be like Jesus, and through his Grace, be humble, prayerful, sober-minded, industrious, reverent and anxious to do good, and finally may I be prepared for the rest which remains for those who love our Lord!

August 21, Anecdote of Schleiermacher—Some one spoke to him of the great audiences of literati, ladies and officers, etc. which listened to his sermons—yes, he said . . . "The students come to hear the sermon—the ladies to see the students—and the officers to see the ladies."

August 25, I called on Dr. Robinson. [He thought] Tholuck had passed his day. Miss R. is intellectual and agreeable, but *very* plain. The mother is plain enough also, in the face, but *good* ...

October 10, Afternoon with Leo ... He said the American people are not *ruhig* enough for a *wissenschaftlich* life.

October 11, Fabyan called. He wished to ask me what "a Revival of Religion" is! He had ... an American newspaper giving an account of the Revival in Brown University in 1846—1847! ...

November 24, Went to Leipzig to have a tooth extracted ... Dr. Weissenborn—his German friendliness is very flattering. He says "I shall learn the English ... merely and solely to read your essays which may appear in *The Bibliotheca Sacra* ..."

December 4, Weissenborn ... asked me if I wanted to take back a German wife. "Oh yes"—he spoke of several of his acquaintances, of one who is determined never to marry, unless she marries an Englishman or an American, but she has a stiff *Bein!* alas!—then another who is the best among all his acquaintances who are *"heiraths-lustig"*—at this expression ... his wife remonstrated. He described the lameness in Latin.

December 6, 1852, Yesterday, Sunday, heard Ahrendts in the N. W. *Kirche* ... Spoke of the heathenism of the last cetnury and of some Christians who still cling to Goethe and Schiller ...

December 8, Long walk with Tholuck. He was especially talkative and agreeable—began by asking what was the most difficult Christian virtue to practise, which he thought to be *Demuth*, humility ... Spoke of Schleiermacher—of his commanding person, of his eyes—"before which one would fear"—of his habit of *"ausspannung"* (unbending) himself in society and talking of general subjects; would turn to a Piano in a little party and play a march, and one would sometimes see tears in his eyes. He mentioned Strauss' remark on Schleiermacher—"he pulverized Spinozism and Christianity so finely and mixed them so closely, that it requires a sharp eye to distinguish them." Tholuck then spoke with admiration of Schleiermacher's studying of Jesus Christ and his doctrine, with his family—The impression of Schleiermacher on him was different than that of Hegel. Hegel was clumsy in appearance, speech, walk and manner—But he had, nevertheless, a sort of religious feeling—the feeling that he was the organ of the *Weltgeist* ... He was always pleased to hear the Gospel preached ... When Tholuck was called from Berlin to Halle, he passed an evening with Hegel, just before he was to leave—Hegel touched glasses with him and said, *"Pereat das hallische Rationalismus"* —Hegel encouraged his wife to go to Pastor Gessner with her children, etc. She once asked him to pray in his family. "My prayer," he replied, "is Logic." ... Göthe, says Tholuck, was a man of the world. Faust contains deep truth—but Shakespeare is a hundredfold greater than Göthe ... Tholuck said there is a revival in Brunswick, one of the two chief seats of Rationalism. Weimar is the other ...

December 12, Friday evening, I spent with Professor Müller ... We talked of the Catholic Church—which ... is now very active in Germany, and constitutes our greatest danger for the future—of the question whether the Catholic Church discourages or fosters Revolutions—He inquired as to our sects in Massachusetts—said that Hase, who denied the *Gottheit des Christus* were hardly *christlich* ... I told them of the Women's Rights Convention—at which they were much amused.

December 17, I spoke with young Licentiat Müller on Christmas ... The Germans generally felt the utmost astonishment that we have no Christian year and no Christmas in our church ...

January 3, 1853 ... I called on Rödiger ... Spoke of the gratification which he once had in celebrating Christmas Eve with guests, when his *Selige Frau* was alive—how once their tree was surmounted with the stars of the American banner—his description of their mode of celebrating Christmas—sending packages one after another into the room, with verses or some joke on the envelope ...

January 5, On Monday, I called on Müller ... Strauss now lives in Weimar, has given up Theology and will write a life of Göthe. Schleiermacher's *Glaubenslehre*, said the Professor, is the most important of the new books in the *Dogmatik* ...

January 9 ... had a walk with Tholuck. He spoke of ... Chalmer's enthusiasm and of his expressing a determination to read Strauss, as Tholuck assured him that Strauss' book contained new historical material on Christianity. "I will get it tomorrow," said Chalmers ... We spoke of prison discipline. Elizabeth Fry did not please him ... She paid too much attention to the nobility and royal family—meeting in Berlin. Her wish to appoint a Quaker meeting for the next day. Tholuck's refusal to give the notice—he felt that it did not become a *Consistorialrat* to give such a notice for a Quaker meeting ... With respect to Scotland ... it is no use —Scotland will not change—will have everything as it was in the days of John Knox ... Tholuck's speaking of travelling in Switzerland. He would gladly spend his old age there. But there would be a difficulty in carrying his library over the mountains ...

I had a talk with Stämer on Baur and his school. The students in Tübingen do not generally follow Baur ...

February 1, Weissenborn told me much of Gesenius. Tholuck was, when younger, much more of a Pietist than afterward, and he and Gesenius were cool toward each other. At last, however, they were not unfriendly ...

February 21, Walked with Tholuck ... Spoke of mystics and mysticism; of the want of it in America—of the Americans' curiosity to see great men ...

March 29, I had a talk with Madame Müller, her husband and family ... I told them of the cost of travelling to America. "Herr Gott"— "Herr Jesu!"

March 31, Called on Tholuck ... He wrote my note of introduction which is a very warm commendation. Then he says, "Do not let your *deutsches Wissen* make you *hochmütig*... with *inniger Liebe, ich scheide von ihnen und wünsche ihnen,* etc. etc. Then called upon Mrs. Tholuck, her beautiful manners. I told her that I should tell my mother how kind she had been to me, etc. Goodbye!"[6]

These Yale men, on their return to Germany, formed, together with some students who had acquired the language from reading, a club with the imposing title *Kaiserthum von Hohenzollern-Etwas.* The association was apparently a pure diversion. The members were decorated with pretentious titles poking genial fun alike at their German teachers and at themselves. Here is the title of George Park Fisher. (The inclusion of Wrentham is a reference to his birthplace, a town of that name in Massachusetts) : Seine Durchleuchtigste Kaiserliche Königliche Apostolische Resplendent-Majestät, Georgius Parkus der 57ste, Kaiser von Hohenzollern-Etwas; König von Anhalt-Nichts, von Mühlhäuser, von Nachweisung; Erzherzog von Wrentham; Fürst von Tapferkeit; Unüberwindlicher Verteidiger der Freiheit des deutschen Bundes; und so weiter. Wohlgeboren. So! Ei! Was!!

A newspaper was conducted by the group in manuscript. One of the redactors was Timothy Dwight, later President of Yale, who had studied at Bonn and Berlin from 1856 to 1858. The paper included a summary of world events. Under Germany there is this entry for February 1, 1860.

In der heutigen Sitzung des Abgeordnetenhauses, in welcher das gesammte Staatsministerium anwesend war, machte der Minister der auswärtigen Angelegenheiten der zungendnacherische Winkeladvocat, Heinrich Taylor von Blake, folgende Mittheilung:

Meine Herren! In dem Augenblick, in welchem die hohenzollern-etwas'eshe Landesvertretung sich versammelt, um ihre Arbeiten, nach kurzer Unterbrechung, wieder aufzunehmen, gehen in der Ferne verhängnisvolle Ereignisse vor sich. Der Kaiser Napoleon von Frankreich hat einen eigenhändig geschriebenen Brief an den Papst geschickt, worin er sagt dass *etwas* ein "fait accompli" ist. Was für ein Etwas dieses Etwas sein kann ist uns bis jetzt unbekannt, weil die Telegraphischen-Depeschen aus Rom vom ersten Februar noch nicht angekommen sind.

[6] Manuscript, Divinity School Library, Yale University.

Under the United States there is this entry. The reference is to the Reverend Joel Hawes of the Congregational Church in Hartford, Connecticut.

Am letzten Sonntag hielt der vortreffliche Prediger, Herr Dr. Joel Hawes, eine Rede über das Tabakwesen in Neuhafen [New Haven], einer kleinen Stadt in Connecticut, welchs ungefähr 15 deutsche Meilen von New York liegt. Derselbe glaubt dass die Menschen gar keinen Tabak brauchen sollten, und seine Gründe sind vier: erstens, das Tabakrauchen u.sw. ist denjenigen Personen, welche es nicht lieb haben, unangenehm, zweitens, es kostet viel Geld,—drittens, ein gewisser Herr Theophilus Parsons, aus Boston, Massachusetts, starb in seiner Jugendblüthe, d. h. als er nur drei und sechzig Jahre alt war—bloss desswegen weil er drei hundert Cigarren am Anfang eines Monats und keine einzige am Ende desselben Monats in seinem Koffer hatte,—und viertens, der Doctor selbst bemerkte, als er 1844 in Constantinopel war, dass die Turken die Gewohnheit viel zu rauchen aber nicht viel zu denken hatten. Es thut mir wirklich leid—denn der Doctor ist auch bei Ihnen in Hohenzollern-Etwas sehr wohl bekannt—Ihnen folgendes sagen zu müssen. Am Ende seiner Vorlesung oder nach derselben deutete der Doctor an, dass er sehr wahrscheinlich nur kurze Zeit noch zu leben hätte. Diess aber hat er schon einmal in Hartford gesagt und wir hoffen desshalb, er wird so lange im Leben bleiben dass er es noch einmal in Neuhafen sagen kann.

The concluding notice under the United States is this: "Neu York 1. Jan. [1861] Nachmittags. Die Vereinigten-Staaten hangen noch zusammen und bleiben gesund."[7]

The Civil War and the disruption of the Union were to occur on the 12th of April.

Despite all this persiflage these Americans were devoting their lives to the cultivation and dissemination of that scholarship which they had acquired in Germany. Noah Porter translated Kuno Fischer's *History of Modern Philosophy* (1887) and made additions to the translation of Ueberweg's *History of Philosophy* (1892). It is interesting also that Porter's own epistemology was the subject of a German dissertation by W. B. Judd, *Noah Porter's Erkenntnislehre* (Jena, 1897). George Edward Day revised the translation of Gustav Friedrich Oehler, *Theology of the Old Testament* (1883) and translated J. J. van Oosterzee, *The Epistle*

---

[7] Manuscript, Memorabilia Room, Sterling Library, Yale University.

of Paul to Titus, from the German (1869). Timothy Dwight wrote prefaces and supplementary notes to several volumes of Heinrich A. W. Meyer's Biblical commentaries, and George Park Fisher, if he did not translate, yet devoted his entire career to the exemplification of that *deutsches Wissen* which Tholuck hoped would not make him too *hochmütig.*

What these American students carried away from their years in Germany is nostalgically described by Newman Smyth, pastor of Center Church in New Haven and for many years member of the Yale Corporation. He wrote,

> The memory of Tholuck... is like a benediction. He was one of the most learned, acutely critical, comprehensively informed, and at the same time the simplest and most spiritual of the evangelical teachers and preachers in Germany. To those students who came under his personal influence he gave himself freely, fully, with a childlike simplicity in his impartation of his learning such as I have hardly known in any one else. In his preaching he was the simple evangelist, but his was the simplicity of wisdom, and when he preached the students flocked to hear him. In his personal conversations with students whom he took under his special guidance, he was the keen questioner and a most stimulating conversationalist. He would be sure to send one back to his studies with a fresh eagerness in the pursuit of truth. And his humility was deep as his faith was high and his knowledge comprehensive. It was a favorite habit of his to ask some student to take his customary walk with him, and suddenly, in the midst perhaps of ordinary conversation, to surprise him with some difficult philosophical or other question. Afterward the student could guess at the professor's estimate of his reply by whether or not he soon received another invitation to walk with him. I think that this was perhaps a deliberate method of his in picking out men to whom he might devote himself, and whom he might train for the future work of evangelical thought and life for Germany. There were many anecdotes of such questionings in these walks with Tholuck. Once, I was told, he suddenly stopped, as was his wont, and threw this question out at the student walking with him: "Why did not the Almighty strike the devil dead?" The youth immediately replied: "Because, I suppose, he wanted to see how the creature would develop."
>
> Tholuck took always a special interest in the American students who came to Halle... A Christmas eve in his study, where he had gathered the little company of us American students, remains to this day one of the happiest recollections of a lifetime. Never before or since have I so felt the simplicity of true wisdom. He spoke so simply that a little

child might have understood every word he said, and yet we knew and felt that behind it all was the knowledge of a great scholar. And the unconscious humility of it! He was talking to us students, and yet he spoke as a little child. So I think Jesus must often have taught his disciples. Tholuck said to us then: "I have but one passion; it is Christ, only Christ!" He gave to each of us some simple Christmas gift, and then sent us away with his blessing.[8]

[8] *Recollections and Reflections* (New York, 1926), pp. 89-90.

19. The Office of the Minister's Wife in New England

The Dudleian lectureship at Harvard was instituted for discussions of the validity of non-episcopal ordination. My two predecessors in the Titus Street professorship at Yale lectured on this foundation and spoke to the point. George Park Fisher in 1888 took as his theme, "The Validity of Non-Episcopal Ordination." Bishop Phillips Brooks jocularly expressed the hope that the lecture would avert episcopal leanings at Harvard.[1] In 1897 the lecture was given by Williston Walker on the history of the theme.[2] By the time I was invited the subject had been so reduced to pulp that latitude was permitted to take a topic which in the days of old New England might have been phrased as: "A seasonable Discourse on the non-episcopally, non-ordained Office of the Minister's Wife in New England." Until very recent times she has not been ordained, but certainly she has exercised an office in the Christian community. Dean Brown of the Yale Divinity School used to say that the minister's wife could not make her husband, but she could unmake him.[3] He was certainly right, on the second score and equally on the first if there were nothing to work on. But given something at the outset, she is able also to make him. The minister's wife must be discreet, guarding those secrets which are committed to her and not inquisitive as to those which are kept back. She must be measured in her friendships, outgoing toward all, but not so intimate with any as to provoke jealousy. Though not

This paper was delivered as the Dudleian Lecture at Harvard University for the academic year 1954-1955. It was given in the Andover Chapel on April 26, 1955, and was reprinted in the *Harvard Divinity School Bulletin*, XXI (November 5, 1956).

[1] *Yale Divinity Quarterly*, I, 4 (March, 1905), 114.

[2] *Validity of Congregational Ordination* (Hartford, 1898).

[3] Charles Reynolds Brown, "The Minister's Wife," *The Making of a Minister* (New York, 1927), Ch. 12.

engaged by the church, she is expected to be active in the woman's work, the Sunday school or the choir. Frequently she is a mother, and her household is under scrutiny. The parish eye will regard her dress. If it be too plain, she will be called slovenly; if too elegant, then extravagant. She is to support her husband under unwarranted attack, to encourage him when depressed, chasten him when inflated, and counsel him wisely in sundry affairs. If the specifications for the minister commonly exceed flesh and blood, no less is this true for the minister's wife.

The examples which I have to offer from New England history range over the eighteenth and the nineteenth centuries. They are not the result of systematic pursuit but have come to attention in the course of other studies. How far some of the instances may be representative, I am not in a position to say, but at any rate they give a vivid picture of the varied, arduous and staunch labors of a number of ministers' wives.

To begin with she was a wife and commonly a mother. In the Colonial period, like other women, she bore numerous children and lost many. The wife of David Hall (Harvard, 1724)' for example, when asked whether the babe in her arms was the first, replied, "Yes, the first of the second dozen."[4] Often the mother succumbed early, and there were more ministers' wives than ministers in New England. A single instance will serve to illustrate this theme. It is the case of Mary, the wife of Thomas Clap, pastor at Windham, Connecticut, and then President of Yale. On the death of his wife he published a tribute from which he omitted the more intimate portions subsequently discovered in manuscript and edited. From this fuller version here are a few excerpts:

> Sometime After I Had Concluded to Settel att Windham... I thought I Wanted one Near friend and Companion.... And among all ye Qualifications of an agreable Consort, I Seemed more Especially to Have In view these two: a Steady Serene Natural temper, and true Piety. ... god In His providence Seemed Already to Have made and Provided one In ye House Where I Was... [Mary Whiting, daughter of his predecessor. Clap married her on the day before her fifteenth birthday.] She was a woman of Such great Prudence and Discretion in ye Conduct of Her Self and Affairs, that She Was Scarce ever taxed with taking a wry

⁴ *Sibley's Harvard Graduates,* VII (1954) , 345.

Step. She was Diligent neat and Saving, and always endeavoured to make ye Best of what She had.... She Endeavoured to treat Her friends and Al that Came in as Handsome and Decent tho not Costly a mannar, as She Could: and was very Kind and Compasionate to ye Poor and all In Distress. She was Adorned with great Humility & meekness, and Never Affected anything above Her Degree, or to Apear fine or gay, but Rather Like the Holy women of old who Trusted in god She Put on ye ornament of a meek and quiet Spirit which is in ye Sight of god a Pearl of great Price.... I Lived In ye House with Her near Eleven years, and She was my wife Almost nine: And Never once Saw Her in any unpleasant temper....

And If it Hapened att any time that we Seemed Not Altogether to Agree in our opinion or Inclination About any Lesser matter we used to Discourse upon it, with A Perfect Calmness & Pleasancy.... And If att any time She Had any Just and necessary occasion to Correct Her Children or Servants She would do it with a Proper and moderate Smartness So as Effectually to Answer yet without the Least Passion or Ruffle of mind.... She was a Faithful friend and monitor to Her Husband and if at anytime She thot I was Overseer in anything She Never upbraided me with it, but ye most Proper and Convenient Seasons....

She Never once omitted her Private Retirement morning and Evening... and she would oftentimes, and Especially under Difficulty Such as Sickness Death of Children, before Her Lyings in and the Like, Desire we to go into my Study with her to pray With Her alone.... I Had a great Dependence on the Prevalency of Her Prayers at ye throne of grace....

She would Sometimes Say to me that Bearing tending and Burying Children, was Hard work, and that She Had Done a great Deal of it for one of Her age (She Had 6 Children whereof she buried 4 and Dyed in ye 24 year of Her age.) yet would Say it was the work She was made for, and what god in His providence Had Called Her to And She Could freely Do it all for him, and that she Should Recon Her Self Well Paid for al Her trouble If She Could be Instrumental of adding Souls to the Kingdom of god.

Though she had been in excellent health during the first seven years of her married life, in the eighth she contracted consumption, which in the following year took its toll following another childbirth. She thanked her husband for his tender love and trusted that after a short separation they would be "Infinitely more Happy together than tis Possible for us to be Here In this world."[5]

[5] "Memoirs of a College President: Womanhood in Early America," ed. Edwin Stanley Welles, *Connecticut Magazine*, XII (1908), 233-239.

The minister's wife was the mistress of a household. This included, of course, her own children, and if she were the second wife there would be also her husband's by the first. Lydia Potwine, for example, the wife of the minister at East Windsor, Connecticut, throughout the second half of the eighteenth century had a household of eleven children of whom eight were her own. In addition there were the laborers and the guests. Sometimes the parsonage was a veritable hostel. Harriet Beecher Stowe observed that in the olden days one could travel all across New England on free hospitality. The parsonage was the most obvious stopping place.

The burden was not inconsiderable for the successor of Mrs. Potwine at East Windsor in the early years of the nineteenth century. She was Fanny Leffingwell, the wife of the Reverend Shabael Bartlett and the daughter of a man of substance in Hartford, who desired to set her up with the elegance on which she had been reared, but she requested him to divide the sum he had in mind, half to go for modest furniture and the other for an adequate dwelling. In 1804 the couple moved into this residence which for fifty years was to be a parish center. They filled it with nine children of their own, and more than once, as the pastor's diary reveals, there were as many as eighteen or twenty overnight guests. If any came in straits, the minister's wife tactfully drew out their tales and sent them away uplifted in spirit and outfitted in body. No wonder that two of the rooms had to wait twenty-two years for lath and plaster.[6]

Funeral sermons would indicate that ordinarily the minister's wife received her due meed of appreciation, but not always. The Rev. Nathan Perkins of Connecticut in 1789 made a tour of Vermont. In his diary he did indeed praise the women of the wilderness who, despite hardship, were serene, contented and loving their husbands. "I asked myself are these women ye same species with our fine Ladies?" But his comments on hospitality were scarcely gracious.

[6] Franklin Bowditch Dexter, *Biographical Sketches,* Vol. II (New York, 1896) on Thomas Potwine and Vol. V (New York, 1901) on Shabael Bartlett. There is a sketch of the latter also in Azel Stevens Roe, *History of the First Ecclesiastical Society in East Windsor* (Hartford, 1857).

came to Rev^d Mr. Badger's, of Blanford. He absent—his wife old-poor-homely-kind. four years older than her husband, & courted him—helped to defray ye expenses of his Education by her own industry. A very poor dinner—bad bread—no sauce—no elegance or good Cookery....reached Pitsfield about Sunset. Put up at Mr. Allyn's, ye presbyterian Minister, of ye town. Introduced myself to him. He is a sociable man,—awkward in his manner,—a handsome woman for his wife,—an infant at ye breast, ye 11 Child, all living. Poor Cookery,—no elegance,—common fare,—bad house-keeping.

At any rate the trip made Nathan Perkins more appreciative of his own home and wife.

O how happy! happy am I at home. I will study to be more contented,—more serene,—more thankful....My wife is not out of my thoughts one half hour.... Every step my horse takes brings me nearer home, & every moment nearer Eternity.[7]

The wife of the minister had thus not only a responsibility for the wayfarer but also for the divinity student who desired to settle perhaps for several years under the tutelage of her husband. In the eighteenth century there were no divinity schools, and after college the theological aspirant served an apprenticeship with the minister of his own choosing. The good man does not appear to have been consulted. The candidate reined up at the door of the parsonage and was taken in. So it was when Samuel Hopkins arrived at Northampton, in his own words, "an utter stranger with a view to live with Mr. Edwards."

When I arrived there, Mr. Edwards was not at home; but I was received
wife received her due meed of appreciation, but not always. The
ment that I might live there during the winter.... I was very gloomy, and
was most of the time retired in my chamber. After some days, Mrs. Edwards came into my chamber, and said, As I was now become a member of the family for a season, she felt herself interested in my welfare; and, as she observed that I appeared gloomy and dejected she hoped I would not think she intruded, by her desiring to know, and asking me what was the occasion of it, or to that purpose. I told her the freedom she used was agreeable to me....I was in a christless, graceless state....Upon which we entered into a free conversation; ... she told me that she had peculiar

[7] Nathan Perkins, *A Narrative of a Tour through the State of Vermont from April 27 to June 12, 1789* (Woodstock, Vermont, 1920).

exercises in prayer respecting me, . . . that she trusted I should receive light and comfort, and doubted not that God intended yet to do great things by me.[8]

If now one compare the characteristic notes of Hopkins' later theology, his emphasis on the divine benevolence and man's duty of utter submission, with Mrs. Edwards' rhapsodies over God's exceeding goodness and her readiness so to efface herself that she would be willing to follow the Negro slaves into heaven, one wonders whether in this instance the minister's wife did not exert a greater influence upon the student than did her husband.

The wife of the Rev. Cotton Mather Smith of Sharon, Connecticut, has given us a lively picture of her trials in looking after a household including divinity students at the time of her husband's service as chaplain in 1775 at Fort Ticonderoga.

In common with many other well qualified Pastors my Husband had been in the habit of receiving into his family from time to time such young men as might wish, after leaving college, to fit themselves for the Gospel Ministry. At this time there were five such students in our house. My Husband provided for them by engaging his beloved friend, the Rev. Dr. Bellamy, of Bethlehem, to come and reside in our house, prosecute the education of the young theological students, supply the Sharon pulpit and attend to pastoral duties; a young friend of Dr. Bellamy engaging to perform like brotherly services for him in his parish. As Dr. Bellamy had two students of his own he brought them with him, which added to those already in our house made my family to consist of twenty-two persons besides servants.

In our present state of peace and plenty [1795] this does not seem so very great a burden; but at that time when the exactions of the Mother Country had rendered it impossible for any but the wealthiest to import anything to eat or wear, and all had to be raised and manufactured at home, from bread stuffs, sugar and rum to the linen and woollen for our clothes and bedding, you may well imagine that my duties were not light, though I can say for myself that I never complained even in my inmost thoughts. . . .And besides, to tell the truth I had no leisure for murmuring. I rose with the sun and all through the long day I had no time for aught but my work. So much did it press upon me that I could scarcely divert my thoughts from its demands even during the family prayers, which thing both amazed and displeased me, for during that hour, at least, I

---

[8] Serano E., Dwight, *The Life of President Edwards* (New York, 1830), p. 159.

should have been sending all my thoughts to Heaven for the safety of my beloved Husband and the salvation of our hapless Country; instead of which I was often wondering whether Polly had remembered to set the sponge for the bread. . .or Billy had chopped light-wood enough for the kindling, or dry hard wood enough to heat the big oven.

Mr. Bellamy on the Sabbath drew tears from those unused to weeping as he spoke of God's fatherly providence, and Mrs. Cotton Mather Smith went to bed more calm, for she had been no little disturbed by reason of Polly's mismanagement which would necessitate baking instead of washing on the following Monday. Mrs. Smith was up at three. By five the bread was ready to be molded, "and the hickery coals were lying in a great glowing mass on the oven bottom, casting a brilliant light over its vaulted top," reminding her of "Nebuchadnezzar's fiery furnace, seven times heated."⁹

The minister's wife was sometimes partner to her husband in intellectual pursuits and literary labors. In fact, a few items gleaned from a century and a half lead one to wonder whether even in the eighteenth century some of the women may not have already been the upholders of cultural interests for which their husbands were too occupied. That was not true apparently in the middle of the eighteenth century, for in 1775 Esther Burr, the daughter of Jonathan Edwards and wife of Aaron Burr, President of Princeton, records in her diary, "We have a French master in the house with us. He is learning the scholar's French. Mr. Burr has a mind I should learn, but I have no time. The married woman has something more to care about than learning French, though if I had time, I should be very fond of learning."¹⁰ By the end of the century the situation appears to have altered. At any rate, Mrs. Cotton Mather Smith was able to serve as an interpreter in French during the Revolution. The women of the Beechers early in the next century were highly instructed, and Lyman, the blacksmith's son, must have appeared uncouth in comparison with his fiancée, Roxana Foote, versed as she was in literature and the natural

⁹ Helen Evertson Smith, *Colonial Days and Ways* (New York, 1901) , pp. 226-229.

¹⁰ Manuscript, Yale University Library, p. 110.

sciences.[11] In the 1840's the wife of Charles Torrey, about to be mentioned, was able to instruct her children in French.

Whether these stray items do or do not warrant any general conclusions, there is abundant evidence that the minister's wife, sometimes along with her husband, engaged in literary labors. Chance has brought into my hand a manuscript letter of Mary, the wife of Elias Cornelius, dated from Andover on the 26 of February, 1827. Her husband had been an assitant to Lyman Beecher at Litchfield, Connecticut, then an agent of the American Board to raise funds for the Indians in the Southwest. In 1819 he became pastor of the church at Salem. In 1826 he was secretary of the American Education Society with residence at Andover, later Boston. He edited the *American Quarterly Register*. His wife wrote one number for the American Tract Society. One may judge from her letter and the list of the society's publications that it was volume I, number 27, on *Parental Duties*. In writing to her husband she is gravely disturbed lest having given counsel to others she should herself be found remiss. She is indeed so deficient that she fears the children may be "permanent sufferers" by reason of their father's frequent absences. She continues,

Since the announcement of my tract, I have had sad forebodings that I should be in the view of the world, added to the long list of those who profess to teach others but do not practice themselves. And how should I wound religion, and neutralize my own endeavors to do good, were our children to be like those of many people quite as good as we are. Dr. Wood last night gave me some pastoral admonitions for which I felt grateful. His object was to guard me from self-approbation on account of my success. . . . In what way could I be so appropriately humbled as in the misconduct of my children. The occasion for vigilance, and for prayer is certainly far greater than ever before. With respect to the publication of my name, you know that I explicitly objected . . . my opinion is that it would have done more good had it been anonymous. . . . I feel sorry to excite anybody's envy or ill will but nothing could mortify me so truly as the prevalence of the idea which your amiable brethren suggested respecting your sermons [apparently that she had written them]. . . . Is it so, that in this free country, a lady may not do good as well as her husband without exposing herself to such shafts as these? If so, then American ladies may never emulate their benevolent and gifted sisters on the other side of

[11] Lyman Beecher, *Autobiography*, I (New York, 1864) , 137f.

the Atlantic. If this troubles you, I shall wish the tract were in the fire—but I will try to care nothing about it so far as I am concerned. I feel less and less complacency in the piece and wonder how it ever was accepted. I am gradually making improvements in it—but alas, I fear it will never embody wisdom enough to make poor parents good ones. Enough of this.[12]

As a sequel to this letter, be it noted that the Corneliuses had four sons and two daughters who did not mortify their parents. The father died in his thirty-eighth year, but the mother lived to be eighty-five, and she did write a little book on matters culinary, entitled *The Young Housekeeper's Friend* (Boston, 1858, an edition of 15 thousand; also editions in 1864 and 1871) [13]

Mary Cornelius was, of course, not the only minister's wife to engage in such pursuits. Mrs. Henry Ward Beecher also published on matters culinary and domestic, treating of topics ranging from the brewing of tea and coffee to the more subtle phases of domestic felicity. Anonymously she published a novel entitled *From Dawn to Daylight; or, the Simple Story of a Western Home, by a minister's wife* (New York: 1859). Here she faced the frustration of an intelligent woman whose life had been reduced to a primitive routine. This minister's wife had experienced

... an unusual amount of sickness and severe suffering ... and added to that a degree of physical labor far beyond her strength.... There had been many hours, ... when her youthful aspirations were brought vividly back to her mind; and the old longing for high intellectual attainments returned with giant strength. Then, contrasting her present life with her girlhood's plans and resolutions, her heart shrank back from the homely reality. To spend a lifetime in this wearisome, unchanging routine—caring only for bodily wants—to cook—to wash and mend—was that all woman was born for? Was a wife who could do *only* that, a meet companion for the husband in whom she gloried?[14]

Mrs. Beecher's answer was that the highest joy of such a wife should be to make of the hearth a resting place for her husband, "I am aware that the *strong minded* females of this progressive age will be exceedingly disgusted with such a sentiment." On the frontier,

[12] Manuscript in the Yale Divinity School Library.
[13] Elias Cornelius in *Yale Biographies*, VI (New York, 1912).
[14] Pages 292-293.

in the home missionary endeavor, the husband probably had little
more time than his wife for high intellectual attainment. Both
partners lived ruggedly. Asa Turner, called "the Father of Congregationalism in Iowa," had always been the sturdy sort. He put
himself through Yale, "rowing with a spade and playing ball with
a bucksaw."[15] He advised prospective home missionaries to ". . . get
wives of the old Puritan stamp, such as honored the distaff and the
loom, those who can pail a cow, and churn the butter and be proud
of a jean dress or a checked apron.[16] In proposing to Miss Martha
Bull he was certainly not modest in his specifications.

July 19, [1830]

Miss Bull, . . . I presume by this time you will have no doubt that I feel an
interest in you. This has been constantly increased by our acquaintance,
and I think we ought to take every opportunity to render our acquaintance more intimate.

What God designs by this providence we know not now. I was glad
to hear you say that you could submit to His will. . . . There are many
things which ought to be the subject of discussion between us. What are
the qualities requisite to a happy union? Affection, you will answer. But
on what must this affection rest, in order to be permanent? A suitable
knowledge of character and mutual esteem arising from this knowledge.
And of what is this the result? I wish you would give me your opinion in
full. Is similarity of taste, feeling, and mental culture essential? Is similarity of views on religious subjects necessary?

I gave you an abstract of my history. I told you I was a farmer, and
the son of a farmer. And in consequence of this there was a neglect of my
early education, a want of that refinement and ease of manners which
would make me acceptable to most young ladies of your advantages. But
I have so long been admitted to refined society that the change in my
feelings is greater than in my person. My advantages in this respect have
been very great, if I had been susceptible of improvement. I have some
ideal notion of what a gentleman *ought* to be, to be *worthy* of the affection
of such a lady as I wish for a companion. Now I want my wife to take me
just as I *am,* and make me what *I ought to be.* Do not shrink from the task!
I will be as tractable *as possible.* Another thing I wish her to do is to criti-
cize the matter and the manner of my sermons. Here there will be a wide
field for labor, and she will be obliged to prune off excrescences with an
unsparing hand. So much for style. I have quite a taste for metaphysics,

[15] George F. Magoun, *Asa Turner* (Boston, 1889) , p. 59.
[16] Colin Brummitt Goodykoontz. *Home Missions on the American Frontier* (Caldwell, Idaho, 1939) , p. 250.

but my powers are growing somewhat rusty for want of use, and I want my wife should bring them into exercise. I want she should be able to detect sophistry in every form—at least all *I* use! and agree to differ with me on some subjects. So, if perchance she should not be a theologian in the outset, I would do all I could to make her one, so that I might have the pleasure of disputation with my beloved wife. I should wish to have her form her own opinions on every subject, and never submit to me, except through the dire necessity of argument founded on truth. You may wonder, *Mary*, at the course I have marked out; but if not a good one, and the best one, you must *correct* me. I will have my mind open to conviction.

You will ask how are domestic duties to be performed? *Indeed, I don't know.* Perhaps it will be best not to have any domestic duties. But at any rate, I could clear off the table as well as Mr. B——, and perhaps set it better. For while I was in college I had a party at my room, and was both cook and master of the assembly. The company praised my johnny-cake and other articles of refreshment. So you perceive I could change with you sometimes.

Another thing: if I am ever rich, my wife must keep the purse strings. Now, although I shall wish her to obey me in all things, according to Scripture, yet I shall wish to have her do as she pleases in a great many. One thing, she must be given to hospitality. I have been into so many ministers' families that sometimes I have been sick of their wives. . . . But in some this picture is reversed, and the good lady renders every body happy who calls. And I wish every body to leave my house feeling that I have the best wife in the world. Again, after all I have said, I am very much afraid that I shall be *too selfish*. Therefore I shall wish my wife to keep an eye on me, and if I will not give according to my ability to benevolent objects, to ward off the reproach *by her own liberality*: that she may have an opportunity to do this, she may have every thing at her own disposal. Don't be discouraged at the task before you. I will not require "bricks without straw"—or stubble; and if I am not susceptible of improvement, I will not require it at your hand.

Yours sincerely,

A. T.

After they were settled at Quincy, Illinois, on December 9, 1830, Mrs. Turner wrote to her sister:

We have but one room for sitting-room, bedroom, study, kitchen, and dairy. We have in it our best bureau, two tables, three trunks, six chairs, two medicine-chests, two writingdesks, cupboard in one corner, and several other pieces of furniture, besides our bedstead. Husband says sometimes: 'Oh, dear! I wish I could get out of the kitchen.' I find that he is so well acquainted with domestic affairs that I am constantly calling upon him to tell me how to do this and that thing. He has, I suspect, become rather wearied, and now he says to every thing: "Do just as you please, my dear." However, we hope to have a room which he can use for a study by spring.

The thermometer yesterday stood at nine below zero. We can keep *nothing* from freezing. . . . We have plenty of wood which costs nothing but the drawing of it from the woods (as Mr. Turner cuts it himself), but still it is not the comfortable heat of Lehigh. I have a cow which gives a fine quantity of rich milk, . . . It is considerable trouble to take care of milk, particularly when frozen.

I do not intend to say much about myself: leave that to husband. We live mostly on wheat batter-cakes and corn dodgers; now and then I bake a 'pone,' or loaf of bread. . . . It requires some skill to make *good bread* out of *bad flour*.

I wish you could only see how comfortably we are situated; it would do you good. So different from what we expected. Our log cabin has proved to be a frame-house.

                                                                    M. T.

Her husband continues:

She makes very good batter-cakes, tea, coffee, and butter, and that is all we live on, except now and then a slice of bread. I can say this much in her praise—she is the best cook I have seen this side of the mountains, and I would not exchange my table with the "first livers" we have. She had made three and a half pounds of butter, a good "heap of pumpkin pies," and some "powerful good" cake. On the whole she is a very good wife, *worth all her transportation,* and I consider her a right smart woman. Our honeymoon still lasts, and I see no probability of failure—for we have "great chance" of bees here. We are blessed with most we need, a tolerable share of contentment, and, I hope, some small desires to do good. When I have time I will write in some other dialect. Till then be assured of my affection and gratitude.

                                                                    A. T.[17]

The minister's wife was called upon to share the anxieties and the trials by which her husband was beset in any battle for truth or right. Horace Bushnell was greatly disturbed as to the course he should pursue with regard to the publication of radical views. His health had suffered a reverse, and if in addition he were to imperil his position, would he be throwing an improper burden

[17] Magoun, *op. cit.,* pp. 67-69, 86-89.

on his wife and children? To his wife he wrote, mentioning first an address lately delivered at Andover:

I said something very cautiously in regard to the Trinity which, perhaps, will make a little breeze. If so, I shall not feel much upset. I have been thinking lately that I must write and publish the whole truth on these subjects as God has permitted me to see it. I have withheld till my views are well matured; and to withhold longer, I fear, is a want of that moral courage which animated Luther and every other man who has been a true soldier of Christ. Then, thinking of such men lately, I have often had self-reproaches which were very unpleasant. Has my dear wife any of Luther's spirit? Will she enter into the hazards and reproaches, and perhaps privations, which lie in this encounter for the truth! Strange, you will say, that I should be talking, in the same letter, of doing more for my family and of endangering all their wordly comforts. But I am under just these contending impulses. However, in what way shall I do more for my family than to connect their history with the truth of Christ? How more, for example, for our dear boy than to give him the name and example of a father who left him his fortunes, rough and hard as they were in the field of truth? But will not God take care of us? These are thoughts which have been urging me for the last few months, or since the shock that has befallen my health. And I have sometimes felt afraid that I should be obliged to leave the world before my work was done. Shall we go forward?[18]

As a matter of fact, Bushnell's church rallied to his support, and his wife was not called upon to endure the ordeal which he had foreseen.

The wife of Charles T. Torrey was not to be thus spared.[19] Her husband resigned his pastorate in Salem, Massachusetts, in 1844 in order to agitate in Washington for the emancipation of the slaves and in Baltimore to assist their escape. He succeeded in aiding nearly 400. Detected, he was condemned to six years of hard labor. His wife, the former Mary Ide, was left at home with two children named for their parents, Charles and Mary. The father intended to provide for their support by writing and by subsisting himself on the scantiest measure of food and fuel. The mother, too, was qualified to write but impeded by the children. The husband

[18] Mary Bushnell Cheyney, *Life and Letters of Horace Bushnell* (New York, 1880) , pp. 90-91.

[19] The following material is taken from J. C. Lovejoy, *Memoir of Rev. Charles Torrey* (Boston, 1847) .

was regretful that he had not been in a position to enable her to devote herself entirely to literary labors. His most severe trial in prison, not less than his rapidly advancing consumption, was the malicious rumor that his wife was seeking a divorce. The arrival of letters proved this insinuation to be utterly unfounded. Here are excerpts from the correspondence:

January 15, 1845

My Dear Husband . . . I hear that you have gone to the Penitentiary! And though I feel it still more even, than I thought I should, still, I would entreat you to be of good cheer. Your imprisonment may be the means of great good, and God grant that it may not be long!

In several of your letters you speak of not hearing from me; and I strongly suspect that my letter has not reached you. . . . But do not think I shall neglect you. I will write as often as I can be allowed to, and shall never cease to speak of you to the children, or remember you in my supplications at the throne of grace; we can meet there, notwithstanding the distance there is between us, and the thickness of the prison wall.

Remember that your health depends upon your spirits and unless you can keep them up, you will not be so likely to endure your captivity. Let then, the determination not to be sacrificed upon the altar of Slavery, keep up your spirits till the joyful day shall come, when the term for which you are imprisoned shall be at an end. *In God* you can do all things; then trust in Him to sustain you till the end. Write to me, if the Warden will permit you to do so, and as often as possible. But let me entreat you *again* in *patience* to *possess* your soul.

Your affectionate wife,
Mary I. Torrey

The next letter has a reference to their daughter:

Mary is not as well as usual to-night, but you need not be alarmed, for I think it will prove to be nothing but a severe cold. She seems to be rather feverish, but I have applied remedies that I think will be successful in relieving it. I wish sometimes that you could look into our room, and see Charles and Mary with your miniature. They take it and talk to it, carry it about, and really seem sometimes as though they thought you had returned. . . . I hope you will be enabled to bear your imprisonment with patience, and I pray God you *may do good while you are in prison.* Try to remember, when you are severely tried, and I presume that will of necessity be quite often, whose ambassador you are! God has, in his providence, called you *to represent* Him, in prison!—try to do it *faithfully!*

April 1, 1845

My dear husband, . . . [a senator] has written to father, that if you will say *to me, or father, that if you get out you will never go into those States* FOR THAT PURPOSE AGAIN, he thinks the most influential member of the senate will petition for your pardon. . . . Now if you will say that you will not go into those States again, for the purposes for which you are now imprisoned, then *you must write immediately and say so.* Now I think you can say that, but I have ever felt doubtful about making these concessions, which would imply any duplicity on your part. When you come out, I want to feel that it is an honorable acquittal; and as dearly as you love liberty, I do not believe you love it better than you do *integrity.* But what the senators wish you to say, is not inconsistent with integrity. . . .

Charles says, tell pa that he braids four yards of straw every day, and almost every day gets it done quick; that he loves you very much; that he went to a fire the other night, and helped put it out by throwing on sand; that he is a pretty good boy, but not very. Mary sends her love to pa, and says, tell him I wish the men would not keep you any longer, but let you come home quick; that she should be happy to come and see you, if she dared.

May 2, 1845

My dear husband, . . . I wrote you several weeks since, asking you to answer it immediately, and tell me if you would be willing to say to me, that you would not go into the States of Maryland and Virginia for the purpose of enticing or assisting slaves away from their masters, if you were liberated. You have not answered the question, and I do not know whether you have not received the letter, or whether you have not been permitted to write. . . .

I feel that my Christian course is so irregular and inconsistent, that I am not fit to bring up our dear children; and I sometimes, yes often, fear that God will think it necessary to remove me from them, if he has designs of mercy toward them.

I know you do not forget them; but let us pray *more* earnestly, not only for *their* conversion and sanctification, but *for our own.* Perhaps when we are more holy, God will again restore us to each other. He can incline the hearts of those who keep you imprisoned to release you. . . . Good night.

June, 1845.

My dearest husband, . . . This constrained correspondence is one of the greatest of my trials. I suppose my letters are a comfort to you, as poor and meagre as they are, because you are glad of any token of remembrance. It is *this thought* only that gives me pleasure when I write. But it is no relief to me. I cannot speak of my joys and sorrows; for my letter must pass through other hands than yours. I do not wish to complain, but I do feel tried....

Your answer to the question proposed by [the senator] is to *me* perfectly satisfactory. It seems to me, that if you had gone any farther, you would have sacrificed your integrity. If you had not said as much as you did, that you would have erred upon the other side. Whether ... the senators are satisfied with your answer, I have not yet learned....

It is very late at night. All in the house have been quietly sleeping for some time, and I must bid you good night. I fully believe that we shall not long thus be separated. Trust in God and he can dispose those who imprison you to release you.

The correspondence, of course, was not one-way. Here is a letter from Torrey to his Mary.

My dearest wife, ... It is now nearly or quite midnight and my poor rheumatic body aches so severely that I *cannot* write, either in prose or rhyme, such a note as I *fancied* I could write, to give with the only lock of hair I ever gave you, that I remember. It looks *so like* taking a memorial of a *departed* friend, or of one we never expect to see again.... Well, my dear Mary, to-day *may open* the way for our union again; or it may separate us for many, many years. If the latter, I trust we shall not *need* memorials, so frail as a lock of hair, to recall each to the other. Yet the hair is the most *enduring* portion of our bodily system. Long after the flesh and bones become small, impalpable dust, the hair, the "glory of the head," retains its color and strength. Nay, it even *grows,* while the rest of the body is decaying; thus seeming to possess an almost independent vitality of its own. So may it be with our affection, when "flesh shall fail" us, and our bodies decay and every memorial of them perish. So may it be with us when *"heart,"* too, shall fail us, and all our earthly relations cease. May God, then, be the strength of our heart, and our portion forever. If, in another world, those undying elements of our spiritual nature are controlled, as I doubt not they are, by the same principles that regulate all *holy* intercourse here, while we may have no *locks of hair,* for a bracelet, we shall not want many a sweet remembrance, in every word and deed of kindness, every mutual prayer, every act of service to our Lord, in which we engaged together; and above all, in the children He has given us to train up for Him. Whether He *frees* me, or not, to help you, may He bless you richly; and may you be a bracelet on His hands, in the day He shall appear "to be glorified *in his saints.*"

Your affectionate husband,
Charles T. Torrey.

Baltimore Penitentiary, Sept. 28, 1845.

My Dearest Wife, . . . I will try to add various things by way of remark on your letters. I thank you again, for every one of them. They have been balm to me, in some very dark hours. I was very happy to hear of your literary engagements. . . . You know it was no fool, but a competent judge, that declared you to be second to no female writer of our country, in *prose;* and, if you would fling your fears to the winds, your poetic powers would soon cause as high and as just praise. *Don't try so hard,* and your attainment of the highest celebrity and usefulness will be very easy. . . . Go on, and God bless you, and guide your pen and mind by His Holy Spirit. Attempt *all* the forms of easy graceful writing such as are common in our literary papers. You will soon learn what you can most *certainly* and rapidly succeed in.

Our dear children are daily in my heart, and on my lips, before God, the Father of the fatherless, and the Judge of the oppressed. Tell them, that when father is too weak to utter the whole of the Lord's Prayer, (as it has often been the case,) he never forgets to pray for them, "Lord, bless them, and make them holy." . . .

Mary answered:

We are all deeply afflicted at your trying state. When I am in such pain nights that I cannot sleep, I think of and pray for you. Do not think I never do it at any other time. Let one thought comfort and animate you. It is this: hundreds and thousands remember you in their prayers at their fireside and their meetings. That is a comfort which every one does not possess. In your afflictions they are afflicted. It is sweet to think we are remembered, but sweeter still, to know that multitudes are daily pleading for us, with that God, who has said, "the effectual fervent prayer of the righteous man availeth much." Mother says she means to write to you a letter of consolation, but I am almost afraid she will put so much—in it, that it will hardly be allowed. . . .

Unbeknownst to her daughter, Mother did write:

May our hearts unite in offering the memorable prayer of our Savior on the cross, for those who refuse to grant you the boon of a pardon—"Father, forgive them—they know not what they do." We all remember you with feelings of tenderest sympathy, and none more so than

Your affectionate mother,
Mary E. Ide.

P.S.   Your wife was in here to-day—your father thinks she looks quite feeble. She does not know I am writing you, or she would send her love. The children are well, and speak of father in terms that show he is not forgotten.

The news of Torrey's death reached the family through one who wrote from Baltimore on May 9, 1846: "His pardon has long been signed and sealed by the King of kings; and this afternoon at three o'clock, a messenger from the Court of Heaven came down and opened the prison doors, and set him free!"

A contemporary journal came out with the verse:

> My countrymen, weep not for him;
> He has passed to the home of the just;
> But gird you with sackcloth, and mourn for the land:
> O, weep, lest beneath the Avenger's strong hand,
> All your hopes sink in shame to the dust.

Torrey's friend, J. C. Lovejoy, wrote a memoir of his life published in 1847. The title page bears the note, "Copy-right secured to Mrs. Torrey." And she did write her book entitled *City and Country Life,* a novel seeking to demonstrate the dangers and responsibilities of inordinate wealth. The edition of 1853 indicated that this was the fourth thousand. Such a sale would scarcely have subjected her to the danger of which she warned.

The brief sketches of ministers' wives in New England surely go to prove that the minister's chief wealth is to be found in her whose price is above rubies.

Selected Bibliography of
Roland H. Bainton

1918 "The Ministry of Thought," *Yale Divinity Quarterly* XV (May 1918), pp. 1-5.

1922 "Church History and Progress," in *Education for Christian Service*, by Members of the Faculty of the Divinity School of Yale University (New Haven, Yale University Press, 1922), pp. 243-266.

1923 "Basilidian Chronology and New Testament Interpretation," in *Journal of Biblical Literature* XLII (1923), pp. 81-134.

1925 "What is Calvinism?" in *Christian Century* XLII (March 12, 1925), pp. 351-352.

1929 "The Development and Consistency of Luther's Attitude to Religious Liberty," in *Harvard Theological Review* XXII (1929), pp. 107-149.

1930 *Debtors to God*, Westminster Departmental Graded Materials. Teacher's Edition (Philadelphia, Westminster Press, 1930), 64 pages. Pupils' edition (Philadelphia, 1930).

"The Immoralities of the Patriarchs According to the Exegesis of the Late Middle Ages and of the Reformation," in *Harvard Theological Review* XXIII (1930), pp. 39-49.

1931 "Sebastian Castellio and the Toleration Controversy of the Sixteenth Century," in *Persecution and Liberty*, Essays in Honor of George Lincoln Burr (New York, Century, 1931), pp. 183-209.

"The Smaller Circulation: Servetus and Colombo," in *Sudhoffs, Archiv für Geschichte der Medizin* XXIV (1931), pp. 371-374.

"William Postell and the Netherlands," in *Nederlandsch Archief voor Kerkgeschiedenis* XXIX (1931), pp. 161-172.

1932 "Methods of Great Religious Teachers," in *International Journal of Religious Education* IX (1932), September, pp. 7-8; October, pp. 6-7; November, pp. 6-7; December, pp. 19-20.

"The Parable of the Tares as the Proof Text for Religious Liberty to the End of the Sixteenth Century," in *Church History* I (1932), pp. 57-89.

"The Present State of Servetus Studies," in *Journal of Modern History* IV (1932), pp. 72-92.

1935 "Academic Freedom in the Light of the Struggle for Religious Liberty," in *Proceedings of the Middle States Association of History Teachers* XXXIII (1935), pp. 37-44.

Bibliography of the Continental Reformation: Materials Available in English (Chicago, The American Society of Church History, 1935), 54 pages. (Monographs in Church History, No. 1.)

Concerning Heretics, by Sebastian Châteillon: Now First Done into English, by Ronald H. Bainton (New York: Columbia University Press, 1935), xiv, 342 pages. (Records of Civilization.)

1936	"Changing Ideas and Ideals in the Sixteenth Century," in *Journal of Modern History* VIII (1936), pp. 417-443.

"Servetus and the Genevan Libertines," in *Church History* V (1936), pp. 141-149.

1937	*David Joris, Wiedertäufer und Kämpfer für Toleranz im 16. Jahrhundert* (Leipzig: M. Heinsius Nachfolger, 1937), vi, 229 pages. (Archiv für Reformationsgeschichte. Texte und Untersuchungen. Ergänzungsband, VI.)

Ulrich von Hutten and the German Reformation, by Hajo Holborn, translated by Roland H. Bainton (New Haven: Yale University Press; London, H. Milford, Oxford University Press, 1937), viii, 214 pages. (Yale Historical Publications. Studies, XI.)

1938	"New Documents on Early Protestant Rationalism," in *Church History* VII (1938), pp. 179-187. Review of *Per la Storia Degli Eretici Italiani del Secolo XVI in Europa,* Testi Raccolti da D. Cantimori e E. Feist (1937).

"Refugees of Other Days," in *Bulletin of the Story Behind the Headlines* II (December 13, 1938), pp. 14-20.

"Servet et les Libertins de Genève," in *Bulletin Société de l'Histoire du Protestantisme Français* LXXXVII (1938), pp. 261-269.

"Straightforward Speech," in *Yale Divinity News* XXXIV (May 1938), pp. 1-3.

"Technology and Pacifism," in *Christian Century* LV (May 18, 1938), pp. 618-619.

"Unity, Utrecht and the Unitarians," in *Christian Century* LV (October 5, 1938), pp. 1189-1190.

1940	*Bernardino Ochino, Esule e Riformatore Senese del Cinquescesto,* 1487-1563, Versione dal Manoscritto Inglese di Elio Gianturco (Firenze: G. C. Sansoni, 1940), x. 213 pages. (Biblioteca Storica Sansoni, Nuova Serie IV.) "Christian Conscience and the State," with Robert L. Calhoun, in *Social Action* VI (October 15, 1940), pp. 4-42.

"Congregationalism: The Middle Way," in *Christendom* V (Summer 1940), pp. 345-354.

1941	*The Church of Our Fathers* (New York: Charles Scribner's Sons, 1941), vi, 248 pages. Also, an English edition; a special edition for Sunday Schools by the Westminster Press; translations into Spanish, Japanese, Siamese, Hebrew, Chinese and French.

"The Left Wing of the Reformation," in *Journal of Religion* XXI (April 1941), pp. 124-134.

"The Struggle for Religious Liberty," in *Church History* X (June 1941), pp. 95-124.

1942	"Christian Views of Human Destiny," in *Religion in Life* XI (Winter 1941-1942), pp. 96-105.

"A Communication for a More Explicit Declaration of Peace Aims," in *Christian Century* LIX (September 16, 1942), pp. 1122-1124.

"Individualism, Christian and American," in *Vital Speeches of the Day,* VIII, No. 19, pp. 590-592.

"Teaching Church History," in *Journal of Bible and Religion* X, 2 (1942), pp. 103-107.

1943	"Bossuet and Leibnitz and the Reunion of the Church," in *The Chronicle* (Protestant Episcopal); XLIII (February 1943), pp. 102-103.

"The Churches Shift on War," in *Religion in Life* XII (Summer 1943), pp. 1-13.

"Congregationalism: From the Just War to the Crusade in the Puritan Revolution," in *Andover Newton Theological School Bulletin* XXXV (April 1943), Southworth Lecture Number, pp. 1-20.

George Lincoln Burr: His Life, by Roland H. Bainton; Selections from His Writings, edited by Lois Oliphant Gibbons (Ithaca, N.Y., Cornell University Press; London, Oxford University Press, 1943), xi, 505 pages.

"Reconciliation and Reality," in *Fellowship* IX (December 1943), pp. 208-210.

1944   "The Christian and the War," in *Christian Century* LXI (May 3, 1944), pp. 559-561.

Pacifism Under Fire. *The Historic Church and Modern Pacifism,* by Umphrey Lee. Review by R. H. Bainton in *Fellowship* X (June 1944), pp. 113-114.

1945   "The Amistad," in *Highroad* (September 1945), pp. 4-6, 47.

"The Churches and Alcohol," in *Quarterly Journal of Studies on Alcohol,* VI (June 1945), pp. 45-58.

"The Churches and War: Historic Attitudes Toward Christian Participation," in *Social Action* XI (January 15, 1945), pp. 5-71.

"The Cohesive Power of Protestantism," in *The Intercollegian* LXII (January 1945), pp. 8-9.

1944, 45   *The Panorama of the Christian Church in Kodachrome Slides* (Boston, Pilgrim Press, 1944, 1945).

1946   "Early Christianity as a Youth Movement," in *Highroad* (February 1946), pp. 35-37.

"The Early Church and War," in *Harvard Theological Review* XXXIX (July 1946), pp. 189-212. Reprinted without notes in *The Church, the Gospel and War,* ed. Rufus Jones (New York, Harper, 1948), pp. 75-92.

"Our Debt to Luther," in *Christian Century* LXIII (October 23, 1946), pp. 1276-1278.

"Eyn Wunderliche Weyssagung, Osiander—Sachs—Luther," in *Germanic Review* XXI, 3 (October 1946), pp. 161-164.

1947   "Dürer and Luther as the Man of Sorrows," in *The Art Bulletin* XXIX (December 1947), pp. 269-272.

"Let's Agree on the Reformation," in *Christian Century,* LXIV (1947), pp. 237-239.

"*Road to Reformation,* by Heinrich Boehmer," in *Church History* XVI (September 1947), pp. 167-176. Book review.

1948   "The Churches and Alcohol," in *Social Progress* XXXIX (November 1948), pp. 13-15, 18-19. Reprinted.

"Luther's Struggle for Faith," in *Church History* XVII (September 1948), pp. 193-206. Printed by mistake in advance of its appearance in the *Festschrift für Gerhard Ritter* (Tübingen, 1950), pp. 232-243.

"Marriage and Love in Christian History," in *Religion in Life* XVII (Summer 1948), pp. 391-403.

The Martin Luther Christmas Book, with Celebrated Woodcuts by His Contemporaries; translated and arranged by Roland H. Bainton (Philadelphia, Westminster Press, 1948), 74 pages.

"Our Protestant Witness," in *The Pulpit*, XIX (December 1948), pp. 272-274.

1949   "Christianity and Russian Communism," in *Journal of the Industrial and Social Order Council of the Society of Friends* VI (March, April 1949), pp. 6-11.

"Christmas in 1949," in *American German Review* (December 1949), pp. 3-4. (Philadelphia, Carl Schurz Memorial Foundation, 1949.)

"Luther and the *Via Media* at the Marburg Colloquy," in *The Lutheran Quarterly* I (November 1949), pp. 394-398.

"The Puritan Theocracy and the Cambridge Platform," in *The Minister's Quarterly* V, 1 (February 1949), pp. 16-21. Also in: *The Cambridge Platform of 1648*, Tercentenary Commemoration (Boston, 1949), pp. 76-86.

"Sebastian Castellio and the British-American Tradition," in *Het Boek* XXX, 4 (1949-1951).

"Die Stellung der Quäker zu Krieg und Frieden," in *Der Quaeker*, Monatshefte der deutschen Freunde, 23. Jahrg. 1949 (January, February 1, 2), pp. 1-7.

"Without Despairing of the World, The Quaker Attitude Toward Peace and War," in *Friends Intelligencer* 106, 7 (Second Month 12, 1949), pp. 87-89.

1950   "The Genius of Protestantism," in *The Minister's Quarterly* VI (February 1950), pp. 13-18.

Here I Stand; a Life of Martin Luther (New York, Abingdon-Cokesbury Press, 1950), 422 pages. Paperback by Abingdon Press, Apex series; paperback, New American Library, Mentor series. Translations into German, Greek, Italian, Japanese, Spanish and Swedish. Portions of this book have been delivered as the Nathaniel Taylor Lectures at the Yale Divinity School (1946-1947), the Carew Lectures at the Hartford Seminary Foundation (1949), and the Hein Lectures at the Wartburg Seminary and Capital University.

1951   "Ernst Troeltsch—Thirty Years Later," in *Theology Today* VIII, 1 (April 1951), pp. 70-96.

"Michael Servetus and the Pulmonary Transit of the Blood," in *Bulletin of the History of Medicine* XXV, 1 (January-February 1951), pp. 1-7.

"The Querela Pacis of Erasmus, Classical and Christian Sources," in *Archiv für Reformationsgeschichte* XLII (1951), pp. 32-48.

"Sebastian Castellio, Champion of Religious Liberty, 1515-1563," in *Castellioniana: Quatre Études sur Sébastien Castellion et l'Idée de la Tolérance*, par Roland H. Bainton, Bruno Becker, Marius Valkhoff et Sape van der Woude (Leiden, E. J. Brill, 1951), pp. 25-79.

The Travail of Religious Liberty; Nine Biographical Studies (Philadelphia, Westminster Press, 1951), 272 pages. The James Sprunt Lectures (1950). Paperback. Harper Torchbook (discontinued). Translation into Italian.

1952   "Documenta Servetiana," in *Archiv für Reformationsgeschichte*, XLIV (1953), pp. 223-234; XLV (1954), pp. 99-108.

"Forschungsberichte und Besprechungen," in *Archiv für Reformationsgeschichte* XLIII (1952), pp. 88-106.

"Luther in a Capsule," in *Bulletin of the American Congregational Association* III (May 1952), pp. 1-9.

The Reformation of the Sixteenth Century (Boston, Beacon Press, 1952), xi, 276 pages. Also, Beacon paperback and translations into Italian and Hebrew.

1952-53   "Christianity and Sex, an Historical Survey," in *Pastoral Psychology* III, 26 (September 1952), pp. 10-26, 82; IV, 21 (February 1953), pp. 12-29. Reprinted in *Sex and Religion Today* (New York, Association Press, 1953), pp. 17-96.

1953   "The Beginnings of Anabaptism," in *Mennonite Life*, five articles commencing in 1953.

"Burned Heretic: Michael Servetus," in *Christian Century*, LXX (1953), pp. 1230-1231.

Hunted Heretic; the Life and Death of Michael Servetus, 1511-1553 (Boston, Beacon Press, 1953), xiv, 270 pages. Reprinted 1956, Beacon paperback; translated into German. For French see below.

"Man, God and the Church in the Age of the Renaissance" in *The Renaissance*, A Symposium (Metropolitan Museum of Art, 1953), pp. 41-62a; the whole reissued as a Harper Torchbook (1963). The article was reprinted in the *Journal of Religious Thought* XI (1953-1954), pp. 119-133.

"Michael Servetus and the Trinitarian Speculation of the Middle Ages," in *Autour de Michel Servet et de Sébastien Castellion; Recueil*, ed. Bruno Becker (Haarlem, H. D. Tjeenk Willink, 1953), pp. 29-46.

Michel Servet, Hérétique et Martyr, two editions within a few months (E. Droz, Geneva, 1953), the first with inadequate correction to be in time for the commemoration, the second with care as *Travaux d'Humanisme et Renaissance* VI, 148 pages.

They Built for Eternity, by Gustav-Adolf Gedat, translated by Roland H. Bainton (New York, Abingdon-Cokesbury Press, 1953), 175 pages.

"War and Christian Ethic," in *The Church and Social Responsibility*, ed. J. Richard Spann (New York, Abingdon-Cokesbury Press, 1953), pp. 201-219.

1954   *The Covenant in the Wilderness* (1954).

"Friends in Relation to the Churches," The Ward Lecture, Guilford College (November 12, 1954), 16 pages.

"Man, God, and the Church in the Age of the Renaissance," in *The Journal of Religious Thought* XI (Autumn-Winter, 1953-1954), pp. 119-133.

"Protestant-Catholic Relations in the U.S.," in *Advance* CXXXXVI (October 18, 1954), pp. 13-24.

"What About Catholic-Protestant Relations in the U.S.A.?" in *Messenger* XIX (October 1954), pp. 14-17.

1955   "Freedom, Truth, and Unity; Reflections on the Renaissance," in *Theology Today* XII (April 1959), pp. 85-96.

"Freedom's Religious Foundations," in *Christian Century* LXXVI (January 26, 1959), pp. 106-109.

"Patristic Christianity," in *The Idea of History in the Ancient Near East*, ed. Robert C. Dentan (New Haven, Yale University Press; London, Geoffrey Cumberlege, Oxford University Press, 1955), pp. 215-236.

"The School of Divinity," in *A Study of A Generation in Transition* (1955).

"This Grand Errand," in *Yale Alumni Magazine* (October 1955), pp. 22-23.

1956   *The Age of the Reformation* (Princeton, N.J., Van Nostrand, 1956), 192 pages. An Anvil Original paperback.

"The Ministry in the Middle Ages," in *The Ministry in Historical Perspectives,* ed. by H. Richard Niebuhr and Daniel D. Williams (New York, Harper, 1956), pp. 82-109.

"Religious Biography," in *Writing for the Religious Market,* ed. by Roland E. Wolseley (New York, Association Press, 1956), pp. 185-191.

"Yale and German Theology in the Middle of the 19th Century," in *Zeitschrift für Kirchengeschichte,* Bd. 65, Heft III.

1957   "The Anabaptist Contribution to History," in *The Recovery of the Anabaptist Vision,* ed. by Guy F. Hershberger (Scottdale, Pa., Herald Press, 1957), pp. 317-326.

"Luther's Simple Faith," in *Luther Today* (Decorah, Iowa, Luther College Press, 1957), pp. 1-33. (Martin Luther Lectures, 1.)

"The Universal Ministry of All Believers," in *Encounter* XVIII, 2 (1957), pp. 131-140.

What Christianity Says about Sex, Love and Marriage (New York, Association Press, 1957), 124 pages. (An Association Reflection Book.) English edition entitled *Sex, Love and Marriage* (Fontana Books, 1958).

Yale and the Ministry; a History of Education for the Christian Ministry at Yale from the Founding in 1701, Line drawings by the Author (New York, Harper, 1957), xiii, 297 pages.

Vignettes of Men Memorialized in the Buildings of the Yale Divinity School; with Drawings by the Author (1957), 11 pages. Condensed from *Yale and the Ministry.*

1958   "Christian Pacifism Reassessed," in *Christian Century* LXXV (July 23, 1958), pp. 847-849.

"The Making of a Pluralistic Society—A Protestant View," in *Religion and the State University,* ed. by E. A. Walter (Ann Arbor, University of Michigan Press, 1958), pp. 42-57.

Pilgrim Parson, the Life of James Herbert Bainton, 1867-1942 (New York, Nelson, 1958), 166 pages.

"Probleme der Lutherbiographie," in *Lutherforschung Heute,* Hrsg. von Vilmos Vajta (Berlin, Lutherisches Verlagshaus, 1958), pp. 24-31. Internationaler Kongress für Lutherforschung, Aarhus, 1956.

"Sex and Religion," in *Ladies Home Journal* LXXV (August 1958).

"Thomas Hooker and the Puritan Contribution to Democracy," in *Bulletin of the Congregational Library* X, 1 (October 1958).

"Total Abstinence," in *Christianity Today* II, No. 20 (July 7, 1958), pp. 3-6.

1960   "Alexander Campbell and Church Unity" (pp. 81-94) and "Alexander Campbell and the Social Order" (pp. 117-129), two articles in *The Sage of Bethany; a Pioneer in Broadcloth,* by Perry E. Gresham (St. Louis, Bethany Press, 1960).

"The Bible and the Reformation," in *Five Essays on the Bible* (New York, 1960), pp. 20-29. Paper read at 1960 annual meeting of the

American Council of Learned Societies Devoted to Humanistic Studies. *Christian Attitudes to War and Peace: an Historical Survey and Critical Re-evaluation* (New York, Abingdon Press, 1960) , 299 pages. Translations into Japanese and Spanish.

Constantine and Religious Liberty, by Hermann Dörries, translated by Roland H. Bainton (New Haven, Yale University Press, 1960) , 141 pages. (The Terry Lectures.)

Early Christianity (Princeton, N.J., Van Nostrand, 1960) , 192 pages. An Anvil Original paperback.

1961   *El Alma Hispana y el Alma Sajona* (Buenos Aires, Argentina) , 143 pages.

1962   *Collected Essays,* volume one in this series.

Luther's Meditations on the Gospels (Westminster Press) , pp. 155. English edition 1963.

The Medieval Church (Princeton, N.J., Van Nostrand, 1962) , 192 pages. An Anvil Original paperback.

1963   *Collected Essays,* volume two in this series.

"The Bible in the Reformation" in *The Cambridge History of the Bible* (Cambridge, England) pp. 1-37.

INDEX

THE KINGS COLLEGE LIBRARY
BRIARCLIFF MANOR, N.Y. 10510

Date Due

DATE DUE

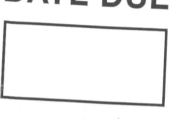

www.tkc.edu
New York, NY
The King's College Library

WITHDRAWN

BR
530
.B34

65383

THE
KING'S COLLEGE LIBRARY
BRIARCLIFF MANOR
N.Y. 10510